Internet Explorer 5
Made Simple

Internet Explorer 5
Made Simple

P.K. McBride

MADE SIMPLE
BOOKS

OXFORD • AUCKLAND • BOSTON • JOHANNESBURG • MELBOURNE • NEW DELHI

Made Simple
An imprint of Butterworth-Heinemann
Linacre House, Jordan Hill, Oxford OX2 8DP
225 Wildwood Avenue, Woburn MA 01801-2041
A division of Reed Educational and Professional Publishing Ltd

℞ A member of the Reed Elsevier plc group

First published 1999
©P.K.McBride 1999

British Library Cataloguing in Publication Data
A catalogue record for this book is available from the British Library

ISBN 0 7506 4627 6

Typeset by P.K.McBride, Southampton
Icons designed by Sarah Ward © 1994
Printed and bound in Great Britain

PLANT A
TREE
BTCV
*British Trust for
Conservation Volunteers*

FOR EVERY TITLE THAT WE PUBLISH, BUTTERWORTH-HEINEMANN
WILL PAY FOR BTCV TO PLANT AND CARE FOR A TREE.

Contents

Preface

Since first appearing four years ago, Microsoft's Internet Explorer has been extensively refined and expanded. Its current version (5) is supplied as part of a suite of tools which, between them, provide just about all you need for any kind of work on the Web. The suite is available for free download from Microsoft's Web site, or can be purchased cheaply on CD. It is also supplied as part of the Windows 98 software, and will be ready-installed in most new PCs.

As well as the browser itself – the key tool and the central part of the system – the suite includes:

- **Outlook Express**, for sending and receiving e-mail messages, and for accessing the many thousands of newsgroups, through which enthusiasts from around the world share their interests;

- **FrontPage Express**, for creating your own Web pages;

- **Wizards** to simplify the initial connection to the Internet and to publish your Web pages;

- **Microsoft NetMeeting** and **Microsoft Chat** for real-time online communications by voice or keyboard.

To use Internet Explorer 5, you need a PC running Windows 95 or 98, a modem and an Internet connection. This book assumes that you are familiar with Windows – if you are not, you might find it useful to read *Windows 95 Made Simple* or *Windows 98 Made Simple* – but no prior knowledge of the Internet is expected.

Internet Explorer 5 Made Simple concentrates on the core components – Internet Explorer, Outlook Express and FrontPage Express. It will show you how to set them up to suit the way you work; how to navigate the World Wide

Web, finding the information and files that you need; how to send and receive messages, articles and files; how to create your own Web pages. Microsoft Chat has been covered briefly, but Net Meeting has been omitted – partly for reasons of space, partly because I doubt that many people will find much use for this software. However, if you do decide that you would like to investigate Net Meeting or have distant colleagues who want to communicate this way, you will find it very simple to use.

1 Introducing Explorer

The Internet Explorer suite

The full Internet Explorer suite consists of a set of tools which between them can handle almost all of the activities that you can do on the Internet.

Internet Explorer 5

IE5 is the browser – the software with which you can explore the World Wide Web. It handles the links between the pages of the Web and can display the text and images, play the sounds and download data files that it finds on Web pages.

It may be the only tool that you need. The usual way to handle e-mail is through an account with your Internet Access Provider, and for this you need Outlook Express (see below) or similar mail software. However, you can get an account with a Web-mail service (see page 82), and here you read and write your mail through the browser.

Connection Wizard (page 26)

This is used to set up your connection to your Access Provider. You will probably only use it once.

Outlook Express (Chapters 6 and 7)

This software handles e-mail and newsgroups – reading and writing messages, and sending them to and receiving them from your Internet Access Provider. Outlook Express can be used to create and display formatted text and embedded images, and can activate IE 4.0 to handle any hyperlinks in messages.

Take note

Your Start menu may well not look the same as mine. When the Explorer suite is installed, programs are placed in the Accessories – Communications and the Internet Tools submenus, as well as in the Internet Explorer submenu. I've grouped them together for simpler access.

2

Address Book (page 98)

Use this to hold the e-mail addresses and other details of your contacts. It can be run separately if needed, but is normally used within Outlook Express.

FrontPage Express (Chapter 8)

If you want to publish your own pages on the Web, this will help you to create them. It can handle almost all aspects of standard HTML – HyperText Markup Language – plus some features unique to Internet Explorer. And when you are done, the **Web Publishing Wizard** (page 143) will help you upload the files to your Internet Access Provider.

NetMeeting

With this you can have audio/video conferences through the Net, sharing files and sketches while you talk. To make use of it, your contacts must also have it (or compatible software) and it works better through an ISDN line, rather than the ordinary dial-up connection.

Microsoft Chat (page 75)

This is used for real-time (typed) communication with other users, working through the 'Chat rooms' that are offered by many large Web sites.

Personal Web Server

This package of tools and documentation is for *serious* Web site developers. There is all you need here to produce a full-blown, all-singing, all-dancing commercial site. It is very much for advanced users, and not covered in this Made Simple book.

Take note

If you intend to download IE5 from Microsoft, read these pages first and decide which components you need. The 'Typical' setup contains only Explorer 5, Outlook Express and the multimedia players. (See page 16 for more on downloading.)

The browser

This is where most of us spend most of our time online, so before we go any further, let's have a look at it.

The main part of the window is used for the display of Web pages. Above this are the control elements. The **Menu bar** contains the full command set, with the most commonly used ones duplicated in the **Standard Toolbar**.

● The **Address** shows you where you are. You can type a URL (page 34) here to open a page (page 36). Typed URLs are stored here, for ease of revisiting.

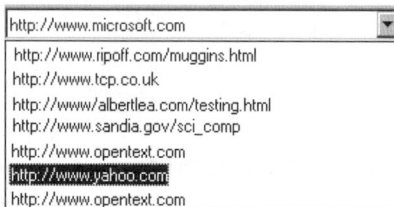

```
http://www.microsoft.com                              ▼
    http://www.ripoff.com/muggins.html
    http://www.tcp.co.uk
    http://www/albertlea.com/testing.html
    http://www.sandia.gov/sci_comp
    http://www.opentext.com
    http://www.yahoo.com
    http://www.opentext.com
```

● The **Links** offer an easy way to connect to selected places. Initially, they connect to pages on Microsoft's site, but you can replace them or add your own (page 60).

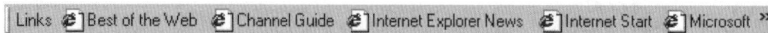

```
Links  🔲 Best of the Web  🔲 Channel Guide  🔲 Internet Explorer News  🔲 Internet Start  🔲 Microsoft  »
```

The Toolbars can be turned on or off as needed, but if you want the maximum viewing area click the Fullscreen icon.

The **Explorer Bar** can be opened on the left of the screen to give simpler navigation when searching the Internet (page 62), or when using the Favorites (page 40) or History (page 38).

The **Status Bar** at the bottom of the page shows how much of an incoming file has been loaded. This can also be turned off if you don't want it.

The Standard toolbar

❑ Navigation tools

Back ▾	Previous page
Forward ▾	Next page
Stop	Stop loading
Refresh	Reload page
Home	Go to your Home page (page 56)

❑ Open in Explorer Bar

Search	Search the Internet
Favorites	Favorites folder
History	History folder

❑ Other tools

Edit ▾	Edit in Notepad or FrontPage.
Print	Print the page
Mail	Mail and News (Chapters 6 and 7)

Tip

You can customise the toolbar display and its contents — see page 30.

Basic steps

❑ Display options

1 Click on View.

2 Point to Toolbar and turn them on (✔) or off from the sub-menu.

3 Click on Status Bar to turn it on or off.

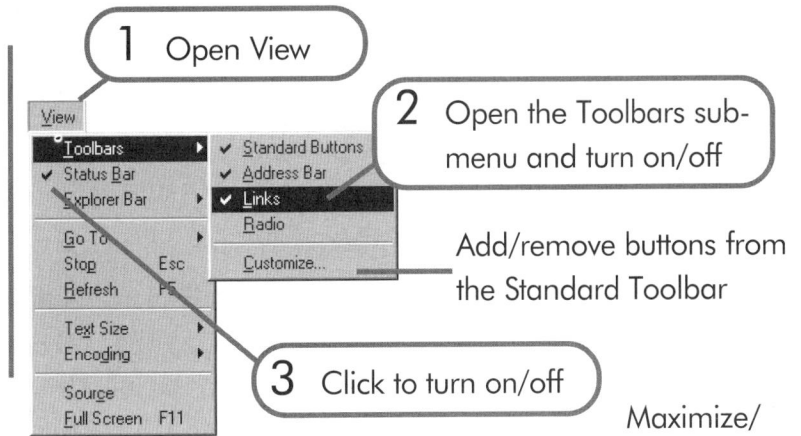

1 Open View

2 Open the Toolbars sub-menu and turn on/off

Add/remove buttons from the Standard Toolbar

3 Click to turn on/off

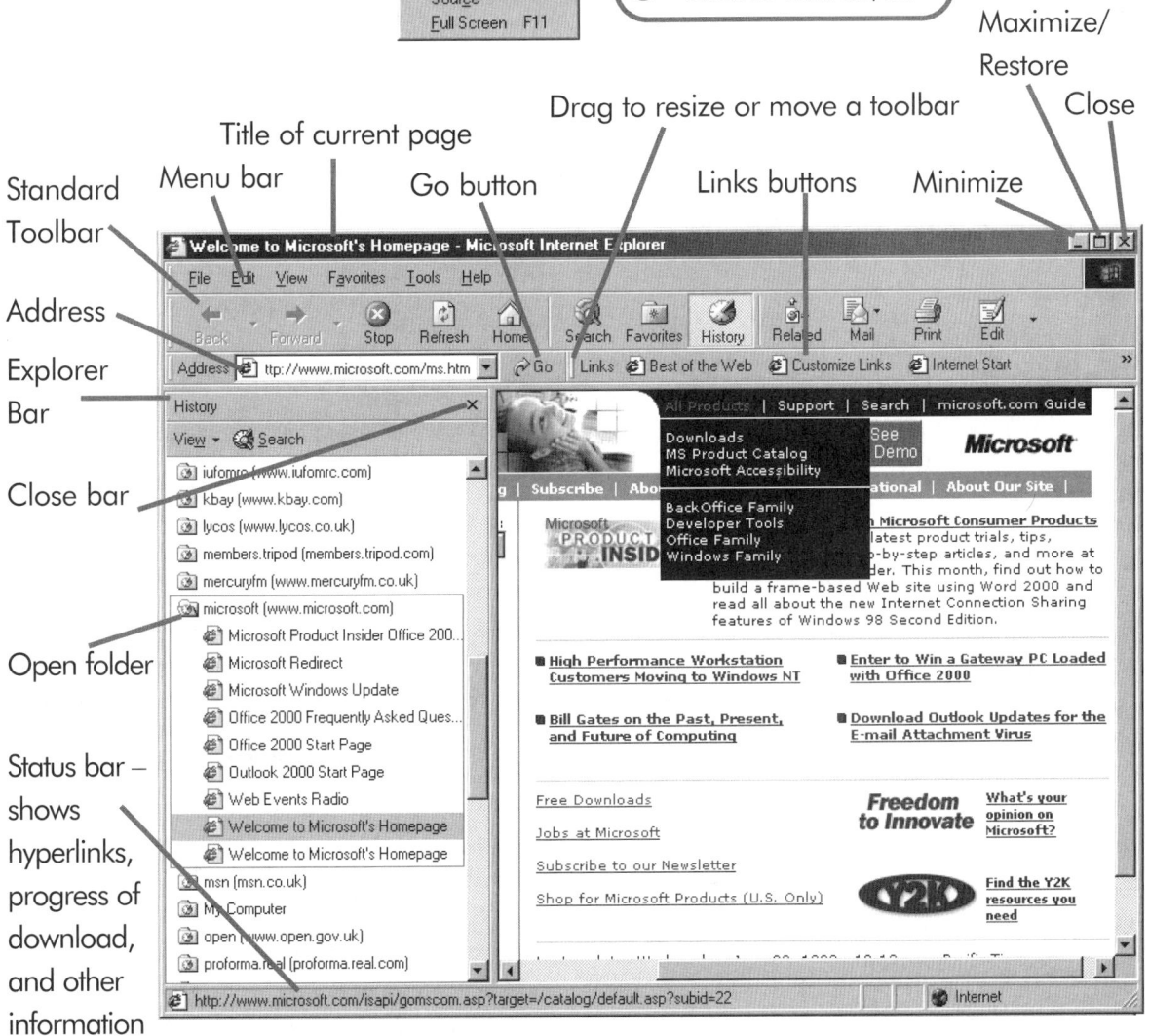

Maximize/ Restore

Close

Drag to resize or move a toolbar

Title of current page

Standard Toolbar

Menu bar

Go button

Links buttons

Minimize

Address

Explorer Bar

Close bar

Open folder

Status bar – shows hyperlinks, progress of download, and other information

Exploring in Windows 98

Internet access is built into Windows Explorer and My Computer in Windows 98. In theory you can open a page on the Web as easily as you can open a file on your hard disk or from within your local network. In practice, of course, getting stuff off the Internet is always far slower and less reliable.

In Windows 98, My Computer and Windows Explorer both have an **Address** box. If you type an Internet address into here, the system will attempt to go online to pick up the link. If it succeeds, then My Computer/Windows Explorer will have its toolbar and menu replaced by those of Internet Explorer.

1 Run My Computer or Windows Explorer.

2 Enter an Internet Address (see page 34).

3 After the page has loaded, you can use the Back button to return to My Computer or Windows Explorer.

1 Run My Computer or Windows Explorer

2 Enter an Address

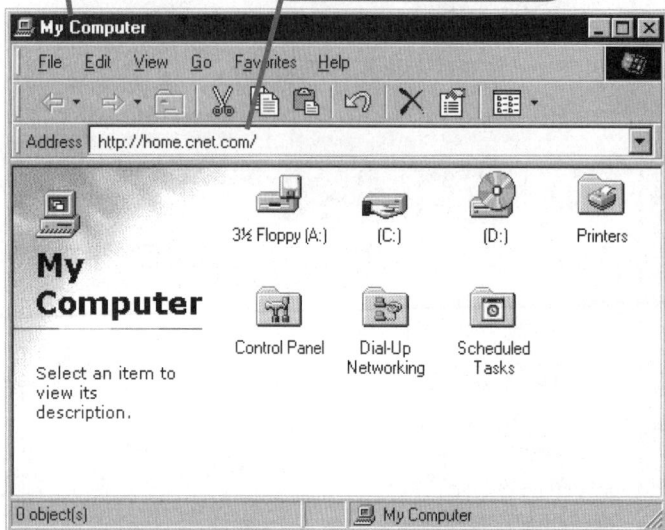

My Computer is seen here in Web page view – Internet access is still there in the alternative 'Classic' (Windows 95 style) display.

Take note

Web/desktop integration has some advantages in an organisation with an intranet (Web for internal use only) and a fast ISDN connection to the Internet. The approach offers far less to home/small business users. If you work through a dial-up connection, and pay by the minute for your online time, exploring the Internet and working with your local files will normally be two separate activities.

6

3 Go Back to My Computer

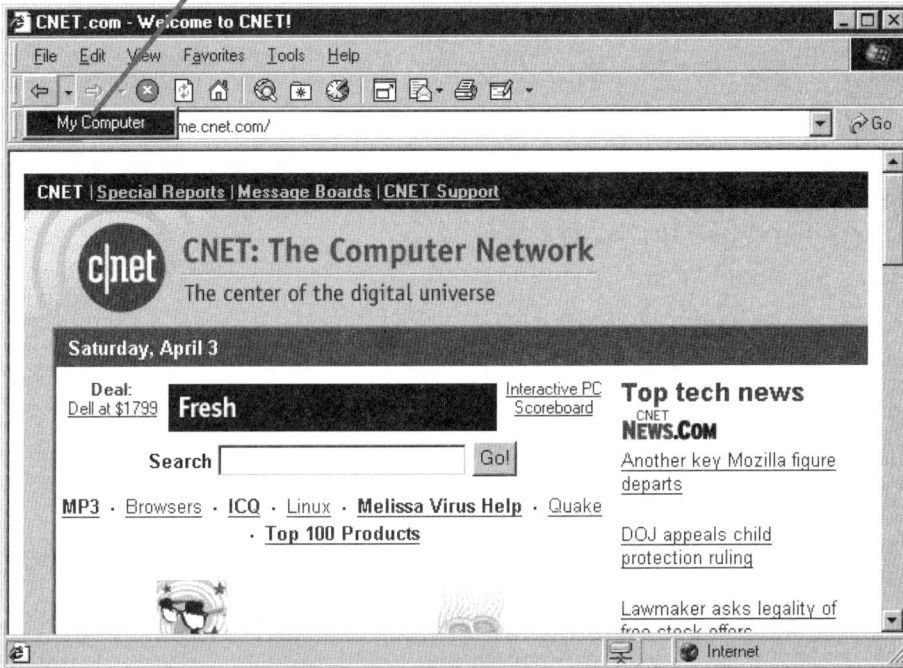

CNET.com - Welcome to CNET!

File   Edit   View   Favorites   Tools   Help

My Computer   me.cnet.com/   Go

CNET | Special Reports | Message Boards | CNET Support

CNET: The Computer Network

The center of the digital universe

Saturday, April 3

| Deal: Dell at $1799 | Fresh | Interactive PC Scoreboard | **Top tech news** |

CNET **NEWS.COM**

Search [   ] Go!

Another key Mozilla figure departs

MP3 · Browsers · **ICQ** · Linux · **Melissa Virus Help** · Quake · **Top 100 Products**

DOJ appeals child protection ruling

Lawmaker asks legality of free stock offers

Internet

Exploring - www.virgin.com

File   Edit   View   Favorites   Tools   Help

Address http://www.virgin.co.uk/

Folders

- psfonts
- Recycled
- temp
- Ulead
- Windows
- Windows Upda
- Xtm
- (D:)
- 09prmcd01 (E:)
- Printers
- Control Panel
- Dial-Up Networking
- Scheduled Tasks
- Web Folders
- My Documents
- Internet Explorer
- Network Neighborhood
- Recycle Bin

Rock, Pop and Funk
The Music channel

RICHARD'S *DIARY*

Thursday, July, 1, 1999
UK site with frames

QuickLink

Virgin Megastores
Virgin Atlantic
Virgin Net
The TrainLine
Virgin Trains
Virgin Holidays
Virgin Radio
Virgin Cola
Virgin Express

Welcome to the Virgin Group's on-line home.

This is the gateway to all our online activities, and your first stop for information about

Internet

In Windows 98, Internet Explorer is in the All Folders list. If the Address bar is displayed, you can use Windows Explorer as if it were Internet Explorer!

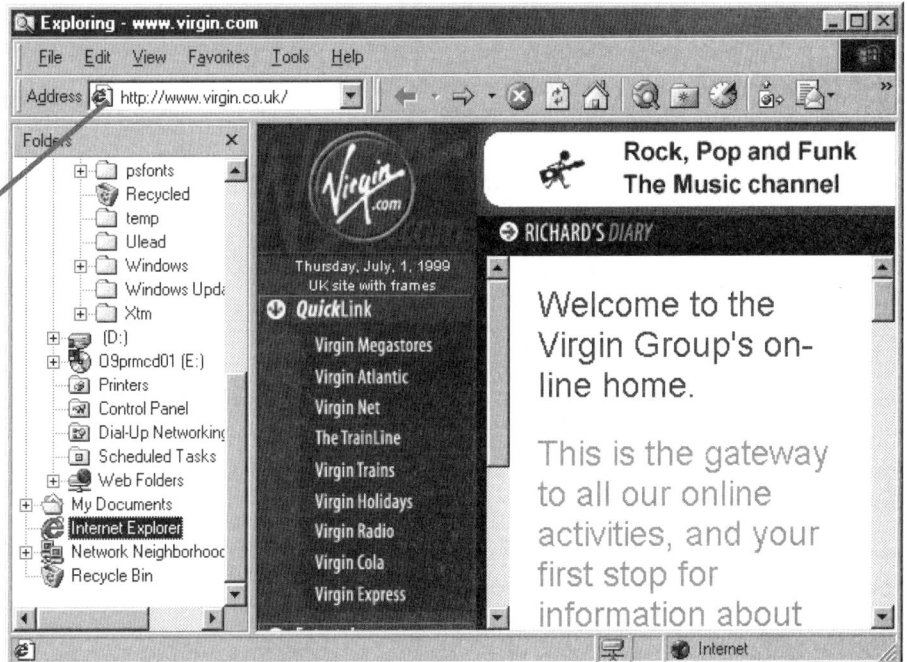

Getting Help

Internet Explorer is supplied with a good Help system. You will find answers to most questions in the local pages, and there's more Help available online if you need it.

Contents

This approach treats the Help pages as a book. You scan through the headings to find a section that seems to cover what you want, and open that to see the page titles.

1 Open the Help menu and select Contents and Index.

2 Click on a 📖 icon or its text to open it.

3 Click on a [?] icon or its text to read a page.

4 Click on underlined topics to reach any linked pages.

5 Click 🗙 to exit Help.

---

1 Select Help – Contents and Index

Help
- Contents and Index
- Tip of the Day
- For Netscape Users
- Tour
- Online Support
- Send Feedback
- About Internet Explorer

2 Open a book

5 Exit Help

3 Open a page

4 Follow up links

Microsoft Internet Explorer Help

Hide | Back | Forward | Options | Web Help

Contents | Index | Search

- [?] Getting started with Internet Explorer
- [?] Taking the Internet Explorer 5 Tour
- 📖 Connecting to the Internet
- 📖 Finding the Web Pages You Want
  - [?] Finding the information you want
  - [?] Listing your favorite pages for quick viewing
  - [?] Change your home page
  - [?] Sharing bookmarks and favorites
  - [?] Find pages you've recently visited
  - [?] Enter Web information more easily
- 📖 Browsing the Web Offline
- 📖 Printing and Saving Information
- 📖 Sending Information over the Internet Safely
- 📖 Protecting Your Computer While You're Online
- 📖 Controlling Access to Inappropriate Internet Content
- 📖 Customizing Your Browser
- 📖 Accessibility

Listing your favorite pages for quick viewing

When you find Web sites or pages that you like, you can keep track of them, so it's easy to open them in the future.

- Add a Web page to your list of favorite pages. Any time you want to open that page, just click the **Favorites** button on the toolbar, and then click the shortcut in the Favorites list.

  Add a page to your list of favorite pages

- If you have a handful of sites or pages that you visit often, add them to your Links bar.

  Add a page to your Links bar

- If there is one page you visit most, you can make it your home page so that it is displayed every time you start Internet Explorer or click the **Home** button on the toolbar.

  Change your home page

Tip

- If you forget to add Web pages to your Favorites or Links bar, click the **History** button on the toolbar. The History list shows where you've been - today, yesterday, or a few weeks ago. Click a

---

Basic steps

1 Click the Index tab.

2 Start to type a word into the slot.

3 Select an Index entry.

4 Click [Display].

5 If there are several relevant pages, you will get the Topics Found list. Pick one and click [Display].

The Contents are good for an overview of how things work, but if you want help on a specific problem you are better off with the Index.

This is organised through an cross-referenced list of terms. The main list is alphabetical, with sub-entries, just like the index in a book. You can scroll through it slowly from the top, or skip through to find the words that start with the right letters.

● Some entries have only one linked page; others have several, listed in a Topics Found panel.

1 Open the Index panel

2 Start to type

5 Pick a topic

3 Select an entry

Microsoft Internet Explorer Help

Hide   Back   Forward   Options   Web Help

Contents | Index | Search

fi|

File Transfer Protocol, see FTP sites
file types for saved Web pages
files
  (see also downloading)
  accessing from toolbars
  copying information into
  saving Web pages
  temporary Internet files
filtering inappropriate content
financial transaction security
information on the Web
pages you recently visited
people
related Web pages
text on a Web page
age, see home page
essing Web Folders
ng background pictures to
ng to toolbars
vsing from the Address bar

Topics Found

Click a topic, then click Display.

Save a Web page on your computer
Saving pictures or text from a Web page

[Display]   [Cancel]

To save a Web page on your computer

1. On the **File** menu, click **Save As**.
2. Doub... save...
3. In the **File name** box, type a name for the page.
4. In the **Save as type** box, select a file type.

   To save all of the files needed to display this page, including graphics, frames, and style sheets, click **Web Page, complete**. This option saves each file in its original format.

   To save all of the information needed to display this page in a single MIME-encoded file, click **Web Archive**. This option saves a snapshot of the current Web page. **Note** This option is available only if you have installed Outlook Express 5 or later.

   To save just the current HTML page, click **Web Page, HTML only**. This option saves the information on the

[Display]

4 Click Display

Search for Help

On the Index panel you are hunting through the titles of Help pages. On the Search panel, the system looks for matching *keywords* within pages.

● A keyword can be any word which might occur in the pages that you are looking for.

● If you give two or more, the system will only list pages which contain all those words.

Basic steps

1 Click the Search tab.
2 Type a keyword into the slot.
3 Click [List Topics].
4 Pick a page from the Topic list.
5 Click [Display].

1 Open the Search panel

2 Type a keyword

3 Click List Topics

Microsoft Internet Explorer Help

Hide Back Forward Options Web Help

Contents | Index | Search

Type in the keyword to find:

download

List Topics

Select Topic to display:

Topic

Access FTP sites directly
Access FTP sites through a CERN-compliant proxy se...
Correctly display Web pages encoded in any language
Customizing Windows Operating Systems
File Download
Internet Explorer keyboard shortcuts
Make an existing favorite item available offline
Make the current Web page available offline
Microsoft Documentation in Alternative Formats
Microsoft Product Support Services Online
Microsoft Product Support Services Online
Protecting your computer from unsafe software
Using accessibility features in Internet Explorer
Viewing the Readme online document for Internet Expl...
What you need to know about FTP
What you need to know about security zones

Display

To make an existing favorite item available offline

1. On the **Favorites** menu, click **Organize Favorites**.

2. Click the page you want to make available offline.

3. Select the **Make available offline** check box.

4. To specify a schedule for updating the page, and how much content to download, click **Properties**.

Notes

● Before you go offline, make sure you have the latest version of your pages by clicking the **Tools** menu and then clicking **Synchronize**.

● You can also make Web pages available offline without adding them to your Favorites list, by saving the pages on your computer.

Related Topics

Making pages available for offline viewing

Save a Web page on your computer

4 Pick a topic

5 Click Display

Help from the Web

1 From the Help menu select Online Support.

2 Select the user area.

3 Follow the Browse link.

4 Open the folders and see if there is a page that might answer your question.

If you have trouble with any of the Explorer suite programs, or need other technical help, you may be able to find it in **Online Support**. There you can search or browse for help on any Microsoft product – the Troubleshooters are very good.

1 Use Help – Online Support

The Tour is an online tutorial about the Web

2 What kind of user are you?

4 See what's there

Home Users

Microsoft's first priority is to the user of its products. If you've purchased a Microsoft product, we're here to make sure it works perfectly for you. The easiest and fastest way to find the support you need is right here. You'll have access to a variety of online information sites and technical assistance avenues such as e-mail, phone support, Frequently asked questions and troubleshooting databases.

No-charge home user support covers most Microsoft consumer products purchased separately from your local reseller or directly from Microsoft. If your Microsoft product was preinstalled or distributed with your computer, then you must contact your computer manufacturer for product support. For more information on no-charge support, click Support Options on this page's toolbar.

Do you need help now?

Visit the Personal Support Center to search for your answer or to contact a Microsoft support professional.

Business Solutions
Enterprise
Information Technology Professionals
Small Business

Partners & Resellers
Microsoft Certified Solution Providers
Resellers & Consultants

Developers
Home User
Education

Help with Problems Using NetMeeting

What problem are you having?

○ I can't connect to a User Location Service (ULS).
○ I can't reestablish a previously saved connection.
⦿ I can establish connections with NetMeeting, but I can't use the audio features.
○ I can't use full-duplex audio, although I can use the other audio features of NetMeeting.
○ I can't start NetMeeting.
○ The Audio Tuning Wizard reports that my sound card isn't supported.

Next

Tip

If you can't find what you want by browsing, try a search – though this tends to offer loads (too many?) of links.

Net-speak

Access provider An organisation that gives businesses and individuals access to the Internet. Sometimes called *service providers*.

Applet A small Java application, embedded in a Web page. Commonly used to create flashy titles or scroll messages in the status bar.

Browse Move from one place to another on the Web, stopping to pick up interesting bits as you go.

Catalog An organised list of Web sites and other Internet resources. The best catalogs offer comprehensive coverage of what's on the Net, with summaries of what you will find at different places. Also known as *Directories* (Chapter 4).

Directory See *Catalog*.

Download Copy a file from somewhere on the Net, into your system.

FTP *File Transfer Protocol*. The standard way of copying files over the Net. Servers that hold databases of shareware, freeware and other files are known as FTP sites.

Home page The top-level page of a set of related pages.

Host A computer providing some kind of service, such as holding files for users to download.

HTTP *HyperText Transfer Protocol*. The way that Web pages are linked together. Browsers can read HTTP links and use them to find Web pages (page 34).

Java A programming language mainly used to create

Take note

This list of jargon covers only the barest essentials — just enough so that you do not get too confused on your first journeys into Cyberspace.

If you want to learn to speak like a real nettie, surf over to:

http://www.netlingo.com

	applets for Web pages, though it can also produce stand-alone programs.
JavaScript	Based on Java, but much simplified. Its commands are written into Web pages and executed when the page is opened.
Newbie	Newcomer to the Net. When you come across disparaging references to newbies, remember that everyone was a newbie once.
Page	A combination of text, graphics, sound and other files that produce a screen display.
Search engine	A system that maintains a database or index of information, pages and/or files on the Internet, and offers users a means of searching through it (Chapter 4).
Server	A computer providing a service to Internet users. Your access provider will have a mail server to act as a 'post office' for your mail (Chapter 6), and a news server to hold the articles from the newsgroups (Chapter 7).
Shareware	Software that can be downloaded free, for trial use, with the request that you pay (a small fee) if you continue to use it.
Site	An organisation's place on the Internet, holding one or more linked pages.
Surf	Move around the Web – and other parts of the Internet – to see what's happening.
URL	*Uniform Resource Locator*. The address of something on the Internet (page 34).

Summary

❑ The Internet Explorer suite centres around the browser and includes software for handling e-mail and news-groups, creating Web pages or full Web sites, and real-time communication – by typing, voice or video.

❑ The browser window has been designed to make navigating easier.

❑ You can run a search, or open the Favorites or History folders in the Explorer Bar.

❑ In Windows 98 you can reach the Internet through My Computer and Windows Explorer as well as Internet Explorer.

❑ There's plenty of Help available. Use the Contents panel to browse through the topics.

❑ Use the Index or Search panels to go directly to the Help on a specified operation or object.

❑ Microsoft's Online Support site offers detailed technical help on all of their products, and also has a tutorial on using the Web.

2 Setting up

Downloading

If you do not yet have Explorer 5, you can get it from the IE 5 download area at **www.microsoft.com/windows/ie/** or through the Windows Update link on your Start menu. There's a choice of two packages:

● Typical (17Mb), which includes Outlook Express, and multimedia software.

● Minimal (7.5Mb) – the browser only or Customize – where you select the components and take control of the installation. The full set adds around 50Mb of files!

Installation is a two-stage, but largely automated, process. The first download should be set to Run – rather than Save to disk. It will then take over and organise the rest of the download and installation.

Basic steps

1 Select Windows Update from the Start menu or go directly to www.microsoft.com/ windows/ie/download/ windows.htm

2 Select the platform, then the Language.

3 Pick a download site and click Next.

4 Select Run this program – wait for it to download and start (about 5 minutes), then follow the instructions.

1 Go to Microsoft's Download Area

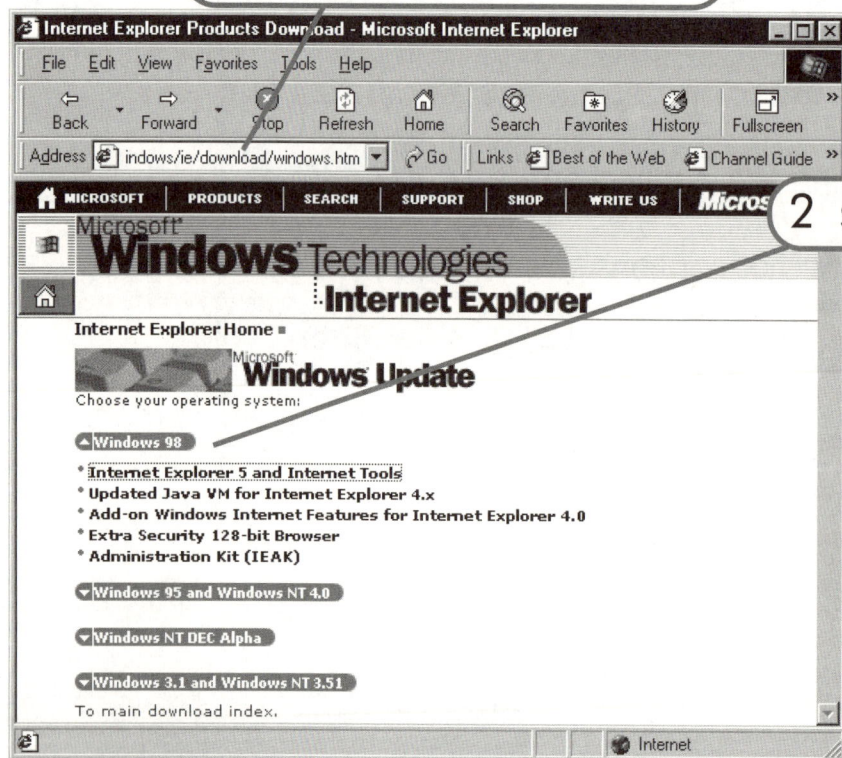

Internet Explorer Products Download - Microsoft Internet Explorer

File   Edit   View   Favorites   Tools   Help

Back   Forward   Stop   Refresh   Home   Search   Favorites   History   Fullscreen

Address indows/ie/download/windows.htm   Go   Links   Best of the Web   Channel Guide

MICROSOFT   PRODUCTS   SEARCH   SUPPORT   SHOP   WRITE US   Micros

2 Select a platform

Microsoft **Windows** Technologies
Internet Explorer

Internet Explorer Home ■

Microsoft
Windows Update

Choose your operating system:

▲Windows 98
* Internet Explorer 5 and Internet Tools
* Updated Java VM for Internet Explorer 4.x
* Add-on Windows Internet Features for Internet Explorer 4.0
* Extra Security 128-bit Browser
* Administration Kit (IEAK)

▼Windows 95 and Windows NT 4.0

▼Windows NT DEC Alpha

▼Windows 3.1 and Windows NT 3.51

To main download index.

Internet

Tip

You can jump to the download area from an
Microsoft Internet Explorer icon if you see one on a Web page.

There are sites all over the world. Try the closest first, but if it is very slow, stop and try another – a good site will download at 3Kb a second or faster.

3 Choose the site

4 Run the program

Take note

Even with a fast modem, the Minimal download can take over 1 hour. If you don't want to spend hours on-line, look for a IE 5 on the front-cover CD-ROMs of computer magazines, or order the CD-ROM from Microsoft.

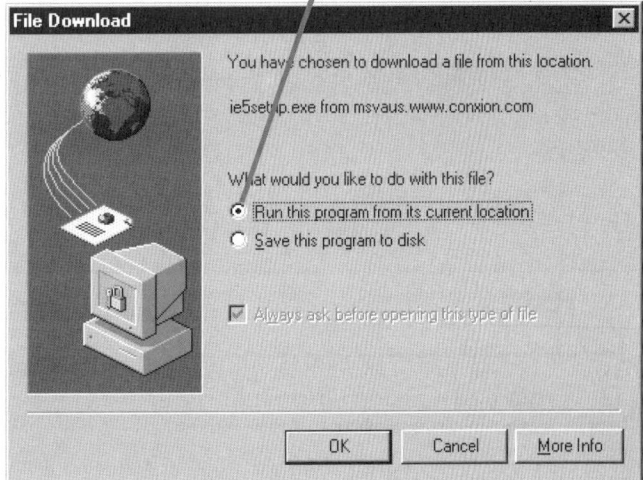

Installation

Whether you are downloading or working from a CD-ROM, the setup routine is much the same – even with a CD-ROM, you may need to go online to collect some updated elements.

You will have to make a few decisions – the key one is whether you want the Typical installation or to choose your own components. Optional components include Microsoft Chat (real-time typed conversation, see page 75), Net Meeting (voice and screen communication, mainly for use by remote work-mates) and FrontPage Express (see Chapter 8).

Basic steps

1 Close down all other applications.

2 Insert the CD into the drive and select Install Internet Explorer 5.

or

3 Run the downloaded setup program.

4 Work through the Wizard, clicking Next at the end of each stage.

5 Do you want the Typical or Minimal/Custom installation?

6 For a Custom installation, tick the components you want.

7 If you are not already online, click Yes to let Setup get stuff from the Microsoft site.

8 Find something to do while it downloads and installs – it'll be a while!

1 Close down other applications

You need Outlook Express to handle e-mail

3 Run Setup

Windows Update: Internet Explorer and Internet Tools

Windows Update: Internet Explorer and Internet Tools
You can update Windows now, or make changes to your installation.

○ **Install Now – Typical set of components – 17.0MB**
(Estimated download time on 28.8 Kbps modem: 2 hours and 24 minutes)
Typical includes: Internet Explorer 5 Web Browser, Outlook Express, Windows Media Player, and other multimedia enhancements.

◉ **Install Minimal, or customize your browser – 7.5MB**
Select only the components you want, the folder in which to install them, choose your default browser, or download the files now and install later.

< Back   Next >   Cancel   Help

4 Click Next at each stage

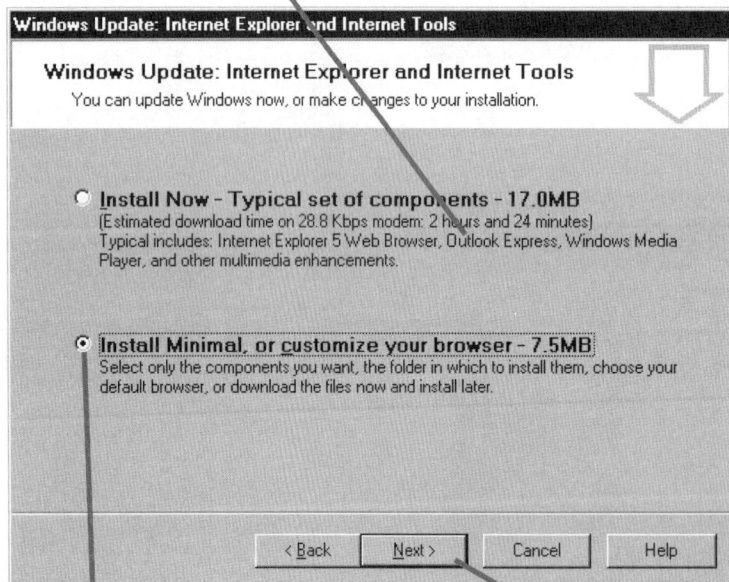

5 Typical or Custom Installation?

Windows Update: Internet Explorer and Internet Tools

Component Options

Choose specific Internet Explorer components or change the installation location here.

Folder to install Internet Explorer to:

C:\Program Files\Internet Explorer   [Browse...]

[Custom ▼]

Description
Microsoft Windows software for Internet connectivity and World Wide Web browsing.

- ☐ Internet Explorer 5
  - ☑ **Internet Explorer 5 Web Browser**
  - ☑ **Offline Browsing Pack**
  - ☐ **Internet Explorer Help**
  - ☑ Microsoft virtual machine
  - ☐ Internet Connection Wizard

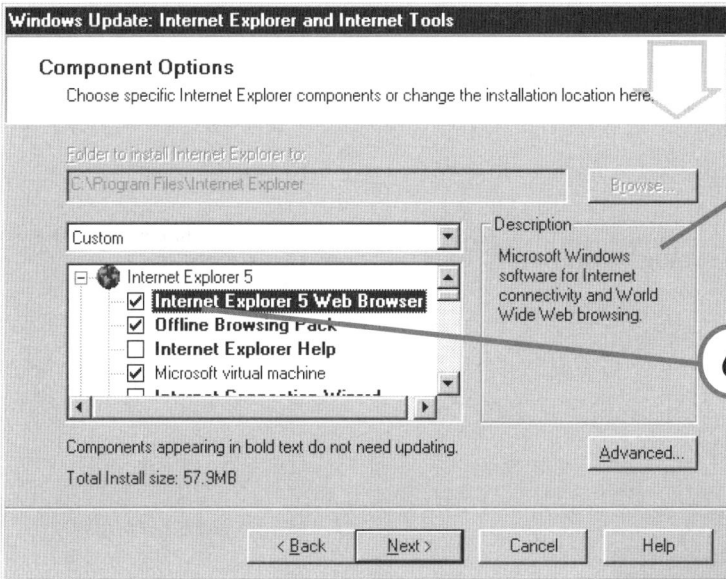

Click on a component to get a description of it

> **6** Tick the components

Components appearing in bold text do not need updating.
Total Install size: 57.9MB   [Advanced...]

[< Back] [Next >] [Cancel] [Help]

> **7** Download files as needed

Windows Update: Internet Explorer and Internet Tools

⚠ Setup needs to download additional files from the Internet to install one or more components you've selected. If you do not have Internet access, please contact your network administrator.

Do you want Setup to download the additional files from the Internet?

[Yes] [No] [Help]

> **7** Relax and wait!

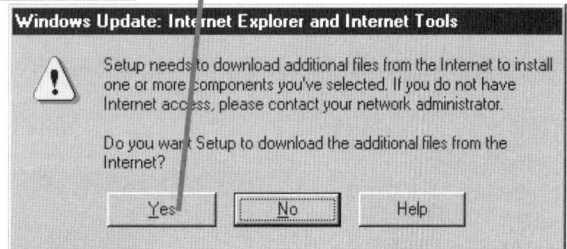

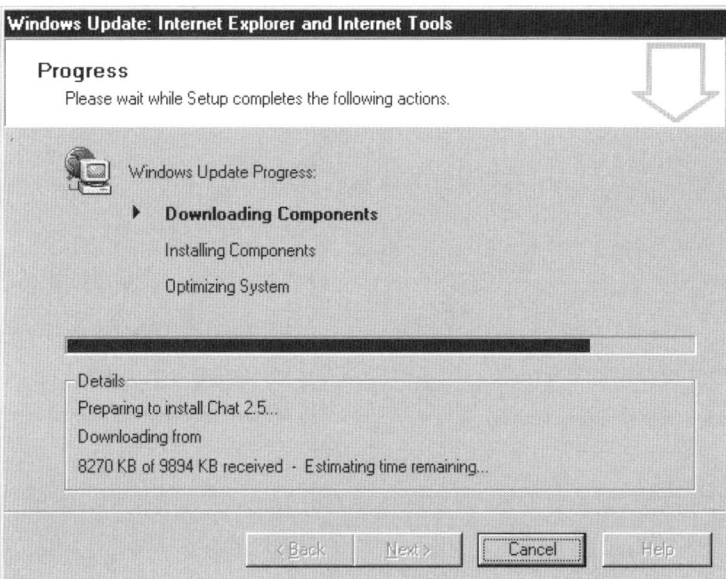

Windows Update: Internet Explorer and Internet Tools

Progress

Please wait while Setup completes the following actions.

Windows Update Progress:

- ▶ **Downloading Components**
- Installing Components
- Optimizing System

Details
Preparing to install Chat 2.5...
Downloading from
8270 KB of 9894 KB received - Estimating time remaining...

[< Back] [Next >] [Cancel] [Help]

Tip

When you run Explorer, it will offer to connect you to your service. Click Cancel if you want to work off-line — perhaps to set options or prepare mail first.

General options

The Internet Options control many aspects of Explorer's display and of how it works. Start on the General panel:

● Choose your **Home page** – this is the one that Explorer will connect to when you go online . It might be at a Web directory or portal (see Chapter 4) – choose 'blank' if you do not want to always start browsing at the same place .

● Set the disk space for storing files of visited pages. When you revisit, Explorer will use these and only download new files if the pages have changed – allocate as much as you can spare for faster browsing.

● Set the **Accessibility** options and choose your own **Colors** and **Fonts** for maximum visibility, if needed.

1 Open the Tools menu and select Internet Options...

2 Go to General.

3 For the Home page, type the URL (or click Use Current if you are on that page), or click Use Blank.

4 Click Settings.

5 Select when to check for new versions of stored pages – Every visit is usually best.

1 Use Tools – Internet Options

2 Open the General panel

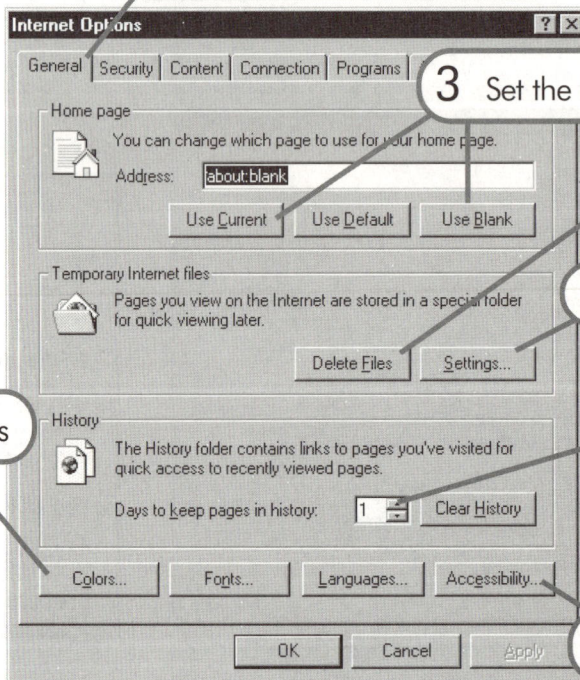

Tools
Mail & News ▶
Synchronize
Windows Update
Internet Options...

Internet Options ? ✕

General | Security | Content | Connection | Programs |

3 Set the Home page

Home page
You can change which page to use for your home page.
Addﾃess: about:blank
Use Current | Use Default | Use Blank

Delete Files to free up disk space

Temporary Internet files
Pages you view on the Internet are stored in a special folder for quick viewing later.
Delete Files | Settings...

4 Click Settings

8 Click Colors

History
The History folder contains links to pages you've visited for quick access to recently viewed pages.
Days to keep pages in history: 1 | Clear History

The History holds links to visited pages – how long do you want to keep them?

Colors... | Fonts... | Languages... | Accessibility...

OK | Cancel | Apply

10 Click Accessibility

20

6 Set the amount of
  space for storage.

7 Click OK.

❑ High visibility

8 Click [Colors...].

9 Set the colours for high
  contrast and click OK.

❑ Set Fonts in the same
  way.

10 Click [Accessibility...].

11 Set Explorer to ignore
   the pages' own colours
   and fonts – so that
   yours are used instead.

12 Click OK.

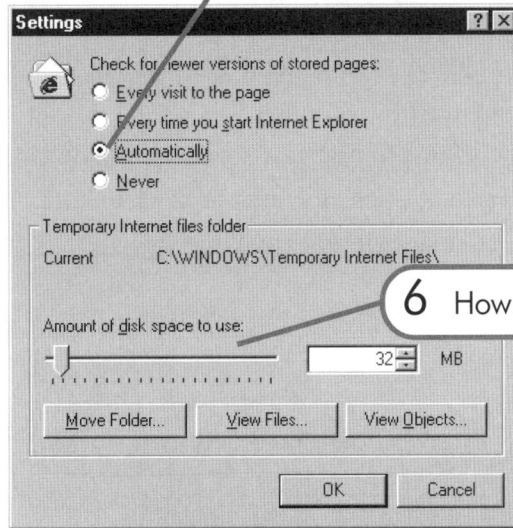

5 Set when to check stored pages

6 How much disk space?

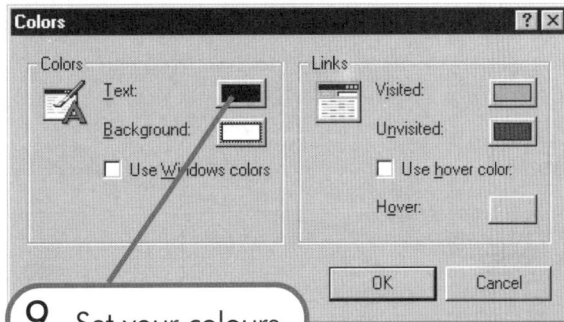

9 Set your colours

11 Use your colours
   and fonts?

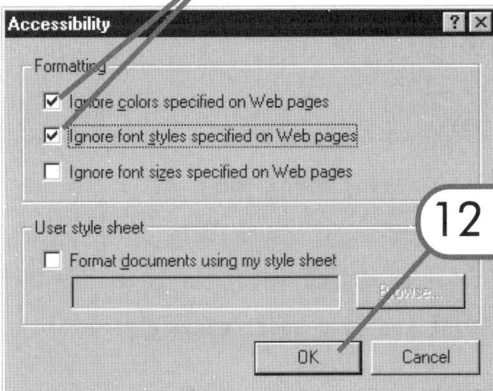

12 Click OK

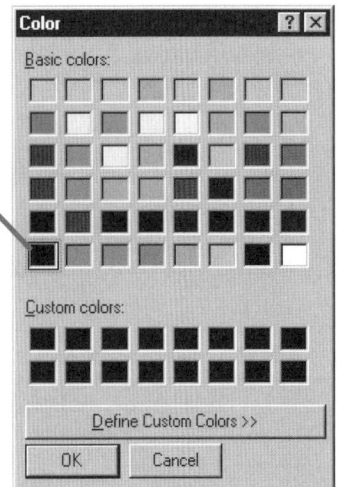

Multimedia options

Pictures, audio and video files are sometimes essential, often merely decorative and always slow to load. Turn them off for faster browsing but pictures often contain links – if you can't see them, you may not be able to navigate some sites. You can turn them back on and reload a page to view the files, or simply click on a non-displayed image (it will appear as 🖻) to load it.

Basic steps

1 Open the Tools menu and select Internet Options.

2 Go to Advanced.

3 Scroll down to the Multimedia section.

4 Click to turn the options on or off as required.

5 Click OK.

2 Open the Advanced panel

4 Tick to turn on

Internet Options

General | Security | Content | Connections | Programs | Advanced

Settings:

- ☐ Use HTTP 1.1 through proxy connections
- Java VM
  - ☐ Java console enabled (requires restart)
  - ☑ Java JIT compiler enabled
  - ☐ Java logging enabled
- Multimedia
  - ☐ Always show Internet Explorer Radio bar
  - ☑ Play animations
  - ☑ Play sounds
  - ☑ Play videos
  - ☐ Show image download placeholders
  - ☑ Show pictures
  - ☑ Smart image dithering
- Printing
  - ☐ Print background colors and images
- Search from the Address bar
  - When searching

Restore Defaults

OK | Cancel | Apply

3 Scroll down to Multimedia

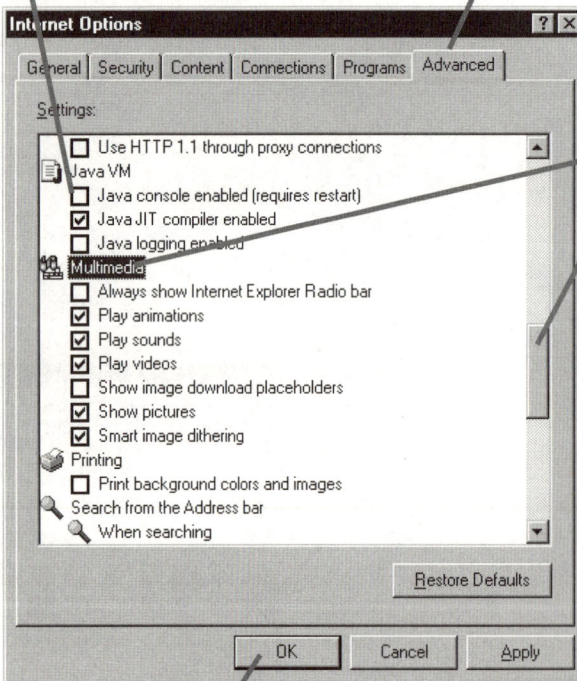

There are lots of other options here – leave these at their defaults until you have more experience of Explorer and the Web.

5 Click OK

Tip

If you have Show Pictures turned off and meet a page where you need to see the pictures it is quicker to turn Show Pictures on and reload the page than to click and load each separately.

Security

1 Go to the Security panel.

2 Pick the Internet zone.

3 Select Custom and click `Settings...`.

4 Tell Explorer how to deal with each type.

or

5 Click Default Level to restore the normal settings.

Many Web pages have **active content**, i.e. they contain multimedia files or applets (small applications) written in Java, JavaScript or ActiveX. These should not be able to mess with your hard disks or access your data, but some hackers have found a way round the restrictions – and anti-virus software is no help here. Active content makes browsing more interesting, and if you stick to major sites, should create no problems. (You can also create your own set of Trusted sites by adding their URLs to the list.)

At first, select the Internet zone (i.e. all Web sites), with the security set to **High**. Use the **Custom** option to fine-tune the settings later, when you have more experience.

1 Go to Security

2 Select Internet Zone

4 Enable/Disable actions

Internet Options

General | Security | Content | Connections | Programs | Advanced

Select a Web content zone to specify its security settings.

Internet | Local intranet | Trusted sites | Restricted sites

Internet

This zone contains all Web sites you haven't placed in other zones

Sites...

Security level for this zone

Move the slider to set the security level for this zone.

Medium

- Safe browsing and still functional
- Prompts before downloading potentially unsafe content
- Unsigned ActiveX controls will not be downloaded
- Appropriate for most Internet sites

Custom Level...   Default Level

OK   Cancel   Apply

Security Settings

Settings:

ActiveX controls and plug-ins
  Download signed ActiveX controls
    O Disable
    O Enable
    ⊙ Prompt
  Download unsigned ActiveX controls
    ⊙ Disable
    O Enable
    O Prompt
  Initialize and script ActiveX controls not marked as safe
    ⊙ Disable
    O Enable
    O Prompt
  Run ActiveX controls and plug ins

Reset custom settings

Reset to: Medium   Reset

OK   Cancel

'Signed' are safer – you know where they came from

3 Customise the settings

5 Click Default Level

Safe Exploring

With Explorer you can protect younger users – or anyone else who might be offended – from the unacceptable material that lurks in various corners of the Net.

The settings on the Content panel allows you to restrict the browser to sites rated by the (RSAC) Recreational Standards Advisory Council – over 50,000 at the time of writing – and to control the levels of sex'n'violence that can be viewed.

If a site's ratings are beyond the limits you have set, access is denied. This can be overriden by the use of the password, should you decide a site has been overrated and is suitable for viewing.

1 Go to Content

2 Click Enable...

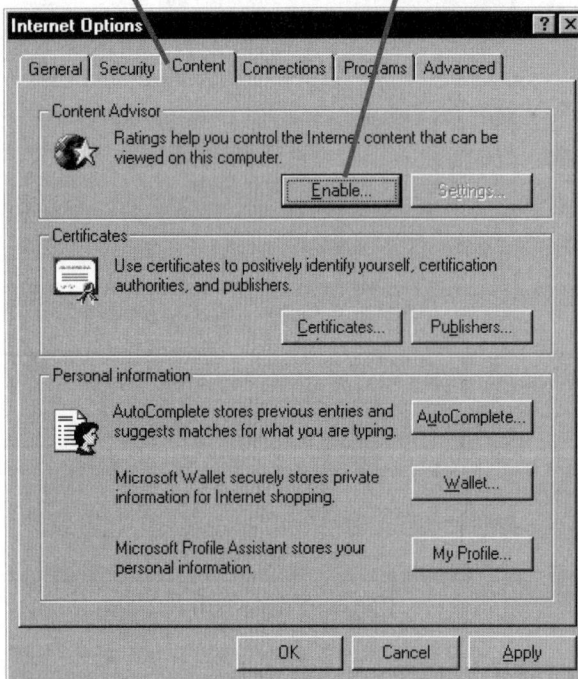

Internet Options

| General | Security | Content | Connections | Programs | Advanced |

Content Advisor

Ratings help you control the Internet content that can be viewed on this computer.

[Enable...] [Settings...]

Certificates

Use certificates to positively identify yourself, certification authorities, and publishers.

[Certificates...] [Publishers...]

Personal information

AutoComplete stores previous entries and suggests matches for what you are typing. [AutoComplete...]

Microsoft Wallet securely stores private information for Internet shopping. [Wallet...]

Microsoft Profile Assistant stores your personal information. [My Profile...]

[OK] [Cancel] [Apply]

Basic steps

1 Go to the Content panel.

2 Click Enable...

3 Decide on a Password and enter it – twice.

4 On the Ratings panel, set the limit for each Category – moving the slider to the right permits higher levels of sex'n'violence.

5 On the General panel, tick the options if you want to allow people to see unrated sites, or to use the password to view restricted sites.

6 Click OK.

Tip

With **Content Advisor** enabled, the Net is a safer place for kids, but for even greater control over their activities on the Net, you should use access control software. One of the best is NetNanny – to find out more about this go to:
http://www.netnanny.com

Create Supervisor Password `? X`

To prevent children from changing their Content Advisor settings or turning it off, you must create a supervisor password.

`OK`
`Cancel`

Content Advisor settings can be changed or turned on or off only by people who know the password.

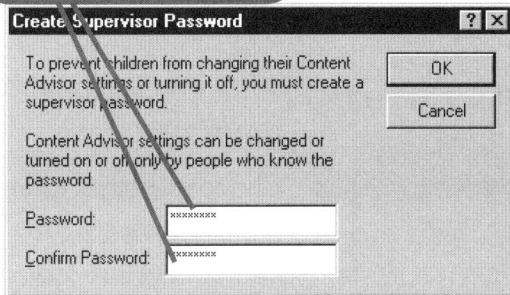

Password: `********`

Confirm Password: `********`

In this panel you can set up your own list of sites that are always – or never – accessible, whatever their rating

Content Advisor `? X`

Ratings | Approved Sites | General | Advanced |

Select a category to view the rating levels:

RSACi
- Language
- Nudity
- Sex
- Violence

4 Decide your limits

Adjust the slider to specify what users are allowed to see:

Level 1: Revealing attire

Description

Revealing attire.

To view the Internet page for this rating service, click More Info.

`More Info...`

`OK`   `Cancel`   `Apply`

5 Set the General options

An unrated site is not necessarily unsuitable

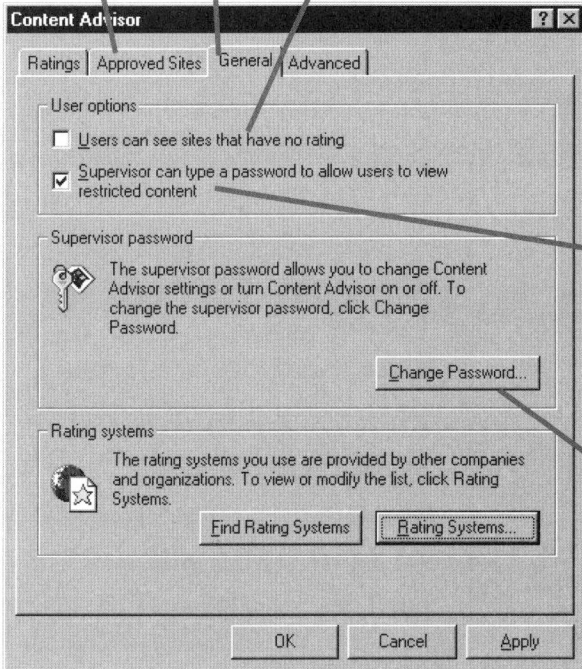

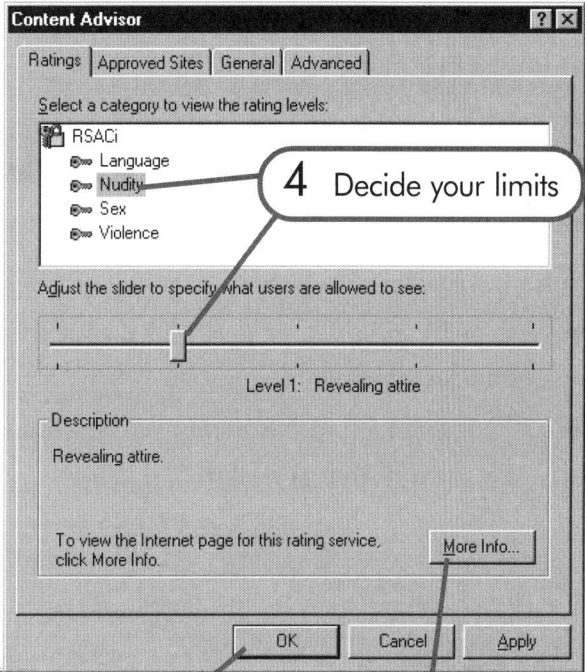

6 Click OK

Click here while on-line to find out about the RSAC

Content Advisor `? X`

Ratings | Approved Sites | General | Advanced |

User options
- ☐ Users can see sites that have no rating
- ☑ Supervisor can type a password to allow users to view restricted content

Supervisor password

The supervisor password allows you to change Content Advisor settings or turn Content Advisor on or off. To change the supervisor password, click Change Password.

`Change Password...`

Rating systems

The rating systems you use are provided by other companies and organizations. To view or modify the list, click Rating Systems.

`Find Rating Systems`   `Rating Systems...`

`OK`   `Cancel`   `Apply`

Turn this on to allow yourself – or any other authorised person – to override a restriction

The password can – and should – be changed regularly

Making the connection

Before you can get on-line, you must tell Explorer about your service provider. The Connection Wizard makes this simple – but you must have the necessary information to hand at the start. You need to know:

- your provider's phone number;
- you provider's Mail and News servers' names;
- your user name, e-mail address and password.

You may also need to know:

- your IP address – or not! Many systems allocate a new address when you log on;
- your provider's DNS Server Addresses – they will be in the form of four sets of digits, like this: 190.99.134.29

1 Run the Wizard

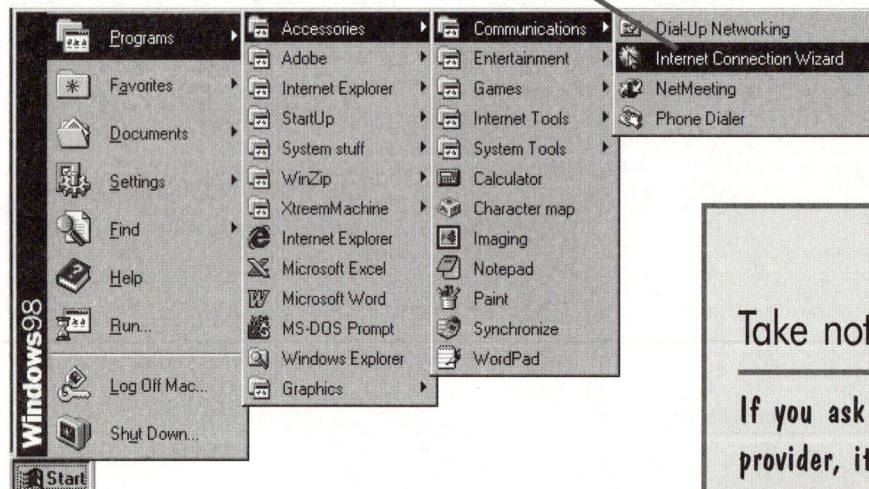

Your Start menu may be different. If you cannot find the Connection Wizard anywhere, run it from My Computer. The program is iwconn1.exe and it will be in the Internet Explorer/Connection Wizard folder.

Basic steps

1 Click on Start, point to Programs – Accessories – Communications and select Internet Connection Wizard.

2 Choose whether to find a provider, set up a new connection to your provider or use an existing connection.

3 Work through the Wizard, clicking Next after each stage. Watch for the panels shown opposite.

Take note

If you ask the Wizard to find a provider, it will try to connect to Microsoft's online service to get the information. When tested, this was a poor service, with slow and unreliable connections.

Use the Wizard to find
a service provider

Quick configure for an
existing connection

Use if you have a provider,
but have not yet connected

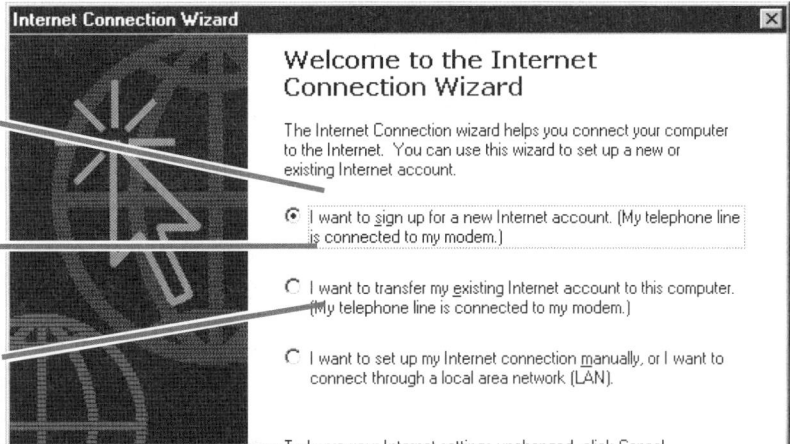

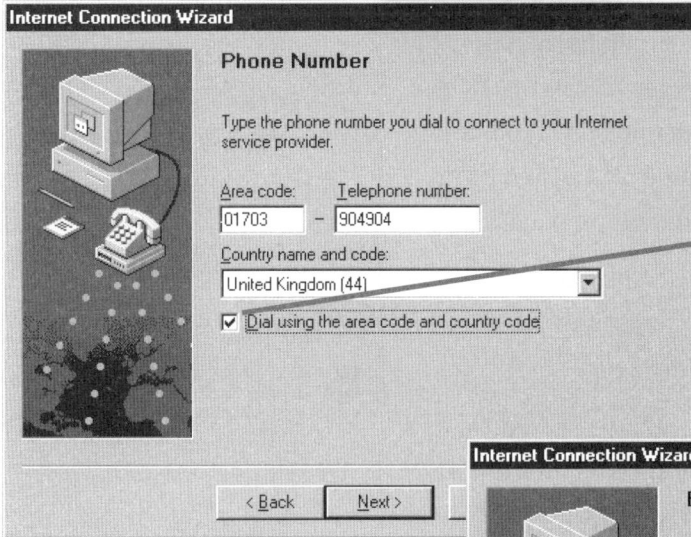

Internet Connection Wizard

Welcome to the Internet Connection Wizard

The Internet Connection wizard helps you connect your computer to the Internet. You can use this wizard to set up a new or existing Internet account.

○ I want to sign up for a new Internet account. (My telephone line is connected to my modem.)

○ I want to transfer my existing Internet account to this computer. (My telephone line is connected to my modem.)

○ I want to set up my Internet connection manually, or I want to connect through a local area network (LAN).

To leave your Internet settings unchanged, click Cancel.

To learn more about the Internet, click Tutorial. [Tutorial]

[< Back] [Next >] [Cancel]

Internet Connection Wizard

Phone Number

Type the phone number you dial to connect to your Internet service provider.

Area code: Telephone number:
01703   –   904904

Country name and code:
United Kingdom (44)

☑ Dial using the area code and country code

[< Back] [Next >]

Uncheck this box if you
can reach your provider
on a local number.

Internet Connection Wizard

E-mail Server Names

My incoming mail server is a [POP3 ▼] server. Type the name of your incoming mail server.

Incoming mail (POP3 or IMAP) server:
mail.tcp.co.uk

An SMTP server is the server that is used for your outgoing e-mail. Type the name of your SMTP server.

Outgoing mail (SMTP) server:
mail.tcp.co.uk

[< Back] [Next >] [Cancel] [Help]

The incoming and outgoing
servers are probably the same
– the name will be something
like *mail.myprovider.co.uk*

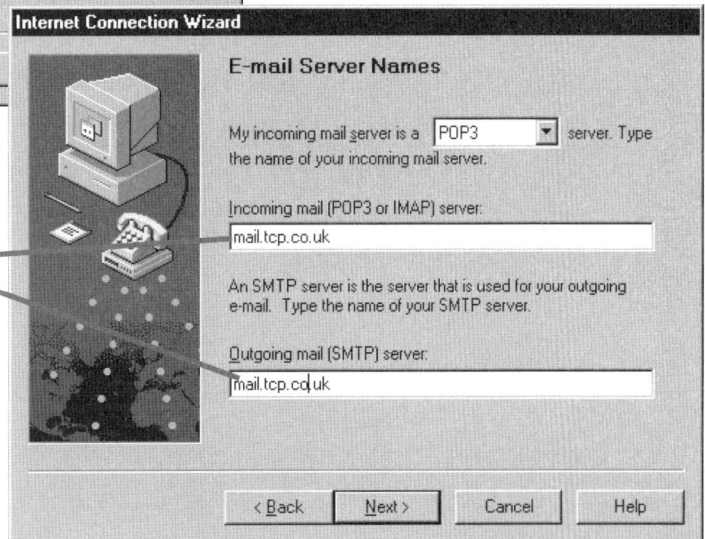

Connection options

Running the Connection Wizard will have filled in the essential information on this panel, but there are a couple of options that need your attention. These are on the Dial-Up Settings panel, which is reached from the Connection panel of the Internet Options.

- Set the number of times to try to connect, and how long to wait before retrying. Mine is set to 5 retries at 30 second intervals – experience will show what is best with your service provider.

- Turning on the **Disconnect if idle...** option will stop you running up unnecessary phone bills should you get involved in something else and forget to disconect. But don't set too short a time. Explorer thinks it is idle if it is actually not transferring data over the phone, and it could cut you off while you were reading a long page!

- If you access the Internet through a local area network, the **LAN settings** and the **Proxy** settings will need to be configured – consult your LAN manager.

- Those network users who normally have shared folders on their computer should turn on the **Perform system security check** option. If a folder is open to other LAN users, it may be accessed by others on the wider Internet. For best security, sharing should be turned off before you go online. This security check will warn you if you have left folders open for sharing.

1 Open the Tools menu and select Internet Options.

2 Switch to the Connections panel.

3 Select the connection and click Settings... .

4 Enter your user name and password.

5 Click Advanced .

6 Set the number of redial attempts, and the delay between trying.

7 Turn on Disconnect if idle and set the time limit.

8 Click OK to close the dialog box and again at the Settings panel.

28

2 Switch to Connections

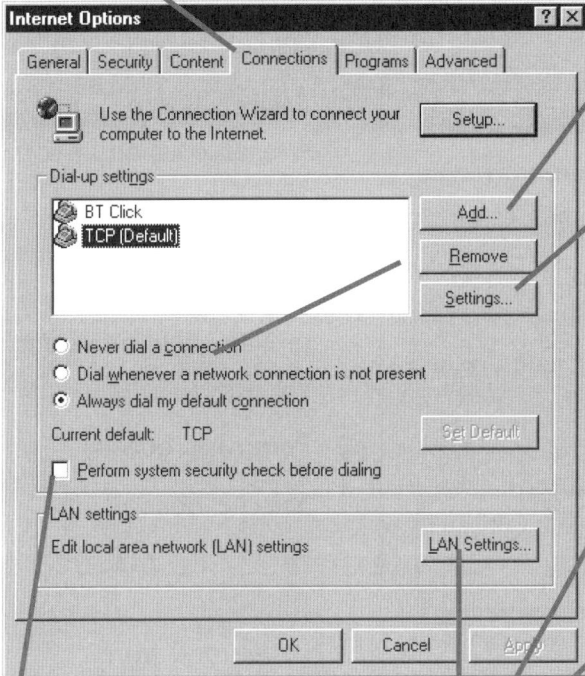

If you change your service provider, use Add... to set up the connection

3 Click Settings

4 Enter user name and password

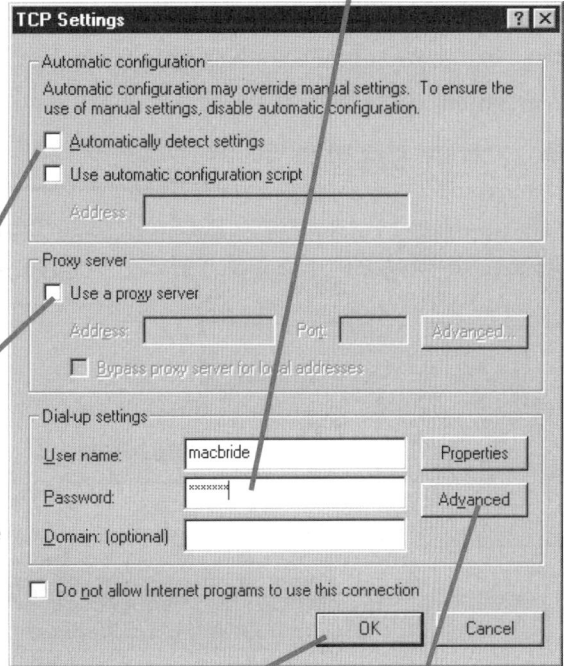

Internet Options `? ×`

General | Security | Content | Connections | Programs | Advanced |

Use the Connection Wizard to connect your computer to the Internet.   Setup...

Dial-up settings

BT Click
TCP (Default)

Add...
Remove
Settings...

○ Never dial a connection
○ Dial whenever a network connection is not present
◉ Always dial my default connection

Current default: TCP   Set Default

☐ Perform system security check before dialing

LAN settings

Edit local area network (LAN) settings   LAN Settings...

OK   Cancel   Apply

Check for shared folders?

If you are working from a LAN, you may need to set these – see your network manager.

TCP Settings `? ×`

Automatic configuration

Automatic configuration may override manual settings. To ensure the use of manual settings, disable automatic configuration.

☐ Automatically detect settings
☐ Use automatic configuration script

Address | |

Proxy server

☐ Use a proxy server

Address | | Port | | Advanced...

☐ Bypass proxy server for local addresses

Dial-up settings

User name: macbride   Properties
Password: ××××××××   Advanced
Domain: (optional) | |

☐ Do not allow Internet programs to use this connection

OK   Cancel

6 Set the redial values

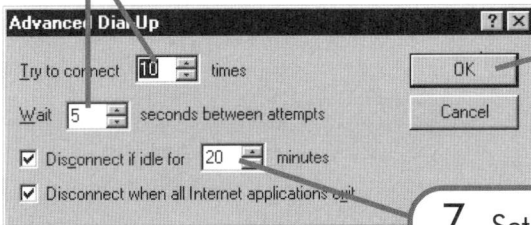

Advanced Dial Up `? ×`

Try to connect 10 ⬍ times   OK
Wait 5 ⬍ seconds between attempts   Cancel
☑ Disconnect if idle for 20 ⬍ minutes
☑ Disconnect when all Internet applications exit

8 Click OK

5 Click Advanced

7 Set idle time limit

Customizing the toolbars

The contents and layout of the toolbars can be adjusted to suit the way you work. It's easily done – and easily undone if you don't like your new display!

Toolbar buttons

There are several buttons which can be added to the toolbar. They don't offer any new functions, but can be more convenient than using the menus. Buttons are added through the Customize panel. You can also use this to:

- remove unwanted buttons to make more space;
- set the text labels to the right of or below the icons, or turn them off;
- set the size of the icons

1 Open the View menu, point to Toolbars and select Customize..

❑ **Adding buttons**

2 Select a button in the Available list and click Add -> .

3 Click Move Up to move it left along the toolbar, or Move Down to move it to the right.

❑ **Removing buttons**

4 Select a button in the Current list and click <- Remove .

❑ **Labels and icons**

5 Set the Text and Icon options from the drop-down lists.

1 Use View – Toolbars – Customize

View
Toolbars
✓ Status Bar
Explorer Bar
Go To
Stop   Esc
Refresh F5
Text Size
Encoding
Source
Full Screen F11

✓ Standard Buttons
✓ Address Bar
Links
Radio
Customize...

2 Select and Add

4 Select and Remove

Customize Toolbar   ? ✕

Available toolbar buttons: Current toolbar buttons: Close
Separator   History   Reset
Folders   Separator
Full Screen   Add ->   Mail
Size   <- Remove   Print
Cut   Edit
Copy   Separator   Move Up
Paste   Move Down

Text options: Show text labels
Icon options: Large icons

5 Set Text and Icon options

3 Move into place

Basic steps

❑ Moving toolbars

1 Point to the vertical line at the left of the toolbar and drag it up or down into position.

❑ Sharing space

2 Drag the line left or right as required.

❑ Hidden buttons

3 Click » to display the missing items.

Toolbar layout

All of the toolbars can be moved around within the top of the window area.

● They can be placed on separate lines, in any order, or share a line with one or more other toolbars.

● Where a line is shared, you can allocate as much space as you like to each bar.

● If there is not enough space to display all the contents of a toolbar, you will see » at the end.

3 Click to display the rest

2 Drag left or right

1 Drag into place

If you hold the mouse over a button, a 'tooltip' will pop up to tell you what it is

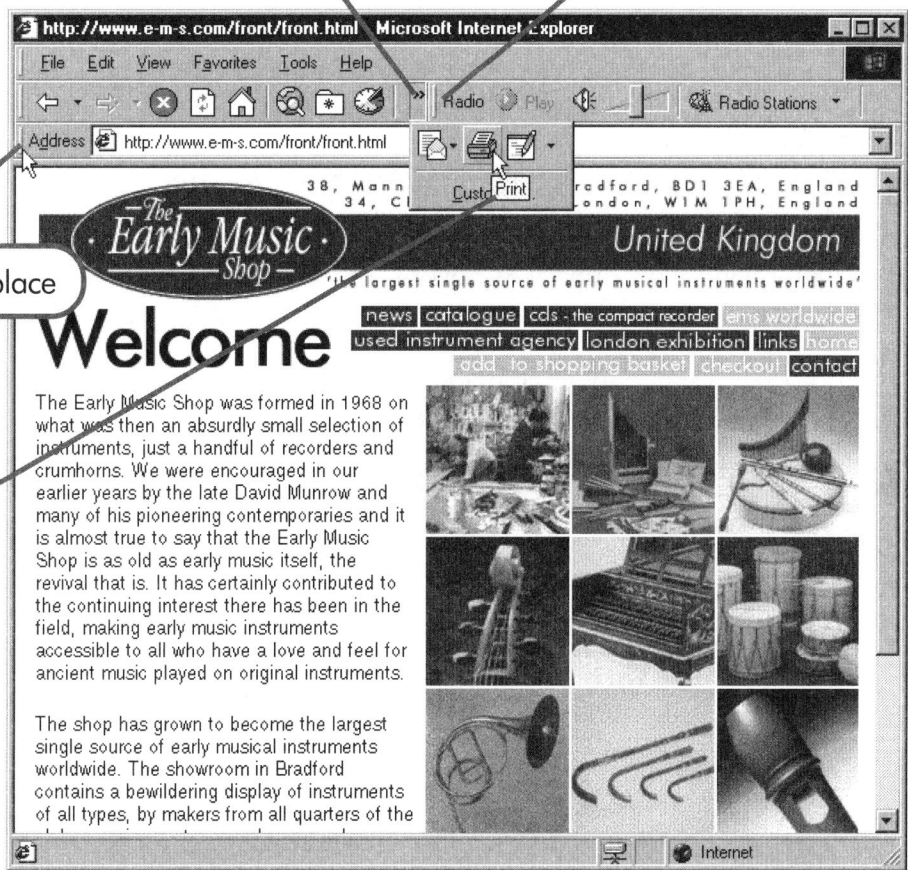

Summary

❑ Explorer is available in versions for most types of computer and operating systems.

❑ The software can be downloaded from Microsoft's Home Page, or wherever you see an Internet Explorer button. Microsoft also supply the IE suite on CD.

❑ Explorer is largely self-installing and does some of the necessary configuration for you.

❑ To get Internet Explorer working just the way you want it, spend some time on the options panels.

❑ Multimedia and active content make Web pages more interesting, but will slow down your surfing.

❑ The Security options help to keep your system safe from on-line dangers, and to restrict the sites that can be reached by other users of your system.

❑ The Connection Wizard makes it simple to set up your connection to your Internet access provider.

❑ When setting the Connection options, you will need addresses and other details from your service provider.

❑ You can customize the toolbars to suit yourself. The Toolbar, Address and Links buttons can be moved or removed, to create a larger viewing area.

3 Browsing the Web

URLs and hypertext

Uniform Resource Locators

Every page on the Web, every file in an FTP site, every newsgroup and every e-mail user have their own Uniform Resource Locator. These tell where and *how* to get to the item.

World Wide Web page URLs look like this:

http://www.heinemann.co.uk/bh/simple/simple.html

http:// (**h**yper**t**ext **t**ransfer **p**rotocol) this is a Web page.

www.heinemann.co.uk – the domain, or address of an organisation

bh/simple – the path to the directory

simple.html – the name of the file that creates the page.

Other URLS that you may meet are:

ftp: (**f**ile **t**ransfer **p**rotocol) – a file that can be downloaded from the archives of an FTP site. The better FTP sites now have user-friendly front-ends and use standard http: links.

news: the name of a newsgroup – linking to this will start Outlook Express to access the group (see Chapter 7).

mailto: an e-mail address – simplifies sending e-mail to the linked user (see page 137).

Hypertext

The World Wide Web is based on hypertext links. These are URLs embedded in the text or images of Web pages. Clicking on such a link makes Explorer try to connect to the identified item. Depending on the nature of the URL, Explorer will jump to a Web page, start to download a file, or open Outlook Express (Chapter 5) so that you can write to the person or read a newsgroup article.

Take note

Web URLs don't always include a page name. It is often missed out for the top page of a set of pages in a site or directory.

Punctuation is crucial. The slashes between the parts of the URL are forward slashes / – not the backslashes \ that are used in DOS and Windows.

Personal home pages will often have a tilde (~) before the user's name. e.g.

www.inet.co.uk/~jo99

E-mail addresses have an at sign (@) between the user's name and the supplier's name. e.g.

jobloggs@inet.co.uk/

Hypertext links

Pointing to hypertext linked images or words, makes the cursor change to a hand and the URL appear in the status bar at the bottom of the window.

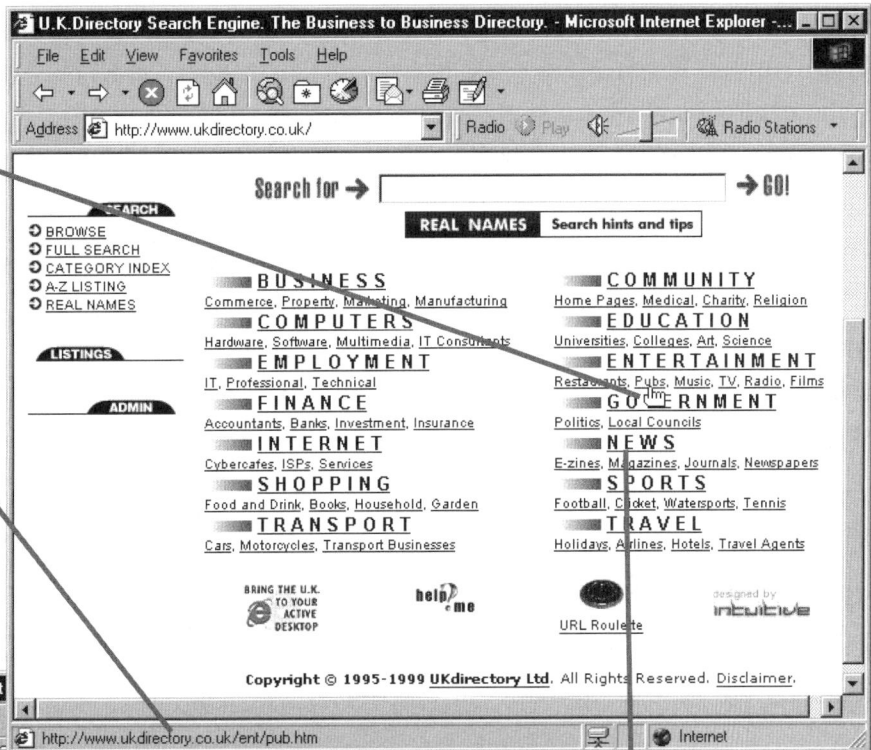

U.K.Directory Search Engine. The Business to Business Directory. - Microsoft Internet Explorer -...

File Edit View Favorites Tools Help

Address http://www.ukdirectory.co.uk/   Radio Play   Radio Stations

Search for →   → GO!

REAL NAMES   Search hints and tips

SEARCH
- BROWSE
- FULL SEARCH
- CATEGORY INDEX
- A-Z LISTING
- REAL NAMES

LISTINGS

ADMIN

BUSINESS
Commerce, Property, Marketing, Manufacturing
COMPUTERS
Hardware, Software, Multimedia, IT Consultants
EMPLOYMENT
IT, Professional, Technical
FINANCE
Accountants, Banks, Investment, Insurance
INTERNET
Cybercafes, ISPs, Services
SHOPPING
Food and Drink, Books, Household, Garden
TRANSPORT
Cars, Motorcycles, Transport Businesses

COMMUNITY
Home Pages, Medical, Charity, Religion
EDUCATION
Universities, Colleges, Art, Science
ENTERTAINMENT
Restaurants, Pubs, Music, TV, Radio, Films
GOVERNMENT
Politics, Local Councils
NEWS
E-zines, Magazines, Journals, Newspapers
SPORTS
Football, Cricket, Watersports, Tennis
TRAVEL
Holidays, Airlines, Hotels, Travel Agents

BRING THE U.K. TO YOUR ACTIVE DESKTOP   help me   URL Roulette   designed by intuitive

Copyright © 1995-1999 UKdirectory Ltd. All Rights Reserved. Disclaimer.

http://www.ukdirectory.co.uk/ent/pub.htm   Internet

Amazon.co.uk - Microsoft Internet

File Edit View Favorites Tools

Address subst/home/home.html/026-1394091-2023408   Radio Play   Radio Stations

BROWSE
by category
All Subjects   Go!

Visit Our Star Wars Hyperstore!

Orange Prize 1999 Shortlist

Join Associates:
sell books from your
Web site

Need a gift today?
Get a gift
certificate!

Join our Staff

Schools@amazon.co.uk
extra books for schools

Amazon.co.uk's Choice
From Portobello to Ministers without Portfolio, W11 is currently London's most talked-about neighbourhood and the inspiration for _Notting Hill_, a wry romantic comedy about what happens when Hollywood's most famous actress literally collides with an English bookseller. Behind-the-scenes photographs and stills illustrate the full screenplay published to accompany the release of the film from the team that swept to success with _Four Weddings and A Funeral_.

Check out the current Amazon.co.uk Hot 100!

In Entertainment
"We reserve the right to contradict ourselves" state the apostles of indie rock. The Manics preach the truth about _Everything_ in Simon Price's detailed chronicle of the Welsh supergroup's small-town roots and rise to fame. Including 10 in-depth essays, a comprehensive discography, a list of fan Web sites and some classic photos (featuring the

Internet

Hypertext links may be listed in a menu or embedded in the text.

They are normally shown underlined and in blue.

If the place has been visited recently, its link will be shown in a different colour – normally magenta.

Opening pages

Clicking on hypertext links is the simplest way to browse the Web, but you have to find some links in the first place, and sometimes will have come across an interesting URL in a newspaper, magazine or on the TV. No problem!

You can go to any place on the Internet as long as you have its URL. Actually, that is not quite true. You will occasionally come across the URLs of pages or files that can only be accessed by authorised people. Within a company or educational site, for example, some places may be open to the public, others restricted to members of the organisation.

1 If you have included the Address slot in your toolbar, type the URL into it and press the [Enter] key.

Otherwise:

2 Open the File menu and select Open.

3 Type the URL into the Open dialog box.

4 Click OK.

2 Select File – Open

File

New	▶
Open...	Ctrl+O
Edit with Microsoft FrontPage Editor	
Save	Ctrl+S
Save As...	
Page Setup...	
Print...	Ctrl+P
Send	▶
Import and Export...	
Properties	
✓ Work Offline	
Close	

1 Enter the URL into Address

The Early Music Shop - Microsoft Internet Explorer

File   Edit   View   Favorites   Tools   Help

Address   www.madesimple.co.uk   Radio ⟳ Play ◁ℰ   Radio Stations ▾

38, Manningham Lane, Bradford, BD1 3EA, Englan
34, Chiltern Street, London, W1M 1PH, Englan

The · Early Music ·

United Kingdom

usical instruments worldwid

We

Open

? X

Type the Internet address of a document or folder, and Internet Explorer will open it for you.

Open: www.madesimple.co.uk

☐ Open as Web Folder

OK   Cancel   Browse...

The Early
what was
instrumen
crumhorns
earlier yea
many of h
is almost true to say that the Early Music
Shop is as old as early music itself, the
revival that is. It has certainly contributed to
the continuing interest there has been in the
field, making early music instruments
accessible to all who have a love and feel for
ancient music played on original instruments.

The shop has grown to become the largest

3 Type the URL

4 Click OK

🕮   💻   🌐 Internet

Basic steps

...and re-opening them

- ❏ Re-using addresses

1 Drop down the Address list.

2 Click on an URL.

- ❏ Returning to a page

3 Click the Back or Forward button.

4 Drop down the Back or Forward list and select a title to visit a page.

Once you have been to a place, you have several simple ways back to it. Here are three:

- ● The **Back** and **Forward** buttons will move you through pages you have visited during the session – click to go to the one before or after, or drop down the list to pick from earlier (or later) pages.

- ● The **Address** drop-down list contains the URLs that you typed in. These are saved between sessions.

- ● The **History** keeps a record of the places that you visit (see next page).

1 Drop down the list

4 Select a page from the drop-down list

2 Select an address

3 Back one page

Made Simple Computer Series & Programm
Yell -
BH.COM
The Early Music Shop
THE EARLY MUSIC SHOP
THE EARLY MUSIC SHOP
Spinet Kit
Mediaeval Fiddle Kit

BH.COM - Microsoft Internet Explorer

File Edit View Favorites Tools Help

Address http://www.bh.com/madesimple/   Radio Play   Radio Stations

http://www.epson.com/
http://www.microsoft.com/
http://www.amazon.co.uk/
http://news.bbc.co.uk/
http://www.ukdirectory.co.uk/
http://www.yahoo.co.uk/
http://www.tcp.co.uk/
http://www.eyp.co.uk/
http://www.halifax.co.uk/
http://www.ukindex.co.uk/
http://www.cardiff.gov.uk/
http://members.cozycabin/screensaver/index.html
http://www.madesimple.co.uk/
http://www.amazon.com/

Site Map

Use these links to find out more about BH and our range of products for technical, management and medical professionals

Business Law, Economics etc).

There has since been a continuous process of updating books in the series in terms of content, and since 1994 titles in the 'blue' series have been published in a new larger, user-friendly format.

The brand was extended in 1994 to a computing series. This highly successful series provides easy to follow, jargon free guides to get you started on computer packages. April 1997 has seen the publication of the first titles from the new Made Simple Programming series.

Take note

The Forward button becomes active after you have gone Back.

37

The History list

As you browse, each page is recorded in the History list and its files are stored in the cache on your hard disk. Clicking the History button opens the list in the Explorer Bar, with the links normally organised into folders, according to site – this view can be changed.

History offline

If you want to use the History after you have gone offline, open the File menu and turn on the Work Offline. If a page actively draws from its home site – typically to get fresh adverts – you will not be able to open it offline.

Basic steps

1 Click the History button to open the list in the Explorer Bar.

2 Click to open a site's folder.

3 Select the page.

4 Click the X at the top right of the Explorer Bar to close it.

You can also view by Date, Most Visited or Order Visited Today

4 Close

1 Click History

2 Open a folder

3 Pick a page

If a link is greyed out, you cannot open it offline

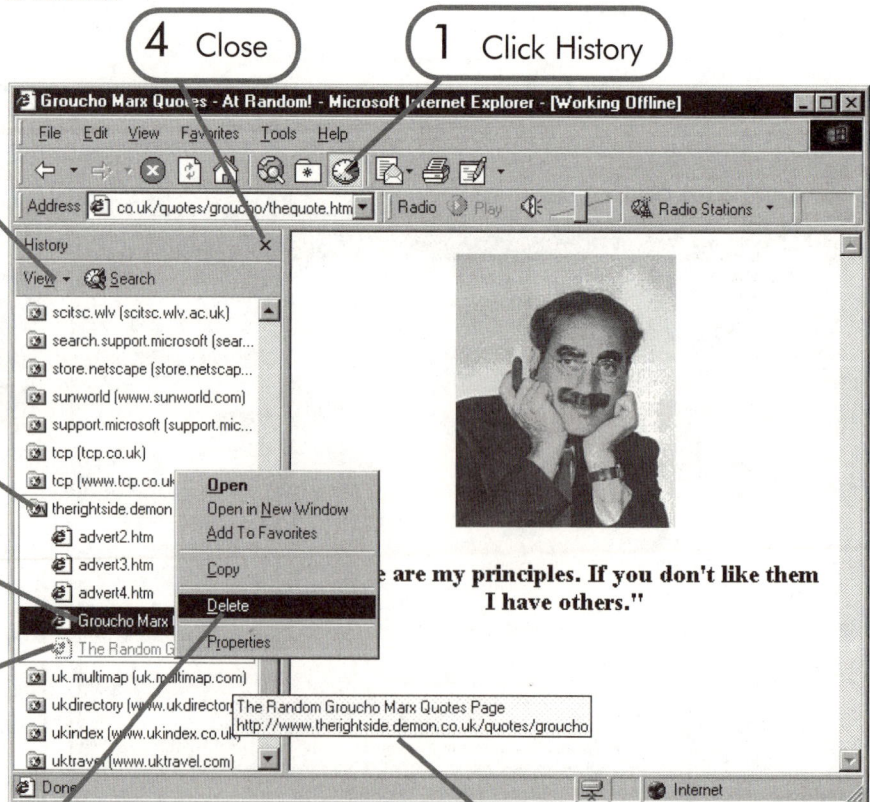

Unwanted items can be removed – right click for the short menu and select Delete

Hold the mouse over a link to see its full URL

38

Basic steps

1 From the File menu select Save As...

2 Set the folder and filename.

3 Set the Save as type – *HTML only* if you just want the page's text, or *Complete* to store all the files that make up the page.

4 Click Save.

Page files are erased from the History list after a while – how long depends on you (see page 20). If you want to keep a page for long-term reference, save it as a file on disk. It can then be opened from there at any time later.

If a page contains images, or it uses frames, use the **Web Page Complete** save option – this stores all the associated files in a folder of the same name.

1 Use File – Save As...

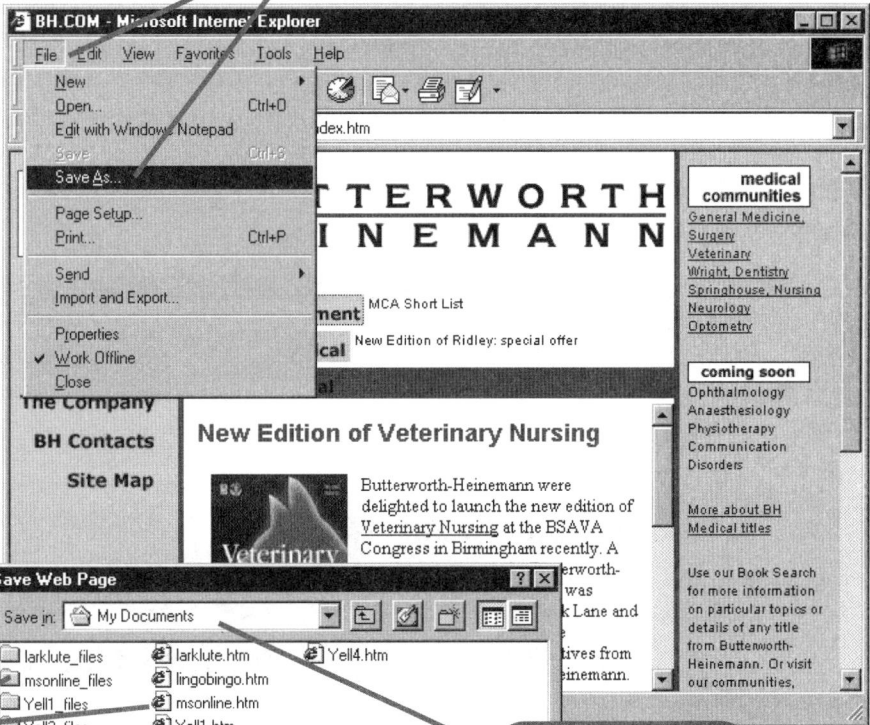

Tip

To re-open a saved page, use File—Open and Browse for it.

When a complete page is saved, there will be a matching folder for its extra files

3 Set the Save as type

2 Set the folder and filename

4 Click Save

Favorite places

Some good places are easy to find; others you discover over a long and painful search or by sheer chance. If you want to return to these pages in future, the simple solution is to add them to your Favorites. This stores the title and URL of the page as an *Internet Shortcut*, and puts the title onto the Favorites menu.

● If you want to go back to a page in a later session, you can simply pick it from the Favorites menu.

● You must have the page open to be able to add it to the Favorites – but you can do this offline by opening the page from the History list (page 38).

● The Favorites are stored in a folder. If you have a lot of entries, you can organise them (page 42) into new folders within this, creating submenus of Favorites.

1 Click ⊞Add... in the Explorer bar.

or

2 Open Favorites and select Add to Favorites.

3 Edit the name if needed.

4 To add it to the main menu, click OK.

or

5 To store it in a folder, click Create in>>.

6 Select the folder.

7 Click OK.

1 Click Add

about:blank - Microsoft Internet Explorer

File Edit View Favorites Tools Help

Add to Favorites...
Organize Favorites...

Address about:bl

Favorites
Add...   Organ
Links
Media
Software Updates
My Documents
Computing

PAGECOUNT
PCHTML Edito
The Common
TheJava(tm) C

directories
html
music
press
schools

music
ArthurRobb - L
Lute Tab
Guildof Americ
LarkIn The M
Musicmaker'sh
Olympic Music
SEMF _ South
The Big Mand
THE EARLY MUSIC SHOP
Worldwide Internet Music ...

RH.COM
Radio Station Guide
Web Events
Business information sources
CCTA Government Information Service
Department of Trade and Industry

LTG software_ LT XML
Management Web Resources Database
Netscape Browser Distribution
Permisison Request
The British Computer Society
The Linux Home Page at Linux Online
Extensible Markup Language
W3C's HTML Home Page
Welcome to MailExcite!
The Computer Information Centre

http://www.linux.org/

press

http://www.linux.org/

Open the menu or the Explorer bar and select the title to go to the page

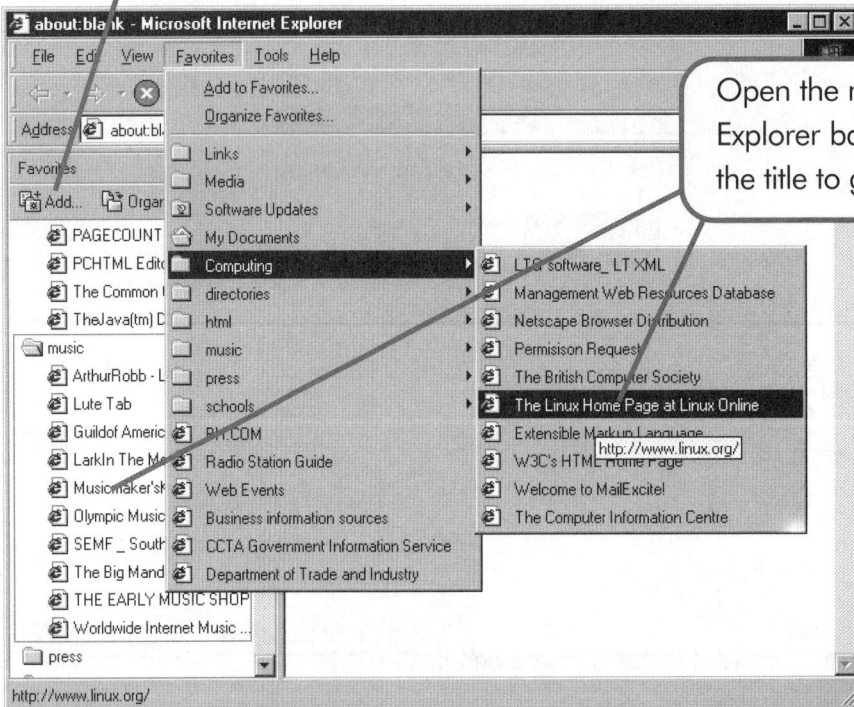

Click the toolbar button to open the Explorer Bar and work from there, or select from the drop-down Favorites menu.

40

Links to the site for
offline working –
see page 47

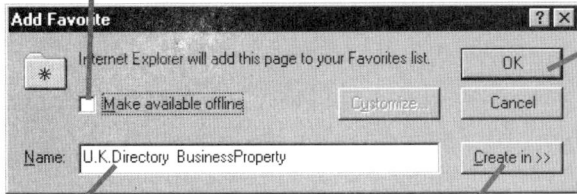

2 Choose Favorites –
Add to Favorites

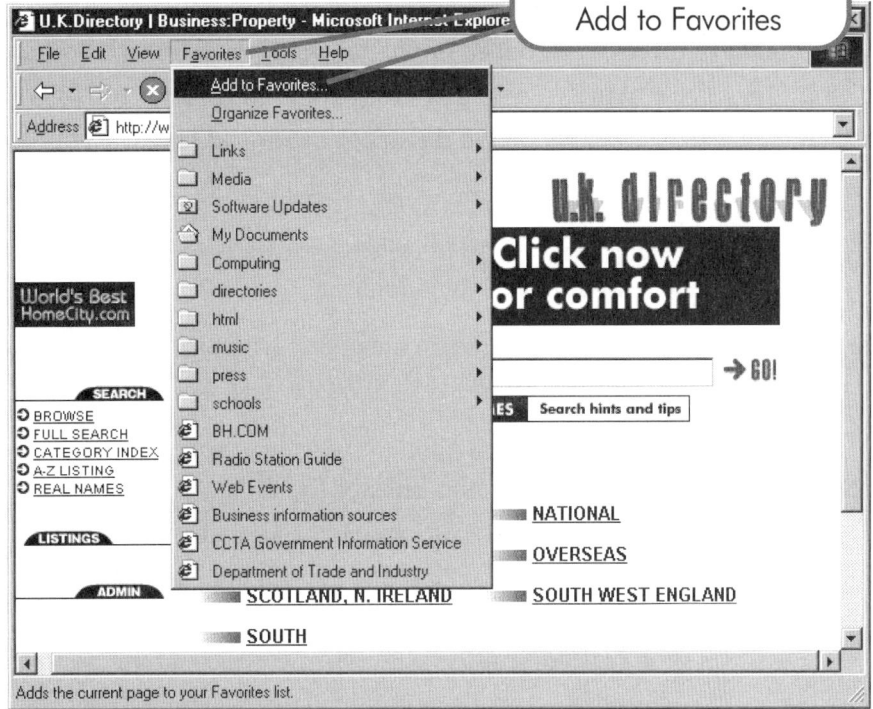

Adds the current page to your Favorites list.

4 Add to main menu?

7 Click OK

3 Edit the name?

5 Store in a folder?

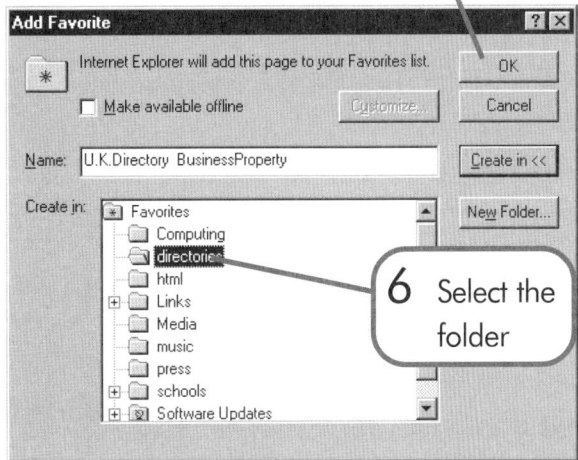

6 Select the
folder

Organising Favorites

The more titles you have on the menu, the harder it is to spot one. Once you have more than a dozen or so, they need organising. If you **Organize Favorites**, you can group them into folders, which then appear as items on the Favorites menu and lead to submenus.

● Before you start, decide which ones have something in common, and what to call their folders;

● Odd ones can be left on the main menu and grouped later.

Favorite names

Favorites take their names from the titles of the linked pages. These may need replacing or editing to produce more meaningful names – remember that the folder name is what appears on the menu.

1 Use Favorites –
Organize Favorites

Favorites
- Add to Favorites
- Organize Favorites
- What's New in IE 5 Beta
- Channels ▶
- Links ▶
- Media ▶
- Software Updates ▶
- My Documents
- Yahoo! UK & Ireland - ScienceBiologyZo...
- Yahoo! UK & Ireland Koi
- aboutblank
- New Folder ▶

Basic steps

1 Open the Favorites menu and select Organize Favorites or click ⌨ Organize... .

2 Click on Create Folder.

3 Change the name from *New Folder* to a more meaningful one.

❑ Renaming Favorites

4 Select the item.

5 Click Rename.

6 Enter a new name or edit the existing one.

7 Click Close.

2 Click the Create Folder button

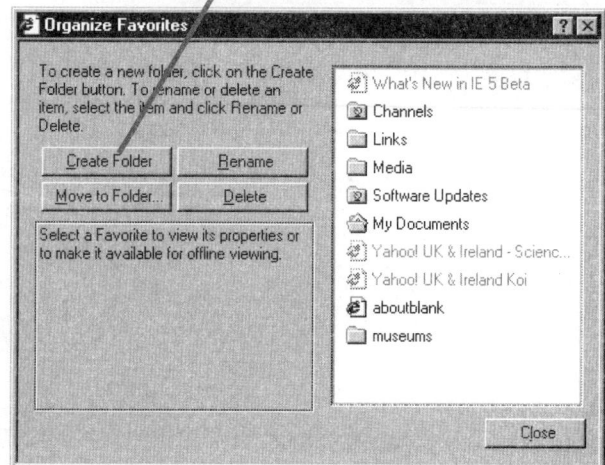

Organize Favorites

To create a new folder, click on the Create Folder button. To rename or delete an item, select the item and click Rename or Delete.

| Create Folder | Rename |
| Move to Folder... | Delete |

Select a Favorite to view its properties or to make it available for offline viewing.

- What's New in IE 5 Beta
- Channels
- Links
- Media
- Software Updates
- My Documents
- Yahoo! UK & Ireland - Scienc...
- Yahoo! UK & Ireland Koi
- aboutblank
- museums

Close

Take note

The Links folder controls the Links toolbar. Edit it to change the toolbar buttons.

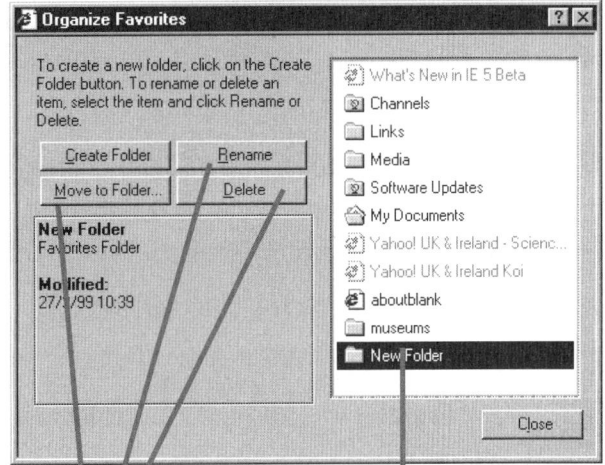

Organize Favorites

To create a new folder, click on the Create Folder button. To rename or delete an item, select the item and click Rename or Delete.

Create Folder | Rename
Move to Folder... | Delete

New Folder
Favorites Folder

Modified:
27/3/99 10:39

- What's New in IE 5 Beta
- Channels
- Links
- Media
- Software Updates
- My Documents
- Yahoo! UK & Ireland - Scienc...
- Yahoo! UK & Ireland Koi
- aboutblank
- museums
- New Folder

Close

3 Give it a meaningful name

You can Move, Rename or Delete files or folders

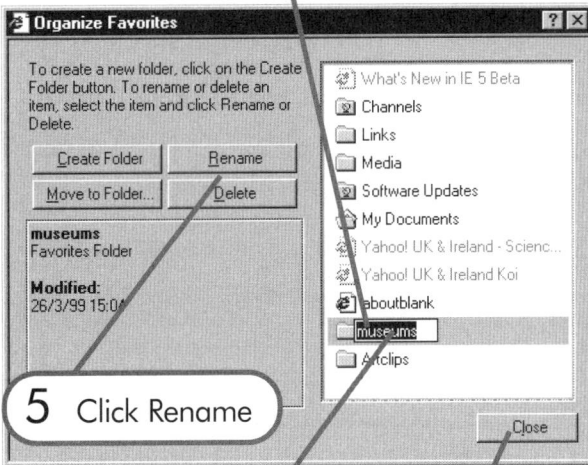

4 Select the item

Organize Favorites

To create a new folder, click on the Create Folder button. To rename or delete an item, select the item and click Rename or Delete.

Create Folder | Rename
Move to Folder... | Delete

museums
Favorites Folder

Modified:
26/3/99 15:0

- What's New in IE 5 Beta
- Channels
- Links
- Media
- Software Updates
- My Documents
- Yahoo! UK & Ireland - Scienc...
- Yahoo! UK & Ireland Koi
- aboutblank
- museums
- Artclips

Close

5 Click Rename

6 Edit or replace

7 Click Close

about:blank - Microsoft Internet Explorer

File Edit View Favorites Tools Help

Address about:blank

Favorites

Add... Organize...

- My Documents
- Computing
  - html
  - Management Web P...
  - Netscape Browser
  - Permission Reques
  - The British Compu
  - The Linux Home P
  - W3C's HTML Hom
  - Welcome to MailE
  - The Computer Info
- directories
- music
- press
- schools
- BH.COM

Open
Create New Folder
Print
Edit

Make available offline

Send To ▶

Cut
Copy

Delete
Rename

Properties

Done   Internet

You can rename, delete – and do other things – with Favorites in the Explorer bar. Just right-click to get the short menu.

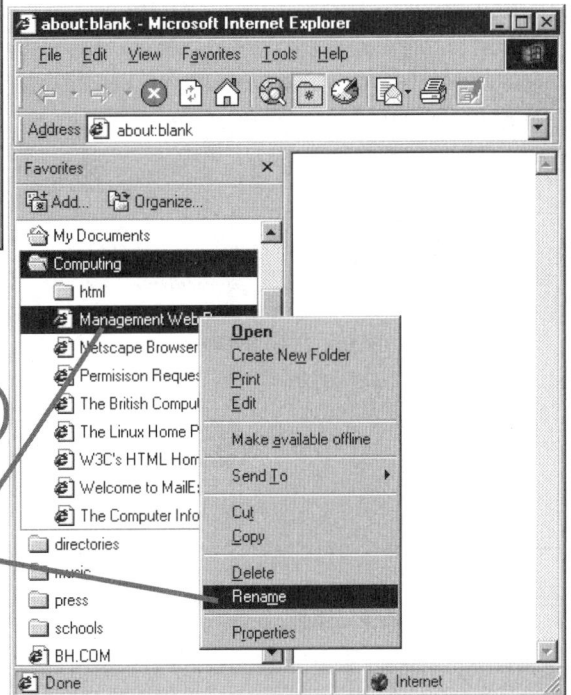

Moving shortcuts

Once you have created your new folders, you can move shortcuts out of the main Favorites folder and into the new ones – i.e. off the main menu and into submenus.

● If the shortcut and its target folder are both visible in the panel – and the window can be lengthened if it helps – you can move a shortcut by dragging it.

● If you cannot easily bring the target folder into view, you can use the Move button in the Organize Favorites panel.

● You can drag-move shortcuts and folders in the Favorites Explorer Bar.

The guideline shows where the shortcut will be inserted

The folder only opens if you pause before dropping the shortcut

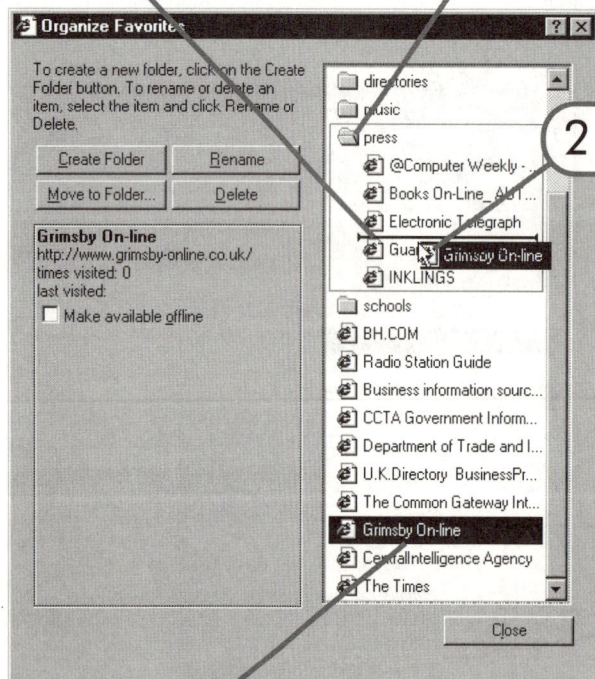

Organize Favorites

To create a new folder, click on the Create Folder button. To rename or delete an item, select the item and click Rename or Delete.

[Create Folder] [Rename]
[Move to Folder...] [Delete]

Grimsby On-line
http://www.grimsby-online.co.uk/
times visited: 0
last visited:

☐ Make available offline

- directories
- music
- press
  - @Computer Weekly - ...
  - Books On-Line_ AUT...
  - Electronic Telegraph
  - Gua Grimsby On-line
  - INKLINGS
- schools
- BH.COM
- Radio Station Guide
- Business information sourc...
- CCTA Government Inform...
- Department of Trade and I...
- U.K.Directory BusinessPr...
- The Common Gateway Int...
- Grimsby On-line
- CentralIntelligence Agency
- The Times

[Close]

2 Drag to the target

3 Release the mouse button

1 Select the shortcut

Basic steps

☐ Move by dragging

1 Select the shortcut.

2 Hold down the left mouse button and drag across the display until the target folder is highlighted.

3 Release the mouse button.

☐ The Move button

4 Select the shortcut.

5 Click Move to Folder.

6 Select the target folder.

7 Click OK.

Tip

If several people share Explorer and the Internet connection, set up a folder for each person's Favorites.

Organize Favorites

To create a new folder, click on the Create Folder button. To rename or delete an item, select the item and click Rename or Delete.

[Create Folder] [Rename]
[Move to Folder...] [Delete]

The British Monarchy
http://www.royal.gov.uk/
times visited: 0
last visited:

☐ Make available offline

📁 press
📁 schools
  📁 Links pages
  📁 Sites to see
    🔗 CCTA Governmen...
    🔗 EduWeb- The Le...
    🔗 First for Education...
    🔗 GCSE Answers
    🔗 GlobalClassroom
    🔗 NASA Photo Gallery
    🔗 National Museum ...
    🔗 NCET home page
    🔗 Netball Resources...
    🔗 Rigby Heinemann ...
    🔗 TheBritish Monarc...
    🔗 UK NetYear Web-...
    🔗 Welcome to MailE...
🔗 Educational Links
🔗 Learning Station

[Close]

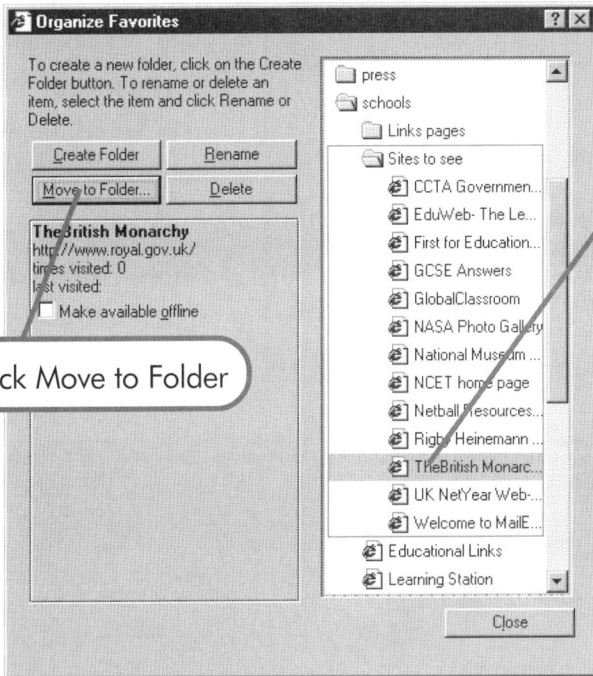

4   Select the shortcut

5   Click Move to Folder

6   Select the target

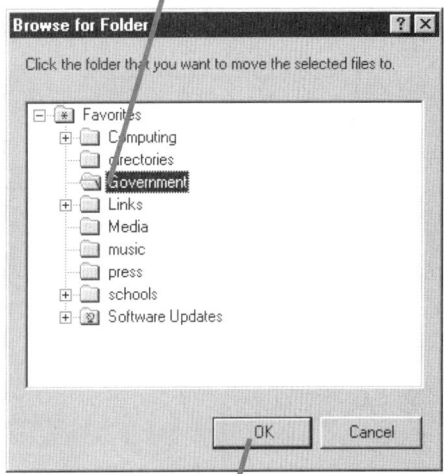

Browse for Folder

Click the folder that you want to move the selected files to.

☐ Favorites
  ☐ Computing
  ☐ directories
  ☐ Government
  ☐ Links
  ☐ Media
  ☐ music
  ☐ press
  ☐ schools
  ☐ Software Updates

[OK] [Cancel]

7   Click OK

Exploring - Favorites

File Edit View Go Favorites Tools Help

Address: C:\WINDOWS\Favorites

Folders

☐ Windows
  ☐ All Users
  ☐ Application Data
  ☐ Applog
  ☐ Catroot
  ☐ Command
  ☐ Config
  ☐ Cookies
  ☐ Cursors
  ☐ Desktop
  ☐ Downloaded Progra
  ☐ Drwatson
  ☐ Favorites
    ☐ Computing
    ☐ directories
    ☐ Government
    ☐ Links
    ☐ Media
    ☐ music
    ☐ press
    ☐ schools

Name	Size	Type
☐ Computing		File Folder
☐ directories		File Folder
☐ Government		File Folder
☐ Links		File Folder
☐ Media		File Folder
☐ music		File Folder
☐ press		File Folder
☐ schools		File Folder
☐ Software Updates		File Folder
🔗 BH.COM	1KB	Internet Shortcut
🔗 Business informati...	1KB	Internet Shortcut
🔗 CCTA Government...	1KB	Internet Shortcut
🔗 CentralIntelligence...	1KB	Internet Shortcut
🔗 Department of Tra...	1KB	Internet Shortcut
🔗 My Documents	1KB	Shortcut
🔗 Radio Station Guide	1KB	Internet Shortcut
🔗 The Common Gate...	1KB	Internet Shortcut
🔗 The Times	1KB	Internet Shortcut
🔗 U.K.Directory Busi...	1KB	Internet Shortcut

2 object(s) selected   95 byt 🖳 My Computer

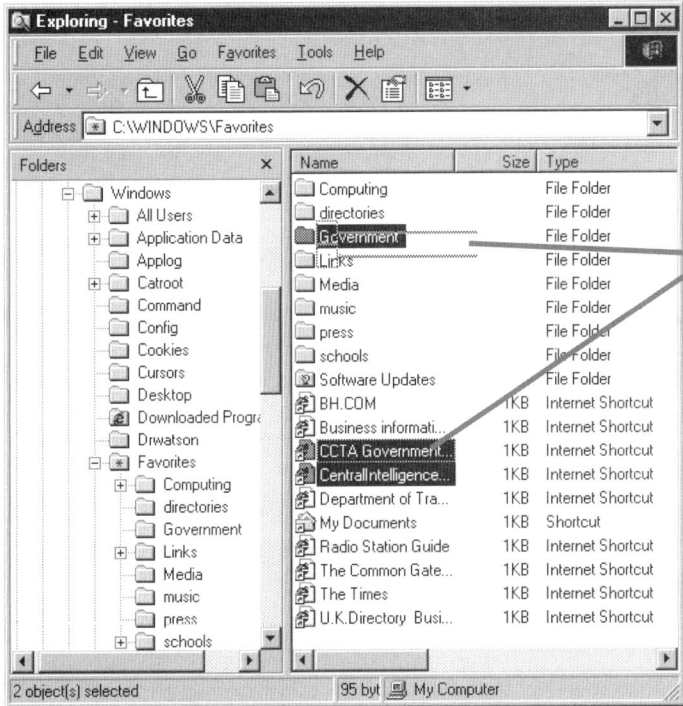

You can organise shortcuts in Windows Explorer by dragging them into folders

Take note

Favorites is a folder in C:\Windows. Open it in Windows Explorer, and you can delete or move files and sub-folders in the usual ways.

Desktop shortcuts

Do you use desktop shortcuts to your most-used applications, or to documents that you want to reopen in a hurry? You can also create desktop shortcuts to Internet sites. One click on the shortcut will then start the browser and make the connection.

● If you want to edit the shortcut's name, right-click and select Rename from the menu, or click twice – separately – into the name and retype or edit it.

1 Go to the page.

2 Drag the 🗐 icon (on the left of the Address) onto the desktop.

Or

3 Right-click and select Create Shortcut.

4 Click OK to confirm.

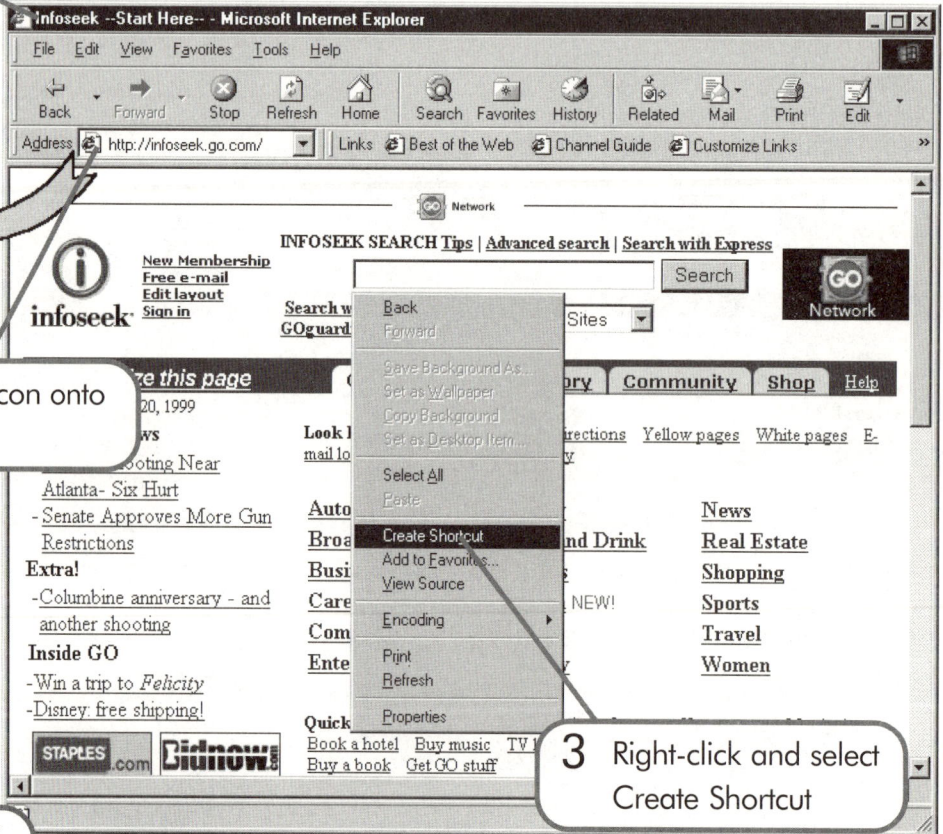

1 Go to the page

2 Drag the icon onto the desktop

3 Right-click and select Create Shortcut

4 Click OK

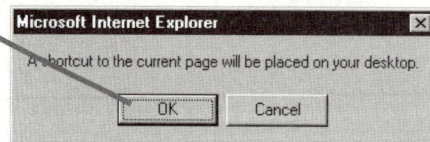

Working offline

1 Go to the top page of the site.

2 Start to addthe site to your Favorites.

3 Tick Make available offline.

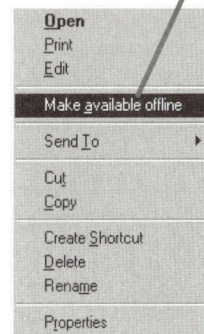

4 Click Customize.

❑ From a desktop shortcut or Favorite

5 Right-click and select Make available offline.

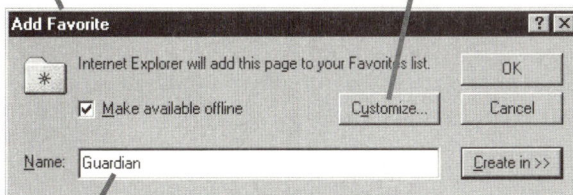

❑ However you start, you'll be taken into a Wizard to set things up – see the next page.

With IE 4.0, Microsoft intro... ...designed to provide a simpler way to get inform... ...urite sites. Instead of you having to go to the... information from them, the site would 'push' it... channel concept was not a huge success and has been dro...ed from IE5. In its place, we have Working offline, which is similar, but more flexible. You could only get a channel from a site if it provided information in channel form; you can set up a Working offline link to any site.

Once you have made a site available offline, IE5 will connect to it – either at scheduled times or on demand – and download any new or changed pages, which can then be viewed offline.

The system works best where you have a permanently open line to the Internet through your organisation – the updating can then be done automatically at set times. If you get online through a dial-up connection, you can get Explorer to do the updating in the background while you surf elsewhere. But there's not much bandwidth in a dial-up line, so other pages tend to come in slower while you are updating.

2 Add it to your Favorites

4 Click Customize

5 Right-click and select Make available offline

3 Tick Make available offline

Offline Favorite Wizard

Set up the following page:

Name: Welcome

URL: http://www.guardianunlimited.co.uk/

If this favorite contains links to other pages, would you like to make those pages available offline too?

○ No
◉ Yes

Download pages 1 links deep from this page

Note: If you have limited hard disk space or you want to reduce synchronization time, it's a good idea to limit the number of linked pages you store.

> 1 How many levels?

Offline Favorite Wizard

You can synchronize this page any time you are connected by choosing Synchronize from the Tools menu. You can also set up a schedule to synchronize this page automatically.

How would you like to synchronize this page?

◉ Only when I choose Synchronize from the Tools menu
○ I would like to create a new schedule

> 2 When you want or scheduled?

Offline Favorite Wizard

When would you like to synchronize this page?

Every 1 days at 00:30

Name: Guardian Update

☐ If my computer is not connected when this scheduled synchronization begins, automatically connect for me

> 3 Set the days and time

You can edit the name here

Do you want it to connect for you, if you are not online?

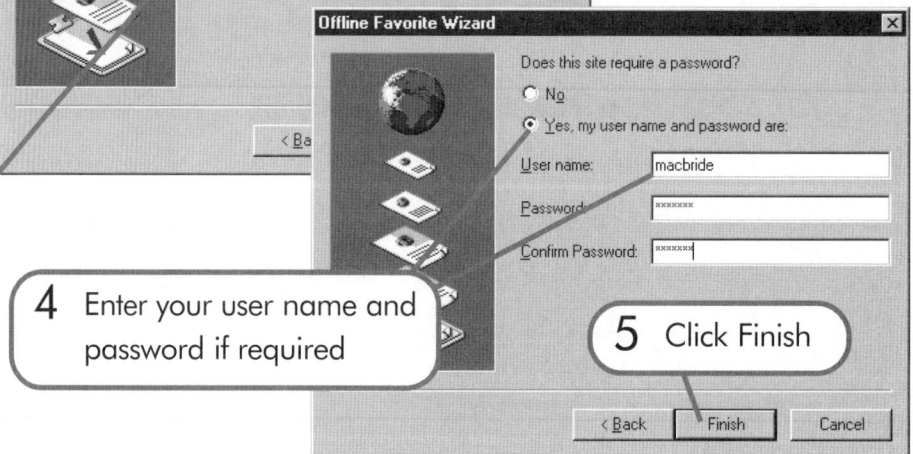

Offline Favorite Wizard

Does this site require a password?

○ No
◉ Yes, my user name and password are:

User name: macbride
Password: ×××××××
Confirm Password: ×××××××

> 4 Enter your user name and password if required

> 5 Click Finish

< Back | Finish | Cancel

Basic steps

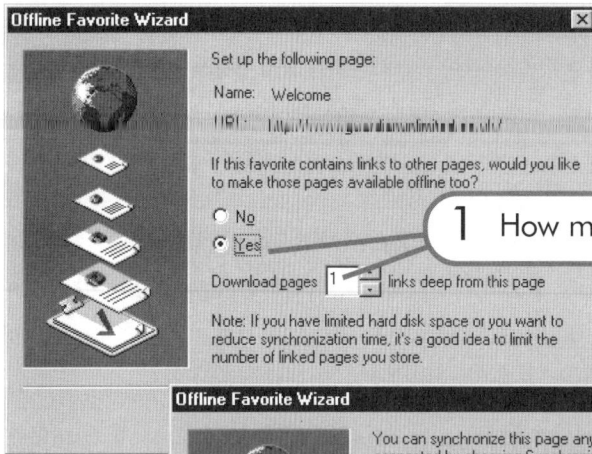

1 If you want the pages linked from the top page, tick Yes and set the number of levels.

2 If you want to update at set times, select create a new schedule.

3 For the schedule, enter the frequency and time of day.

4 Enter a user name and password if required.

5 Click Finish and the pages will download for the first time.

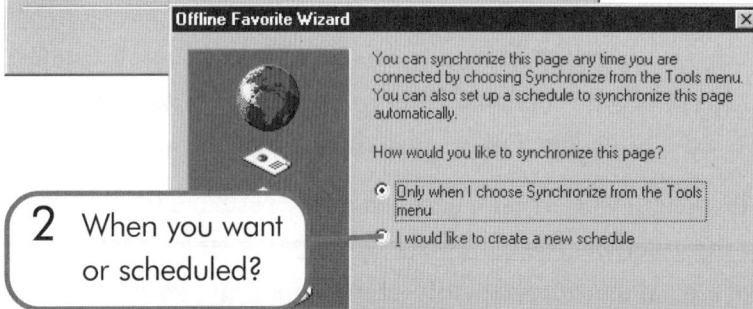

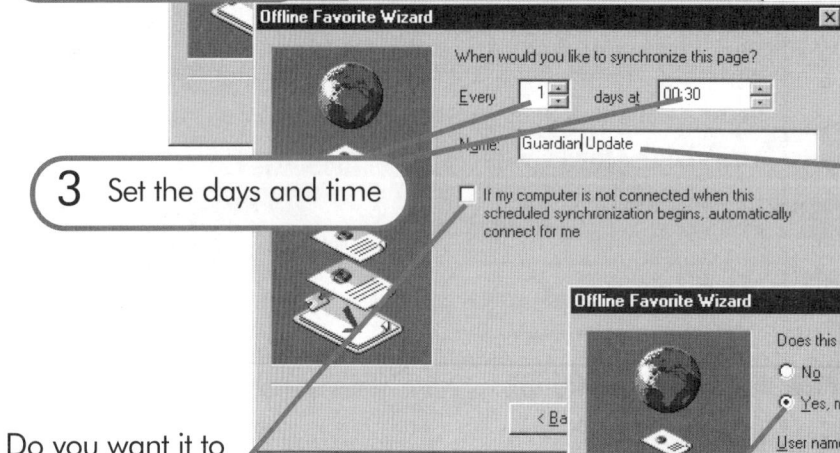

Basic steps

Fine-tuning the schedule

1 Right-click on the link and select Properties.

2 On the Schedule tab, select the link and click Edit.

3 On the Update panel, switch to Settings.

4 Set the Task Completed and Idle Time options as required.

5 Turn on one or both Power Management options if yours is a portable PC.

If you open the Properties panel for an offline link, you can edit the schedule, adjusting its times or setting how the update interacts with your other work – this is well worth checking if you want the update to run when the PC is otherwise idle.

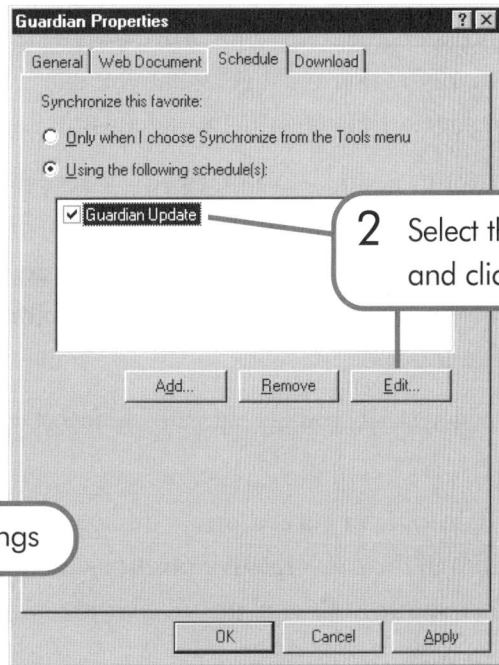

2 Select the link and click Edit

Adjust the times here

3 Go to Settings

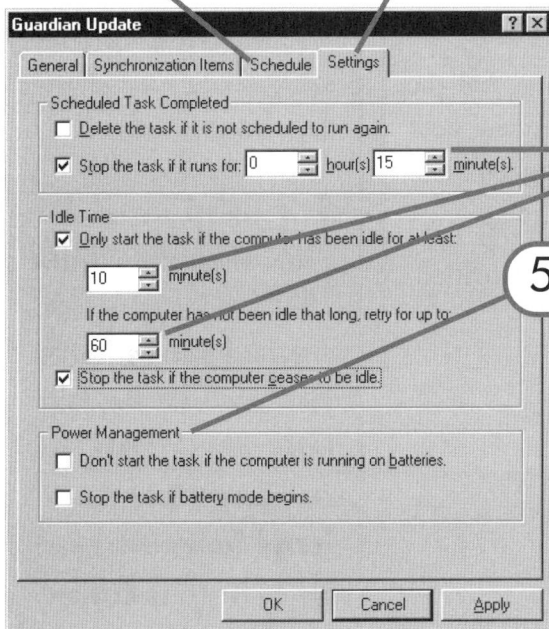

4 Set the Completed and Idle Time options

5 Portables need Power Management

In your own time

To manage updating for youself, turn off the schedule and click **Tools – Synchronize** when you want to update.

Printing

One of the beauties of HTML – the coding system used to create Web pages – is that it translates very well to paper. When you print a Web page, you get all the formatting and the same overall layout of text and images. There will be some minor differences in layout, but only because paper is a different width from a screen – just as the layout varies when you resize the browser window. And you don't just get what you can see on screen – the whole page, of however many screensful, can be printed.

When you print a simple – unframed – page, the options are much the same as for printing a word-processed document. You can choose your printer, the number of copies and which pages to print, though this last option is largely guesswork when going from screen to paper!

On a framed system, you also have a choice of which parts of the frame to print.

- **As laid out on screen** prints the entire page, with the frames in the same relative positions, and their contents shown in full – beyond the visible screen if appropriate.

- **Only the selected frame** prints only the one that the cursor is in. If you are not sure which is selected, hold down the left mouse button and drag to highlight a bit of text – the highlight won't show up on the printing.

- **All frames individually** gives you all the information, but without the layout.

Basic steps

1 Open the File menu and select Print…

2 Select the Printer and set its Properties as needed.

3 Set the Print range and number of Copies.

4 If it's a framed display, choose a Print frames option to print what you need.

5 Click OK.

Tip

On a typical framed display, one frame holds adverts or the site's logo, a second has navigation tools and only the third holds content that you really want. **Only the selected frame** is the best option for these displays.

BH.COM - Microsoft Internet Explorer

File Edit View Favorites Tools Help

New
Open...   Ctrl+O
Edit with Microsoft FrontPage Editor
Save   Ctrl+S
Save As...

Page Setup...
Print...   Ctrl+P

Send
Import and Export...

Properties
✓ Work Offline
Close

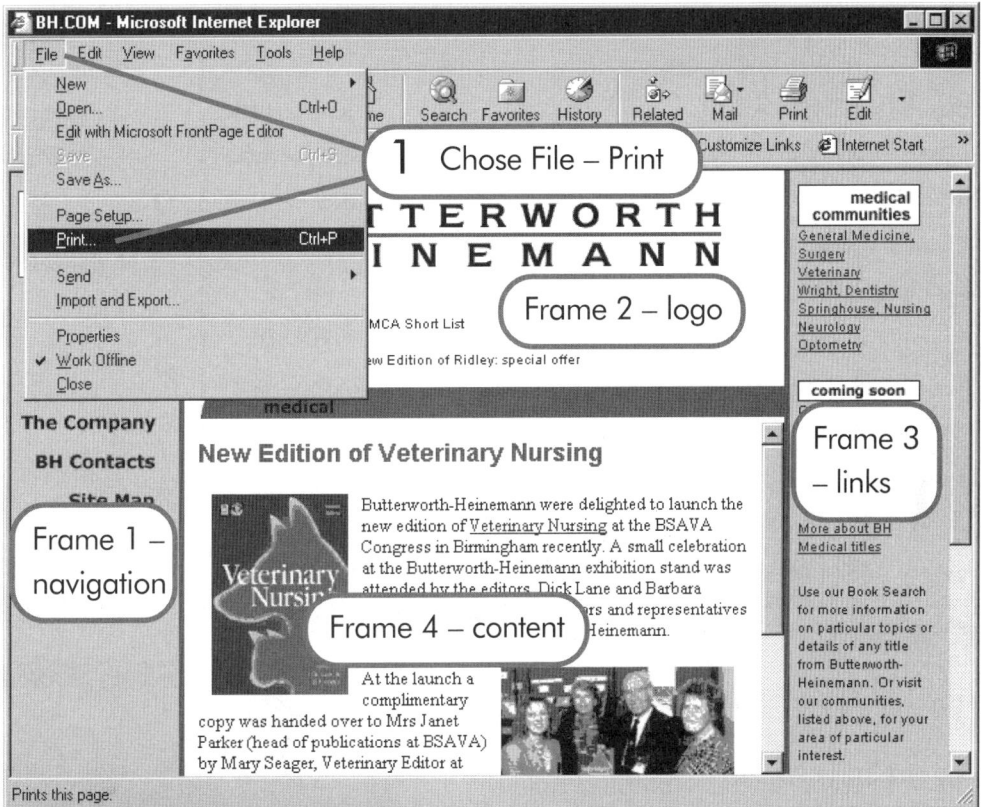

1 Chose File – Print

Frame 2 – logo

Search Favorites History Related Mail Print Edit

Customize Links   Internet Start

medical communities
General Medicine,
Surgery
Veterinary
Wright, Dentistry
Springhouse, Nursing
Neurology
Optometry

coming soon

Frame 3 – links

**TTERWORTH
INEMANN**

MCA Short List

ew Edition of Ridley: special offer

medical

The Company

BH Contacts

Site Map

Frame 1 – navigation

New Edition of Veterinary Nursing

Butterworth-Heinemann were delighted to launch the new edition of Veterinary Nursing at the BSAVA Congress in Birmingham recently. A small celebration at the Butterworth-Heinemann exhibition stand was attended by the editors, Dick Lane and Barbara rs and representatives Heinemann.

Frame 4 – content

At the launch a complimentary copy was handed over to Mrs Janet Parker (head of publications at BSAVA) by Mary Seager, Veterinary Editor at

More about BH
Medical titles

Use our Book Search for more information on particular topics or details of any title from Butterworth-Heinemann. Or visit our communities, listed above, for your area of particular interest.

Prints this page.

Print

Printer

Name: Brother HL-760   Properties

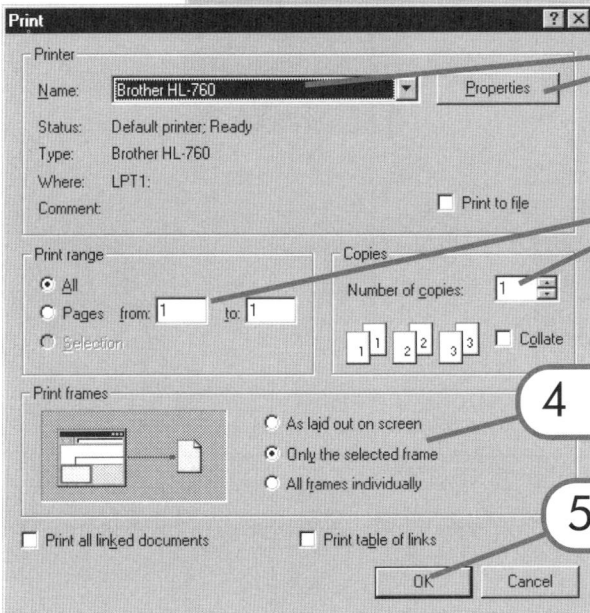

2 Set up the printer

Status: Default printer; Ready
Type: Brother HL-760
Where: LPT1:
Comment:

☐ Print to file

3 How much and how many?

Print range
◉ All
○ Pages from: 1 to: 1
○ Selection

Copies
Number of copies: 1

☐ Collate

Print frames
○ As laid out on screen
◉ Only the selected frame
○ All frames individually

4 Which parts?

5 Click OK

☐ Print all linked documents   ☐ Print table of links

OK   Cancel

Tip

Some pages might print better Landscape (sideways) – Click Properties to change the Orientation.

Active Desktop

The Active Desktop can hold interactive links to sites. You will find 'Add to Active Desktop' links at many sites, but the biggest source is at Microsoft's Active Desktop Gallery. The example shown here – the Search Component – gives you a simple way to hunt through dozens of the different search engines.

Basic steps

1 From Start, point to Settings then Active Desktop and select Customize...

2 Turn on View ACtive Desktop as a Web page.

3 Click [New...] and wait for the Gallery to download.

4 Select an element, click [Add to Active Desktop] and wait for it to download.

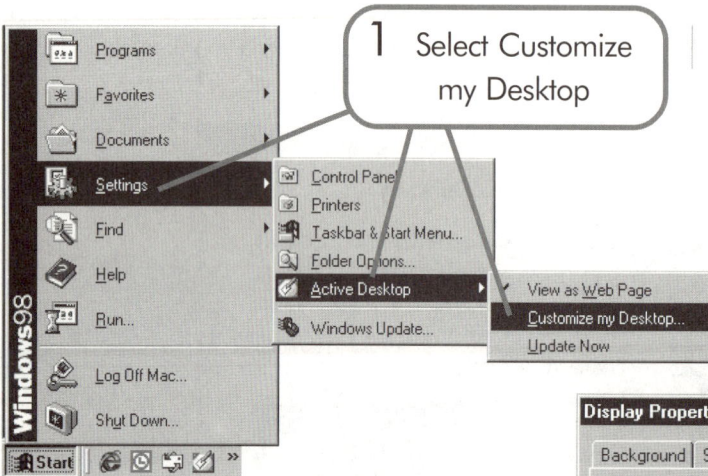

> **1** Select Customize my Desktop

Quick Launch toolbar – created automatically to give fast access to Explorer and related programs.

Mine has shortcuts to 🌐 Internet Explorer, 🔵 Outlook, 📨 Outlook Express and 📝 the Desktop (minimising all aplications)

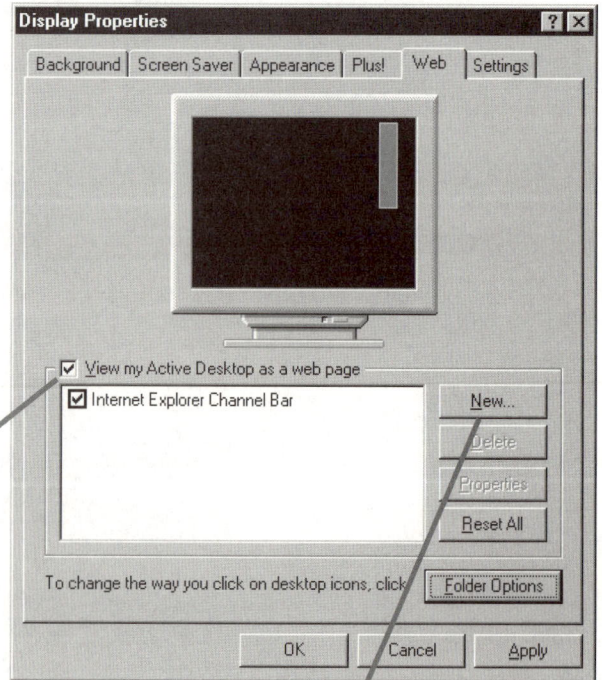

> **2** Turn on

> **3** Click New

- Using the Search component

5 Go online.

6 Select a Search Engine.

7 Type in one or more words to define what you are looking for.

8 Click **Go** ▶. Internet Explorer will open, linking to Microsoft, then on to the search engine, to find and display the results.

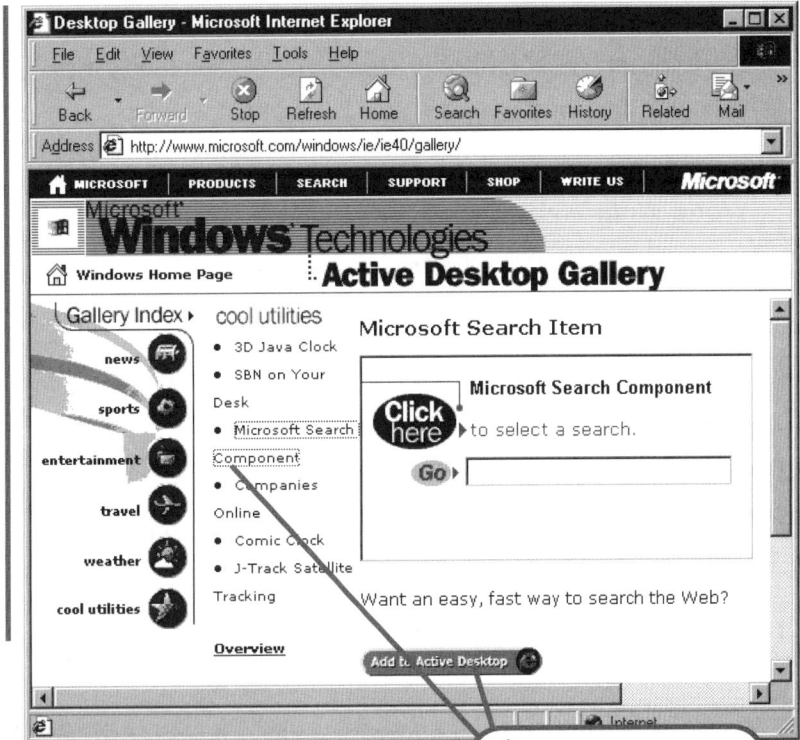

Desktop Gallery - Microsoft Internet Explorer

File Edit View Favorites Tools Help

Back Forward Stop Refresh Home Search Favorites History Related Mail

Address http://www.microsoft.com/windows/ie/ie40/gallery/

MICROSOFT PRODUCTS SEARCH SUPPORT SHOP WRITE US *Microsoft*

Microsoft **Windows** Technologies

Windows Home Page **Active Desktop Gallery**

Gallery Index ▶ **cool utilities** Microsoft Search Item

news • 3D Java Clock

• SBN on Your **Microsoft Search Component**

sports Desk **Click here** ▶ to select a search.

• Microsoft Search

entertainment Component **Go** ▶

• Companies

travel Online

• Comic Clock

weather • J-Track Satellite

cool utilities Tracking Want an easy, fast way to search the Web?

Overview Add to Active Desktop

4 Select and add to the Desktop

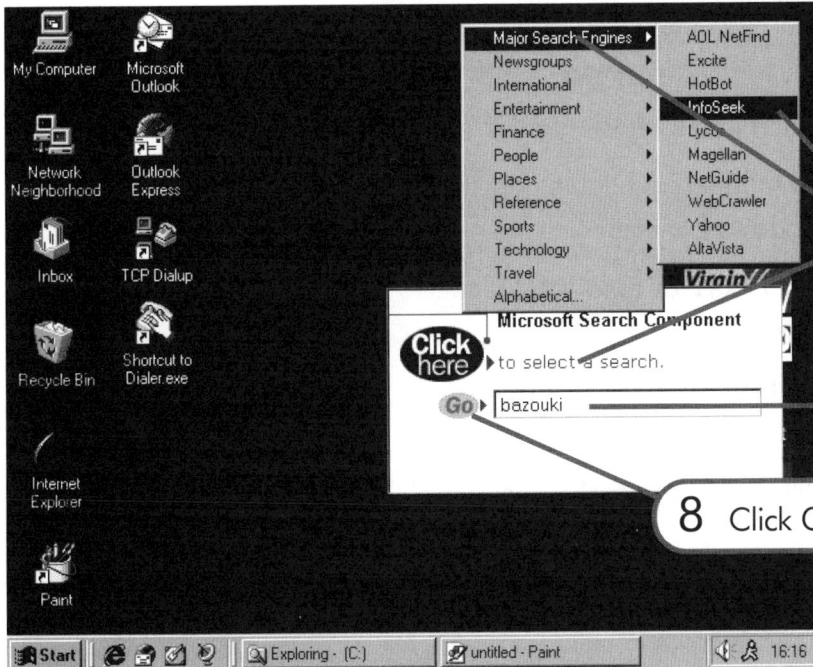

My Computer Microsoft Outlook

Network Neighborhood Outlook Express

Inbox TCP Dialup

Recycle Bin Shortcut to Dialer.exe

Internet Explorer

Paint

Major Search Engines ▶ | AOL NetFind
Newsgroups ▶ | Excite
International | HotBot
Entertainment ▶ | InfoSeek
Finance ▶ | Lycos
People ▶ | Magellan
Places ▶ | NetGuide
Reference ▶ | WebCrawler
Sports ▶ | Yahoo
Technology ▶ | AltaVista
Travel ▶ | *Virgin*
Alphabetical...

6 Pick an engine

Microsoft Search Component

Click here ▶ to select a search.

Go ▶ bazouki

7 Enter keywords

8 Click Go

Start Exploring - (C:) untitled - Paint 16:16

53

Summary

- ❏ Every page on the World Wide Web, and every file on the Internet has a Uniform Resource Locator (URL) that tells you how and where it can be found.

- ❏ Hypertext creates the links between pages on the World Wide Web.

- ❏ If you know the URL of a Web page, you can go direct to it using the File – Open command.

- ❏ The History list keeps a record of where you have been, providing a simple means of returning to a site.

- ❏ Pages can be saved as files for long-term reference.

- ❏ If you add a site to your Favorite places, you will have an easy means to get back to it another day.

- ❏ Favorites can be organised into folders, so that they appear in submenus on the Favorite menu.

- ❏ Favorite take their names from the titles of pages. If these are not clear, you can edit the name as you add the page to your set.

- ❏ New Favorites can be added into a chosen folder.

- ❏ Favorites can be moved into different folders, just as files can be moved in Windows Explorer.

- ❏ You can set up Desktop shortcuts for quick access to Internet sites you use regularly.

- ❏ When a site is set up for offline working, its main pages can be downloaded for later reading.

- ❏ Pages can be printed. With framed pages, you can choose which parts to print.

- ❏ Interactive links to sites can be created on the Active Desktop.

4 Starting to explore

Where do I start?

There are millions upon millions of Web sites – where do you want to go? If you know the address, there's no problem (see page 36), but if not, how are you going to find the way?

There are two main types of sites that can help you to find stuff on the Internet:

Directories, or catalogues, have organised sets of links. You use these as you might browse the shelves in a library. For instance, if you were researching the Battle of Waterloo, you'd head for the Humantities area, then the History stack and look under 19th Century, or Military History. Most directories have some kind of selection process to ensure that sites are in the right categories and not a complete waste of bandwidth. Some have very thorough reviewing and rating systems.

Search engines sites have 'spider' programs that constantly travel the Web, picking up words in the titles, descriptions or text of Web pages, and adding them to a database. The aim is to index the *whole* Web – an impossible task, given the rapid rate of growth and change, though some achieve a coverage of 90% or more. To use them, you enter one or more words to describe what you are looking for, and the site's search routine checks its database and gives you links to any pages where it found a match. These searches can return literally millions of 'hits', but a carefully defined search can produce a manageable number of relevant pages. Search engines are not discriminating – expect to get a lot of junk mixed in with the good stuff!

In this chapter we'll have a look at a few of the major directories and search engines. For more about these, and other aspects of using the Internet, try *The Internet Made Simple*.

Portals

❏ Portals are sites that act as gateways into the Web, each one hoping to be *the* place at which people will start their surfing sessions. They normally offer selected links on popular topics, shopping, travel, financial services, Web mail (see page 106), on-site games and other activities designed to bring you into the site and keep you there as long as possible. (Their income is from advertisers who pay by the number of times the ads are seen.)

Many directories, search engines and other major 'content provider' sites (i.e. those offering news, guidance, shareware, etc.) have turned themselves into portals over the last couple of years.

Basic steps

1 Click Home.

2 Click Personalize My MSN or the ⊃ at the end of the paragraph.

3 Give your name and e-mail address.

4 Tick the options to choose the features.

5 Click 🔵 and wait a few moments.

The default 'Home page', the one linked from the Home button, and where you go at the start of every session, is at MSN (MicroSoft Network) – this can be changed through the General options (page 20). If you decide to keep this portal as your Home page, you can personalise its contents to show the types of news and other features that interest you.

If you have changed your Home page, enter the address msn.co.uk or click Internet Start on the Links bar – that also leads to MSN

1 Click Home

Welcome to MSN UK - Microsoft Internet Explorer

File   Edit   View   Favorites   Tools   Help

Back   Forward   Stop   Refresh   Home   Search   Favorites   History   Related   Mail   Print   Edit

Address http://msn.co.uk/default.asp

msn. Microsoft

What are you looking for?

msn.co.uk home   The Best of the Internet in One Place   Make this your Home Page

Channels
- News
- Computing
- Business
- Entertainment
- Football
- Chat
- Shopping

Today on MSN - Sunday, June 06, 1999

THAT'S ENTERTAINMENT

⊃ WANT TO know What's On and where? Check out our Entertainment Channel and plan your leisure time.

⊃ Cricket World Cup
⊃ Euro 2000 horror
⊃ Drop the Debt Chat Special
⊃ Peace talks continue

New MSN Entertainment Channel

Now on MSN

Promote your website with LinkExchange
○ CLICK HERE

The Gaming Zone on MSN
○ CLICK HERE

Shopping on MSN
○ CLICK HERE

Things to do
⊃ Personalise
⊃ Look up Sh
⊃ Free E-mai
⊃ Free MSN n
⊃ Find a Film
⊃ Search MSN
⊃ Online Wea
⊃ Buy books
⊃ Download S
⊃ Add your F
⊃ Advertise o
⊃ Contact Us
⊃ Feedback

2 Click Personalise My MSN

Index Page ▼ go

Search for

MSN Search ▼ 🔍

? About MSN
? Help
? MSN WorldWide

MSN Hotmail Check E-Mail name:_____ password:_____   🔵 Register for MSN Hotmail

Personalise My MSN

MY MSN   You can tailor this area so it gives you everything that you want from the Web, quickly, everytime you visit.
Just click on the things you like to make this page into whatever you're into. It really is that simple - click here for a step by step guide ⊃

© 1999 Microsoft and its suppliers. All rights reserved.
⊃Terms of use ⊃Privacy Statement ⊃Advertise ⊃Feedback

GET Microsoft Internet Explorer

http://msn.co.uk/personalize/personform2.asp?front=yes&status=never   Internet

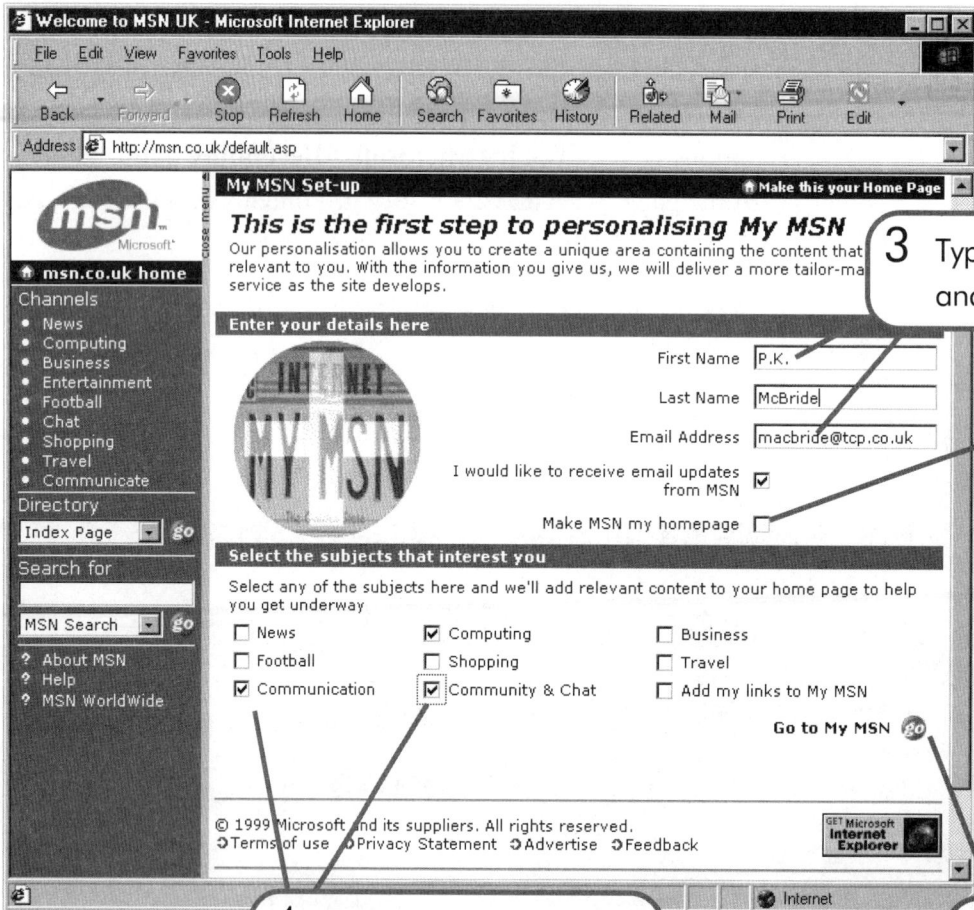

Welcome to MSN UK - Microsoft Internet Explorer

File   Edit   View   Favorites   Tools   Help

Back   Forward   Stop   Refresh   Home   Search   Favorites   History   Related   Mail   Print   Edit

Address http://msn.co.uk/default.asp

My MSN Set-up   🏠 **Make this your Home Page**

This is the first step to personalising My MSN

Our personalisation allows you to create a unique area containing the content that
relevant to you. With the information you give us, we will deliver a more tailor-ma
service as the site develops.

Enter your details here

First Name   P.K.

Last Name   McBride

Email Address   macbride@tcp.co.uk

I would like to receive email updates
from MSN   ☑

Make MSN my homepage   ☐

Select the subjects that interest you

Select any of the subjects here and we'll add relevant content to your home page to help
you get underway

☐ News   ☑ Computing   ☐ Business
☐ Football   ☐ Shopping   ☐ Travel
☑ Communication   ☑ Community & Chat   ☐ Add my links to My MSN

Go to My MSN 🔘

© 1999 Microsoft and its suppliers. All rights reserved.
↺Terms of use ↺Privacy Statement ↺Advertise ↺Feedback

msn. Microsoft®

🏠 **msn.co.uk home**

Channels
• News
• Computing
• Business
• Entertainment
• Football
• Chat
• Shopping
• Travel
• Communicate

Directory
Index Page ▾ go

Search for
MSN Search ▾ go

? About MSN
? Help
? MSN WorldWide

🌐 Internet

---

3 Type your name and address

Set the Home Page on the Internet Options

4 Tick the things you want

5 Click Go

Tip

If you are in an area of MSN that you would like to include on your Home page, look for and click on its **+ Add to My MSN** button.

Take note

MSN is by no means the only site offering personalised Home pages online. Other good sites include Excite (www.excite.co.uk), Lycos (www.lycos.co.uk), Netcenter (www.netcenter.com) and Yahoo (www.yahoo.co.uk).

Basic steps

1 Click the Best of the Web link.

2 Select an area from the Index.

3 Pick a category.

4 Start browsing!

The Best of the Web link leads to MSN's **Web Directory**. This is a collection of links to selected sites, organised into topics and sub-topics. If you are looking for a good place to start your browsing, why not try Microsoft's **Best of the Web**. This is a catalogue of selected links, grouped under topic headings. Just click on the **Links** button to connect.

1 Click Best of the Web

2 Select an area

3 Pick a category

4 Start browsing

Web Directory

| msn.com home | personalize | web directory | microsoft.com | help |

index

best of the web	categories
business	Books and publishing
computers & internet	Film and video
education & reference	Fun and games
entertainment	Music and performing arts
health	TV and radio
home & family	
lifestyles & hobbies	
news	
shopping	
sports	
travel	

search
MSN
go

best of entertainment sites:
El Online
Entertainment Drive
Entertainment Weekly
Hollywood Online
MSBET
NBC
People
Warner Bros. Online

news

MSN Gaming Zone
click to add to your MSN.COM home page
Midtown Madness New Upgrade Playable on Zone
Check Out the Preview Area of Asheron's Call
Backgammon Backyard Barbecue Tourney Signup

MTV
click to add to your MSN.COM home page
Limp Bizkit Taps Kid Rock For Summer Tour
Chili Peppers Give It Away Online; Join Beasties, Others On MOM Benefit
98 Degrees Goes Back To High School

Warner Bros Online
click to add to your MSN.COM home page
Win A Complete Home Theater At "You've Got Mail!"
Build A Free Home Page With The Women Of "Charmed!"
Don't Leave Home Without The Rules Of Dating!

events
Click here to select a different time zone.
broadcast.com Events
click to add to your MSN.COM home page
00:00 GMT - Fancast with Hedwig and The Angry Inch - broadcast.com - Audio
16:00 GMT - 05/27/99 - Young Presidents' Organization Presidents' University -

http://www.msn.com/exploring/subcats/Y8315T4.HTM   Internet

Yahoo

Yahoo was one of the first, and is still one of the biggest and best Net directories. It now has national sites in many countries and offers a wide range of portal services, but its main attraction remains its superb directory, with links to over a million selected Web pages and newsgroups. These are organised into a hierarchy of categories with extensive cross-referencing.

Once you get past the first level, you find a mixture of links to pages and lists of subcategories, with the links increasing as you go down the hierarchy. For specialist topics you may need to work down through three or four levels of menus.

Basic steps

1 Go to Yahoo at
www.yahoo.com
or www.yahoo.co.uk

2 Click on a category.

3 Select a category from the next menu – repeat as necessary.

4 When you reach the links, select one.

1 Go to Yahoo

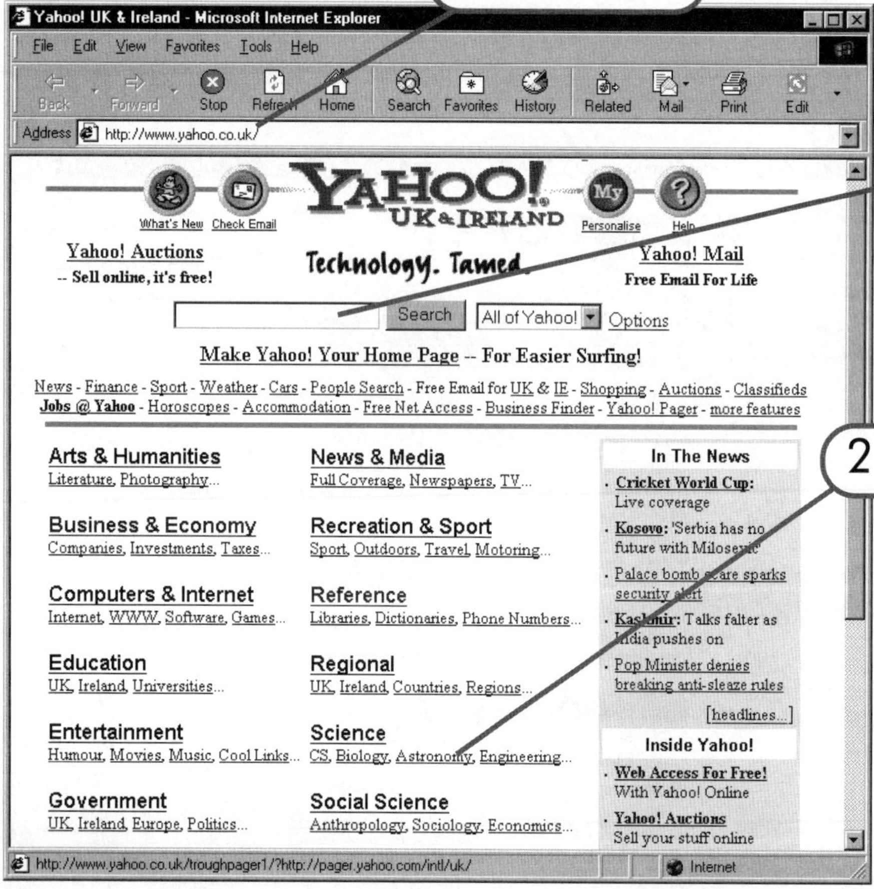

Try searching for a keyword if you are not sure which category to start looking in

2 Select a category

The top menu lists major categories and some of the second level of categories

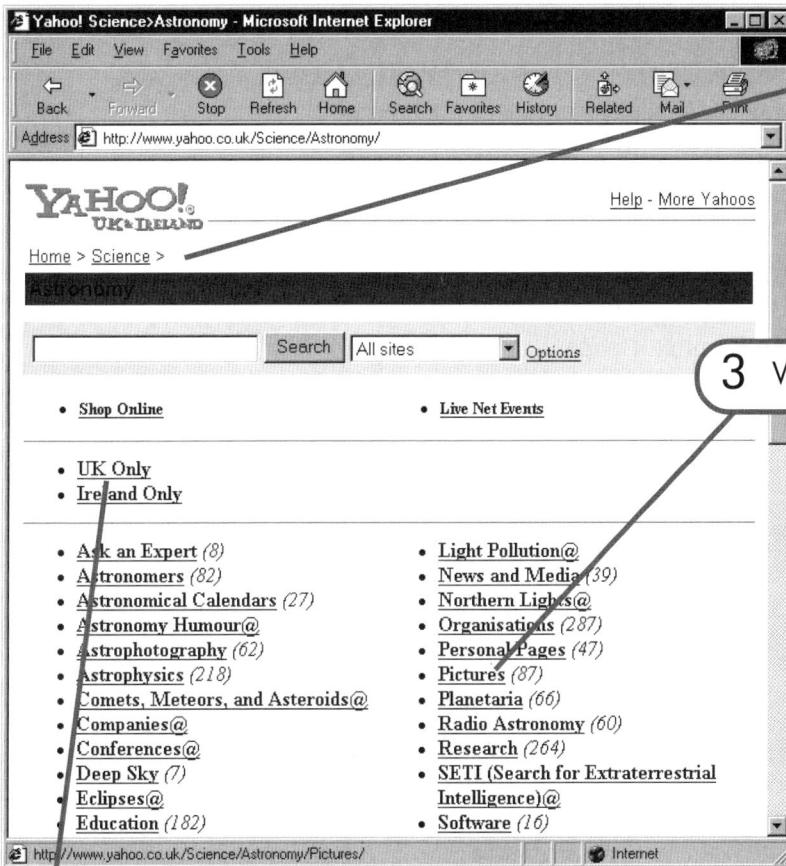

Click Back or use the links to return to a higher level

3 Work through the categories

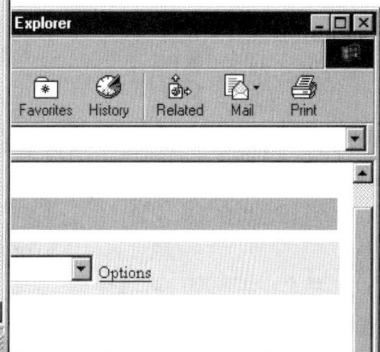

You can limit the display to the UK only, but UK-based sites are listed at the top of the links

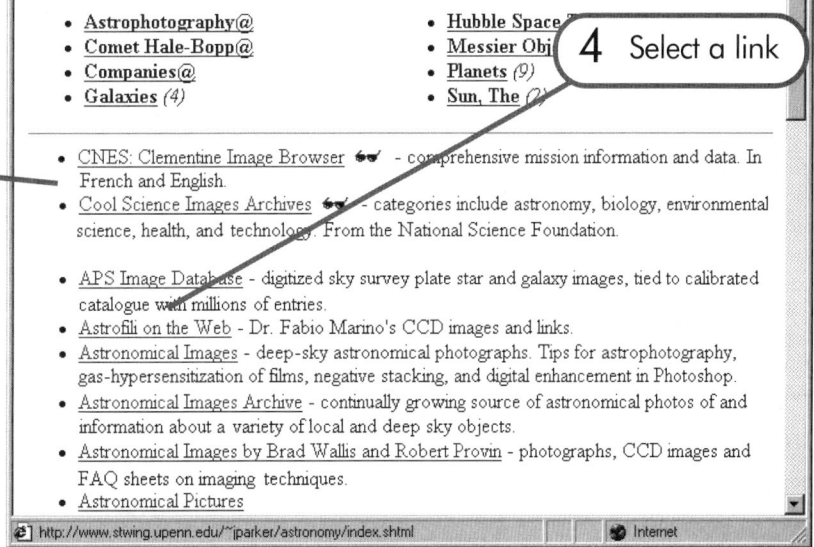

4 Select a link

As you work down through the menus, you usually get more links and fewer subcategories

Searching in Explorer

Directories are good for initial research on a topic, but if you want specific information, you may be better with a search. You can run a search in the Explorer Bar for Web pages, newsgroups, maps and words (in *Encarta*, Microsoft's encyclopedia).

This is a convenient way to handle searches – you can switch easily between viewing results and running new searches – but it may not always work that well. To search efficiently, you should go to the search sites (see the next 4 pages).

Basic steps

1 Click the Search tool.

2 Select a category.

3 Enter a word or phrase.

4 Click Search.

5 You are taken to Excite for the results – click a link to view its page.

6 If you don't find what you want, start a new search at Excite.

1 Click Search

2 Pick a category

Gives the Encarta encyclopedia entry

3 Enter search word(s)

4 Click Search

I happened to be at MSN when I started this search – it doesn't matter where you are when you start

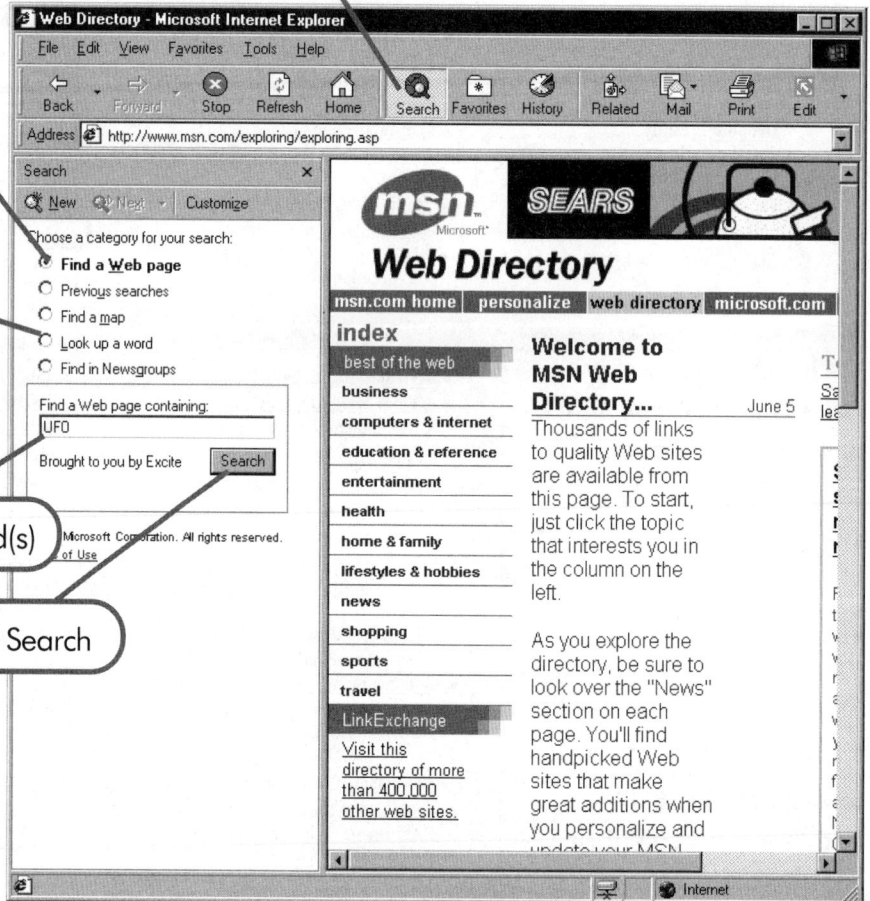

Web Directory - Microsoft Internet Explorer

File   Edit   View   Favorites   Tools   Help

Back   Forward   Stop   Refresh   Home   Search   Favorites   History   Related   Mail   Print   Edit

Address http://www.msn.com/exploring/exploring.asp

Search

New   Next   Customize

Choose a category for your search:

- Find a Web page
- Previous searches
- Find a map
- Look up a word
- Find in Newsgroups

Find a Web page containing:

UFO

Brought to you by Excite   Search

Microsoft Corporation. All rights reserved. of Use

msn SEARS

Web Directory

msn.com home | personalize | web directory | microsoft.com

index

best of the web
business
computers & internet
education & reference
entertainment
health
home & family
lifestyles & hobbies
news
shopping
sports
travel
LinkExchange

Visit this directory of more than 400,000 other web sites.

Welcome to MSN Web Directory... June 5

Thousands of links to quality Web sites are available from this page. To start, just click the topic that interests you in the column on the left.

As you explore the directory, be sure to look over the "News" section on each page. You'll find handpicked Web sites that make great additions when you personalize and update your MSN.

Internet

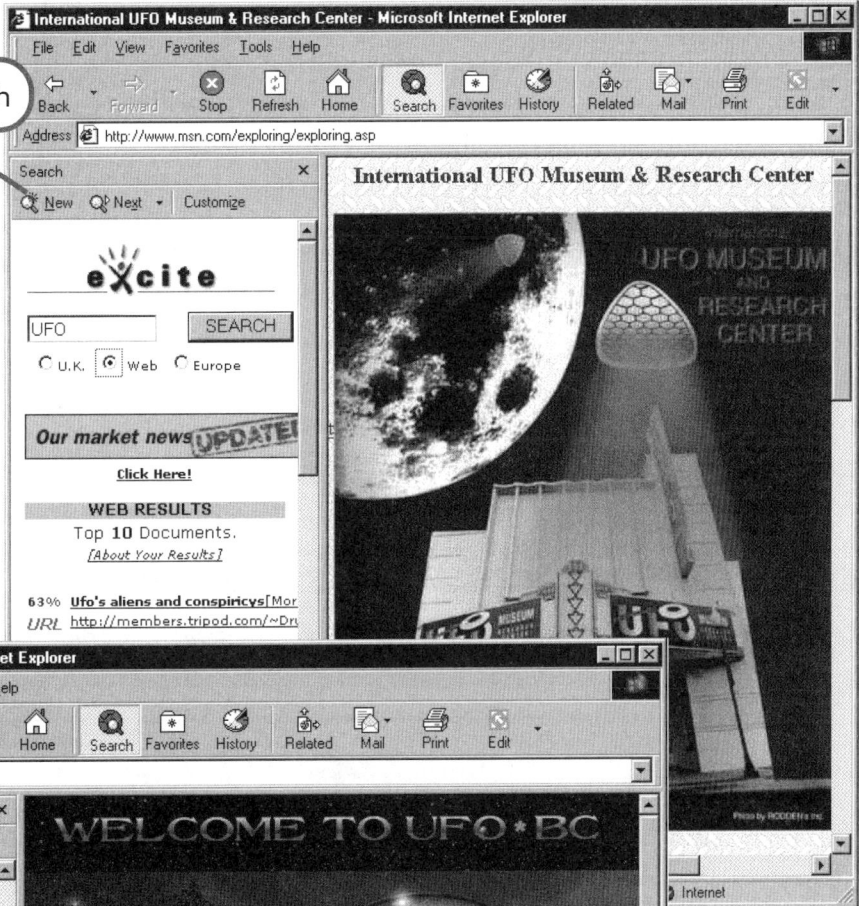

6 Start a new search

The Explorer Bar remains unchanged even if you follow up links in the main display area

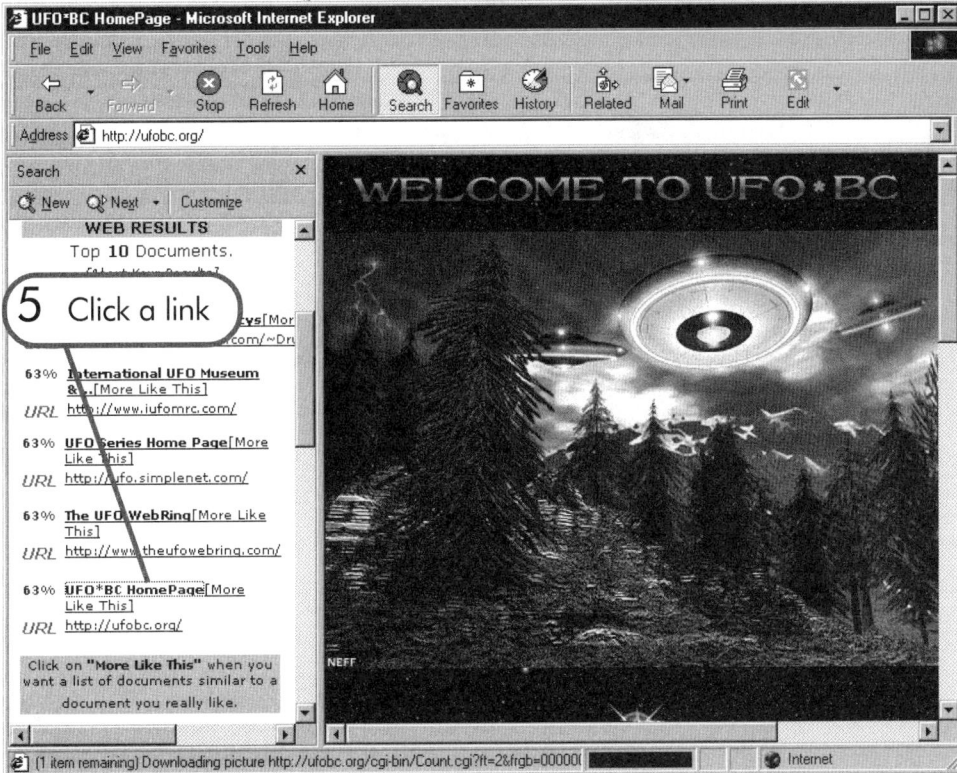

5 Click a link

Excite

Excite is one of the leading portal sites, with a range of services that includes its unique 'Communities' – a flexible alternative to chat rooms (see page 74) for bringing together far-flung family and friends, old and new. It's worth visiting for these, but an even better reason is its powerful search engine.

Excite has one of the most extensive databases on the Web, but is fast and easy to use. A simple search is likely to bring up far more than you want, as words often have more than one meaning. Selecting associated words at the next stage will focus in on the right pages – this filtering can be repeated as often as necessary.

1 Go to Excite at www.excite.co.uk

2 Enter your search word.

3 Click [Search].

4 If you don't see what you want, select other relevant words and click [Search] again.

1 Go to Excite

2 Enter your keyword(s)

3 Click Search

Excite UK Channels - Microsoft Internet Explorer

File Edit View Favorites Tools Help

Back Forward Stop Refresh Home Search Favorites History Related Mail

Address http://www.excite.co.uk/

eXcite
UNITED KINGDOM

EXCITE UK
Tue 8/06/1999

amazon   Entire Web   Search

Today on Excite
· Royal Gossip and News
· Work Out Your Family Tree
· Are You Being Ripped Off?
· Latest Shopping Bargains

Book your Holiday   Find a job   Personals   Share Quotes
Buy CDs   Free Email   Play Games   Weather
Find a Home   People Finder   Power Search   Yellow Pages

Contents

Chat   Entertainment   Lifestyle   Relationships
Classifieds   Games   Money/Investing   Shopping
Communities   Horoscopes   Motoring   Sport
Computers   Jobs/Careers New! News   Travel

Personalisation Manager

CHANGE:
Content | Layout | Look

Login
New My Excite User?
Change my profile
Help

The Cricket World Cup
Click Here!

Add this to My Page
☐ Currency Calculator
☐ Cinema Guide
☐ Restaurant Finder
☐ Favourite Links
☐ International Weather

Add Now!   MORE

My News last updated 08/06/99 23:02   change

Home News

· MILITARY LEADERS MEET TO THRASH OUT PEACE
· FAMILY TEARS AS AITKEN GOES TO JAIL
  More Home News...

Entertainment News

Done   Internet

File Edit View Favorites Tools Help

Back Forward Stop Refresh Home Search Favorites History Related

Address http://www.excite.co.uk/search.gw?trace=a&look=excite_uk&lang=en&search=amazon&c=we

4 Select words and search again

excite
UNITED KINGDOM   Home • help

SEARCH RESULTS
June 8, 1999

You searched for:

amazon rainforest   on Entire Web   Search   Search in other languages

Refine existing search using:

☐ aznt   ☐ usually   ☐ iquitos   ☐ bezos   ☐ amazons
☐ cdnow   ☐ smythe   ☐ manaus   ☐ ships   ☑ rainforest

More Excite Searches	Web Search Results	Do this search on News
· Get your horoscopes	Top **10** Documents.	**View Page Titles only**
· Find a friend		**List by Web Site**
· Find the latest screensavers	*[About Your Results]*	
· Search for shareware		
· What's on at the cinema	**64%** **Amazon City - chat, bulletin b...** [More Like This]	
· Find a restaurant	*URL* http://www.amazoncity.com/	

WELCOME TO AMAZON CITY The progressive online
community for women Not a Member? It's free! Click here!
Strong Women, Strong Words Do not worry about whether

There are a lot of 'Amazon's out there! I just want the rainforest …

… and I found it at the next level – lots of links, including this one to Ask Jeeves

File Edit View Favorites Tools Help

Back Forward Stop Refresh Home Search Favorites History Related Mail Print Edit

Address http://www.ajkids.com/RainforestTour.asp

THE ask Jeeves for kids **Rainforest** TOUR

Introduction to the Rainforest

What are the different types of rainforests? Ask

What is the difference between tropical and temperate rainforests? Ask

Where are there rainforests in South America? Ask

Where can I find information on the ecosystem of tropical rainforests? Ask

Past Tours

Internet

Tip

Ask Jeeves is a fun but effective place to search for information (and much more). Go to: www.askjeeves.com

Infoseek

This is my favourite search engine. It has a very high coverage of the Web, it's quick, and it lets you run searches within the results of the previous search. For example, suppose you want a recipe for tandori chicken. If you enter *tandori chicken recipe* as the keywords, it will find pages that contain all or any of the three – and far too many will be irrelevant. Start with a single word, search for a second word within the results, then do it again and you should have exactly what you want.

When tested, *recipe* found over 2,700,000 pages! Filtering with *chicken* reduced these to 10,590; a further filter with *tandori* brought this down to 12 – all relevant, and some very tasty.

1 Go to Infoseek at:
  infoseek.go.com

2 Enter the first keyword.

3 Click Find.

4 Enter another keyword.

5 Select Search only within these pages.

6 Click Find.

7 Repeat steps 4 to 6 to get down to a few dozen or so results.

1 Go to Infoseek

2 Enter a keyword

3 Click Find

Infoseek also runs a good directory of selected links

4 Enter the next word

5 Limit the search

Address http://infoseek.go.com/Titles?col=WW%2Ccat_RES&qt=chicken&sv=IS&lk=no

GO Network

GO > recipe > **chicken**

6 Click Find

Search ○ New search ● Search within results

tandori   [Find]

Search options | How to search

- **Similar searches:**   • chicken pox   • super chicken   • chicken soup for the
- kentucky fried chicken   • chicken recipe   • kentucky fry chicken   soul
                                                                              • cow chicken

The similar searches and matching topics – may have useful links

Matching topics

- Chickens   • Chicken wings   • Chicken pox   • Chicken soup
- Chicken pot pie   • Chicken recipes   • Barbecue chicken   • Fried chicken
- Nutritional content of • Poultry recipes
  white meat

Web search results 1 - 10 of **10,590**

Next 10 > | Hide summaries | Sort by date

Creole and Cajun Recipes
Celebrate the Creole cuisine of New Orleans,
country").
100% Date: 22 Feb 1999, Size 14.2K, http://www.gumbopag
Find similar pages

Chinese and Japanese Recipes
A selection of Chinese and Japanese recipes t

(i) infoseek℠   Home | Help | **Yellow Pages**
                          This form requires JavaScript

Infoseek Advanced Search

WEB USENET PEOPLE FINDER COMPANIES STOCKS NEWS SHAREWARE REFERENCE

- Click each box to see options. • Enter query terms. • Leave unused boxes blank.

Search the Web for pages in which the:

Document ▼ must ▼ contain the phrase ▼ tandori chicken

Document ▼ should ▼ contain the word(s) ▼ recipe

Document ▼ should not ▼ contain the phrase ▼ restaurant

Show only ▼ results from _____ .com ▼

Show my results: **Number of results:**
Show Summaries ▼   10 per page ▼

Search by collection: **Search by location:**   search   clear form   Tips
Entire Web ▼   Earth ▼

Done   Internet

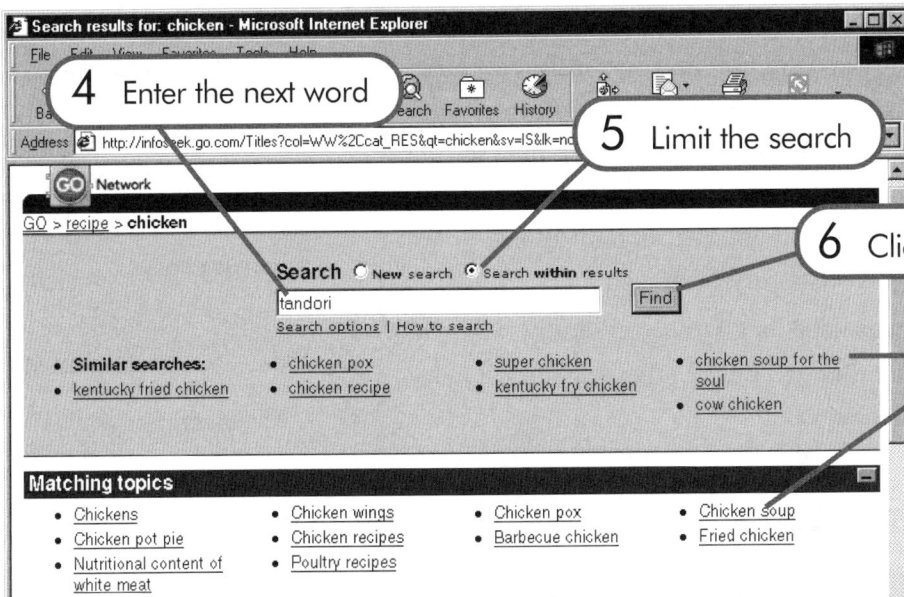

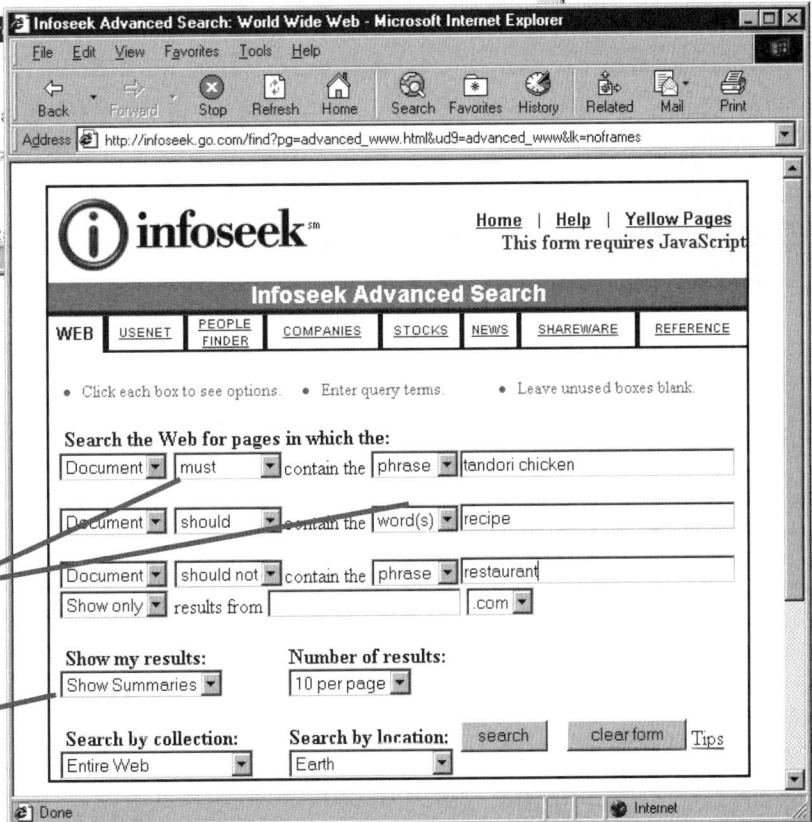

If you are looking for something very specific, try the Advanced search – this lets you choose which words, names or phrases must, should or should not appear in a page. You can also choose where to search and how to display the results.

UK directory

If you want to find local suppliers, clubs, courses, etc. the main Internet directories and search engines may not be the best place to look – simply because you will get too many irrelevant links. If you want local stuff, look in a local directory. In the UK, the first place to try is UK directory. It has links to UK businesses, shops, schools, colleges and government organisations, news, travel, entertainment and other services.

The directory is well-organised, but if you don't know where to start, try a search – note that this only finds sites and category headings within the directory.

Basic steps

1 Go to UK directory at: www.ukdirectory.co.uk

2 Click on a category or subcategory heading and work through the lower menus.

or

3 Enter the search words.

4 Click ➡ GO!

1 Go to UK directory

3 Enter the keyword(s)

4 Click Go!

2 Browse the catalog

Basic steps

1 Go to Yell at
   www.yell.co.uk

2 Enter the business type
   – this must match the
   EYP categories.

Or

3 Enter the company
   name.

4 Enter the location.

5 Click Go!.

If they're in Yellow
Pages, they're in Yell

Yell is primarily a business directory, centred around the Electronic Yellow Pages (all the Yellow Pages directories in the UK). It also has good travel, property and shopping links – and its Film Finder is great for finding what's on locally or for tracking down a cinema that is showing a particular movie.

1 Go to Yell

2 Enter the business type …

3 …or company name

4 Enter the location

5 Click Go

What's on at
the movies?

Yell also has a directory
of UK Web sites

Summary

❑ Directories and search engines can help you to find material on the Internet.

❑ You can personalise the Home page at MSN – and at other portals.

❑ The Best of the Web page is a good place from which to start your browsing.

❑ Yahoo was the first and is still one of the greatest of the Net directories.

❑ If you are looking for specific information, you can find it faster by a Search, rather than browsing.

❑ You can run a search from within the Explorer Bar.

❑ The Excite search engine has indexed most of the millions of sites on the Web.

❑ At Infoseek you can run a series of searches, filtering the results to get just the material that you want.

❑ If you are looking for sites in the UK, try UKdirectory, or Yell for UK businesses.

5 Online Interaction

Gaming Zone

There are tens of thousands of sites catering for all manners of games. Many act as discussion forums for games played offline – use these to find your nearest bridge club, discuss chess strategies or get the cheats to help you survive in a game on your PlayStation. Some hold stores of games for playing on- or offline – there are loads of solitaires, word games, 'arcade action' and computerised board games. Others are devoted to interactive onlines games, and one of the best of these is MSN's Gaming Zone. You must join to play, but membership is free, as are many of the games, though some others incur charges or require you to have commercial software.

Basic steps

1 Go to the Zone at: www.zone.msn.com

2 Sign up (or login if you've already joined).

3 Pick your game.

4 Play!

❑ Some software will download when you first join, and when you first play a game.

MSN Gaming Zone - Home - Microsoft Internet Explorer

1 Go to the Zone

2 Sign up or in

3 Pick a game

4 Play!

Interactive online games

Tip

Yahoo, Excite and other major service providers also run games rooms — check them out and see which suit you best.

Adventure and action games normally require special software, which can sometimes be downloaded free from the game site, but more often must be bought and installed before you go online. All action and some adventure games are played in real-time, though some adventure (and tactical) games are played by turns, with the moves assessed by an online referee – these are normally charged for.

With card and board games, the software is normally free and downloads automatically on your first entry. These can be very competitive and played at a high level, but there are 'social lounges', for those more interested in chatting than playing!

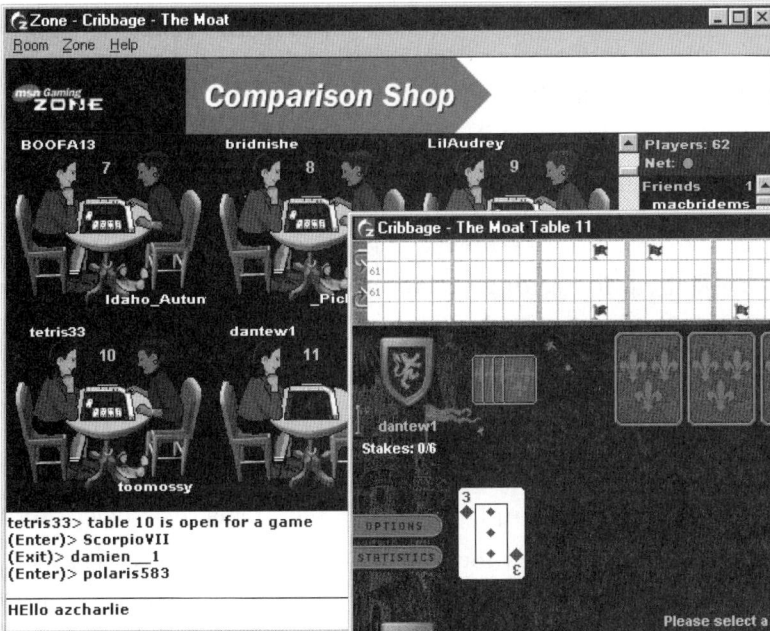

People played cribbage in ale houses of Shakespeare's time, now they play it online – and it is still a great game!

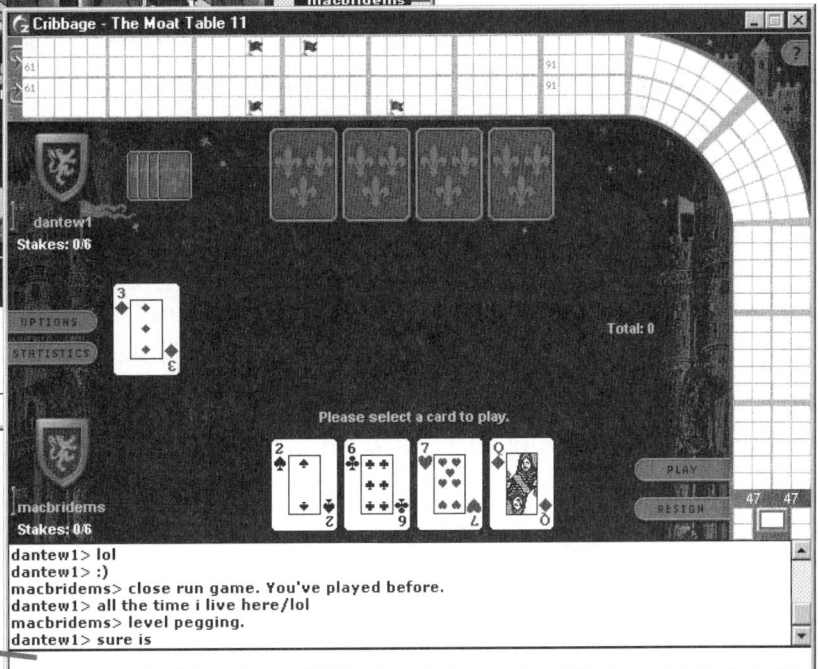

Card games can be sociable. Type here to chat to the other player(s)

Chat rooms

In chat rooms you can communicate with other people in real time by typing messages to each other. There are essentially two types of rooms.

Open chat rooms

These are the CB radio of the Internet. Some people find them a good place to wile away the hours – but I confess I am not one of them. It is very difficult to find a room where you can get a good conversation going. There are some practical problems:

- Most chat rooms will accommodate anything up to 20 or 30 people at a time, which is too many. If you find a room with only a few guests, there's a better chance of starting a sensible conversation.

- The 'chat' is typed and takes a few seconds to reach the screen. In between you reading something that you want to respond to and your response appearing, several other messages could have hit the screen.

- Too many chat users seem to be there for getting off or showing off. This is true even for those rooms that are supposed to be centred on a specific topic.

Private rooms

If you have friends and family scattered around the world, these can be good places to meet – you can set up private rooms at most chat sites. Agree a time and a site (by e-mail or during a meeting once you are organised) and get together online.

Microsoft Chat

1 Go online and connect to a server.

2 Choose a room from the list that appears.

3 Select your expression.

4 Type your message.

❑ Right-click on a person's icon to find out about them or send a private message.

This dedicated chat application – part of the full IE5 package and also available for download from Microsoft – has some neat features, including a 'Comic chat' option. This presents the conversation as a comic strip, rather than as plain text. You can choose your character and pick an expression to match or emphasise your messages.

Setting up is simple, and it comes preconfigured with links to some major chat servers. Once online, you can join in any open rooms or set up your own – making them private if you want to restrict them to invited guests.

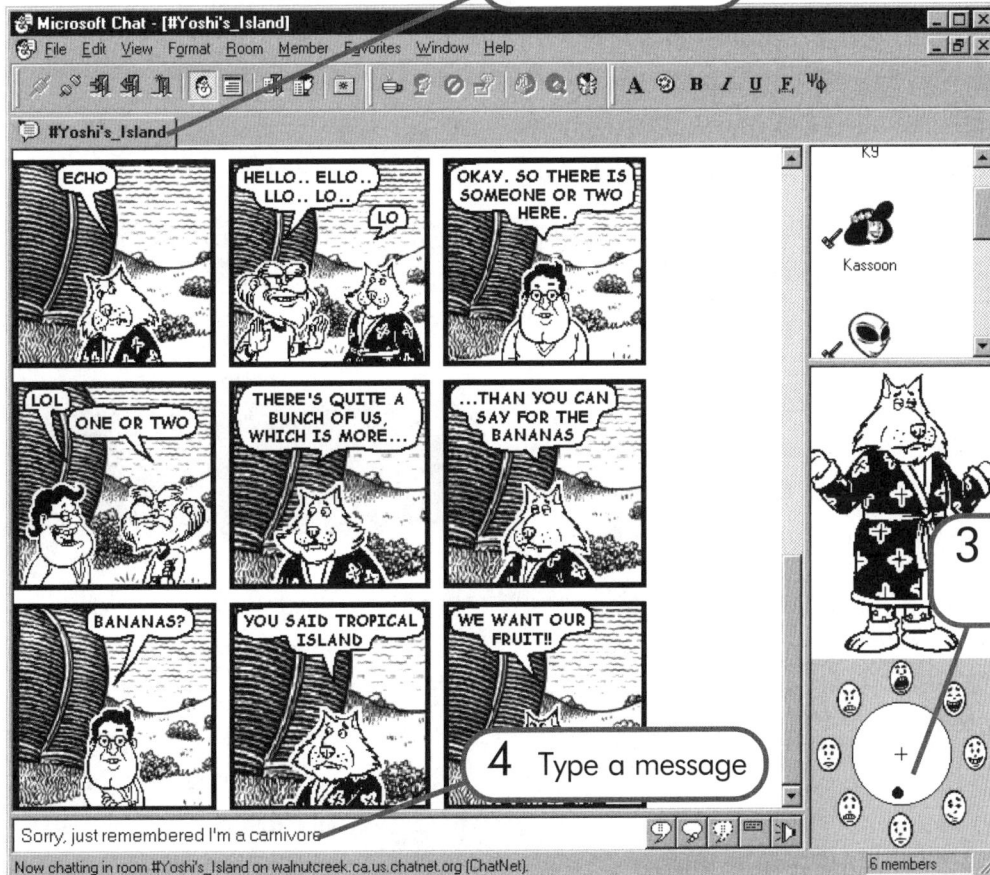

2 Enter a room

3 Pick an expression

4 Type a message

75

Radio stations

One of the most visible new features of Internet Explorer 5 is Internet Radio reception – and it works! Over the last couple of years, new techniques have been developed for transmitting sound in real time. Now you can listen to a 'broadcast' through your browser and the quality is about as good as you would get from a small portable radio. You can browse elsewhere while it plays, though pages will come in much slower. But the key question is, why not just listen to the radio?

If you can get the station on your radio, then it makes little sense to listen through your browser, but can you get American Family Radio, KBAY of San José, Dallas Police Scanner, OzRock? You can through the Web.

Radio broadcasts are in two formats, and you should have players for both Windows Media Player and RealNetworks RealPlayer already installed along with IE5. They seem to be equally effective and are used in the same way.

When you link to a radio station, its Web page will normally download and the audio may follow directly – starting up the appropriate player. At some stations you have to click a 'Listen here' link, and these links are generally offered in both formats. You will see a 'buffering' message as the initial file comes in, and you may occasionally have to click the Play button to start. In all cases, the player can be minimised out of the way once it has started.

Basic steps

1 Display the Radio toolbar.

2 Click Radio Stations and select Radio Station Guide.

3 Click a radio button.

Or

4 Pick a Country from the drop-down list.

5 Select a station from the list that will appear.

6 Click ⬛ Stop to turn the radio off and it replacement ⬤ Play to restart.

RealPlayer is perhaps the most common format

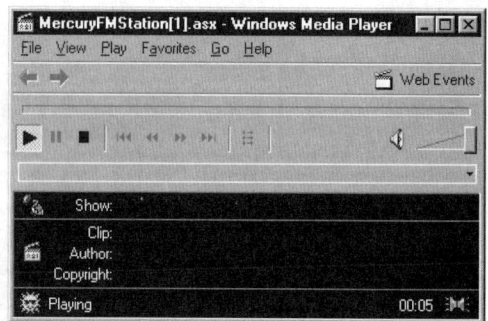

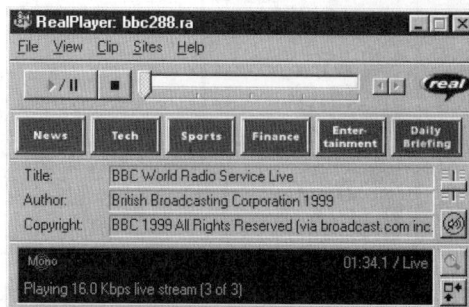

Windows Media Player is closely integrated with IE5

If you need a player, you will find a download link at most radio stations

Web Events Radio - Microsoft Internet Explorer

File   Edit   View   Favorites   Tools   Help

Back   Forward   Stop   Refresh   Home   Search   Favorites   History   Related   Mail   Print

Address   http://webevents.microsoft.com/iradio/en_gb/Radio.asp

Radio   Stop   Radio Stations

1   Display the Radio toolbar

2   Select Radio Station Guide

Add Station to Favorites...
Radio Station Guide

duct... | Support | Search | Microsoft UK Guide

Web Event

experience online audio and *video*

Microsoft

Web Events Home

Welcome! Here you can browse
hundreds of stations sorted by
location, program format, or
language. **Note**: When you "push" a
radio tuner button, the station's
Web site appears while the station
is loading.

Click a button to hear a radio station's direct webcast.

Search for audio & video content

jazz

3   Click a button

radio
station
guide

Download
Windows Media
Player.

Get
Windows
Media Player

| BBC News | Classic FM | Virgin | WRN1 | JazzFM |
| RELEASEradio | Premier | Classic Gold | Mercury FM | |

56k or higher is recommended

4   Pick a country

History   Related   Mail   Print

Browse radio stations or personalize your tuner:

● Language   ● International   ● Format   Australia

Canada
Czech Republic
Germany
Greece
Hong Kong
Italy
Japan
Korea
Latvia

○ FOX FM
○ MIX 106.5
○ OzIndig
○ OzRock
○ PMFM
● Radio Australia
○ Radio Capital City

SIC *f*M

commercial radio
f programming 24
n a range of
frequencies between 100-102 FM.

Buy your favourite music
online using

iMVS.com

Classic Newsnight
e-business
In Association With

IBM

5   Select a station

Magazine
Technical
Information

Launched in September 1992, Classic FM is now
well established and attracts over 5.1 million
listeners per week.

Classic FM's premise is that classical music is, and
always has been, popular music. The station's aim is
to make classical music accessible to as wide an
audience as possible.

Currently on-air is **Smooth Classics at 7** with **John
Brunning**

The weekday musical wind-down, featuring music
from throughout the ages. Sponsored by Vauxhall
Omega

CLASSIC *f*M
Present in Concert

Lesley
Garrett

FREE

tickets

Some Web stations
provide information and
features to accompany
their broadcasts

Shareware sites

There are literally megabytes of shareware (and freeware) programs available through the Web – and one of the best places is **shareware.com**. This is run by CNET which also provides a range of other services to Internet users.

● If you are looking for particular software – and know its name – use the Quick Search facility.

● If you are just starting to build your shareware collection, try the Most Popular selection.

Basic steps

1 Go to: http://www.shareware.com/

2 In the search for slot type the (common) name of the program.

3 Select your operating system.

4 Click Search and wait.

5 Read the descriptions to find the right file.

1 Go to shareware.com

2 Type the name

3 Which platform?

4 Click Search

You can also search by type and description on the Power Search page

78

6 Click on the filename to start the download.

7 Save the file as usual.

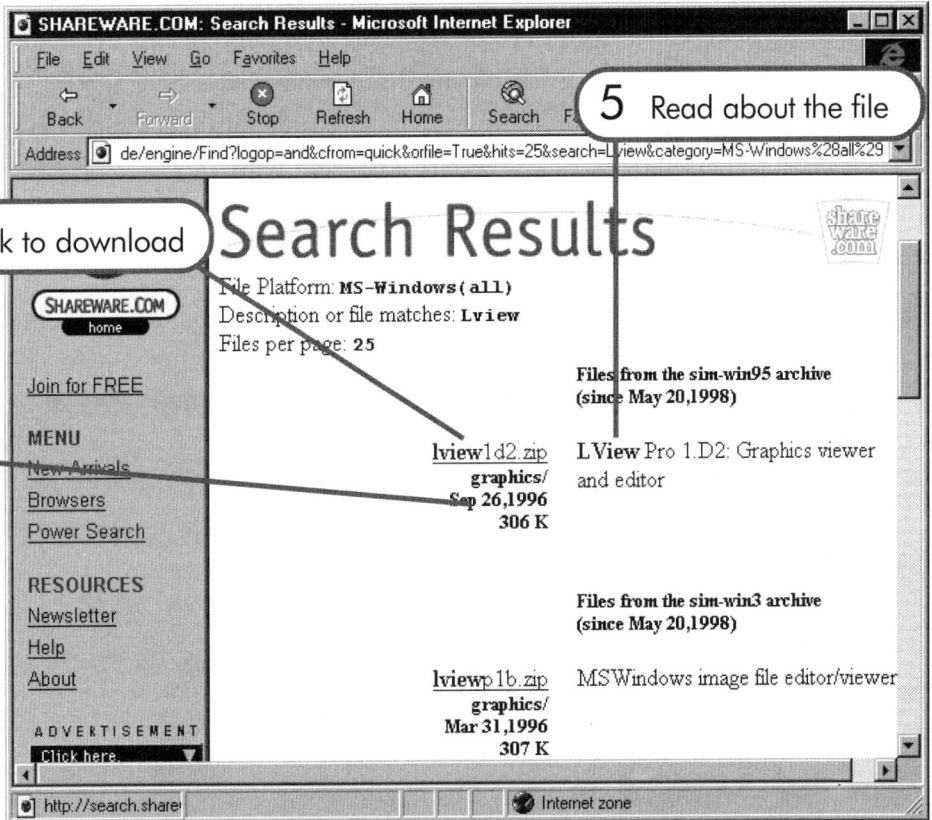

Check the size – is it worth the download time? (lview is!)

5 Read about the file

6 Click to download

Search Results

File Platform: **MS-Windows(all)**
Description or file matches: **Lview**
Files per page: **25**

Files from the sim-win95 archive (since May 20,1998)

lview1d2.zip
graphics/
Sep 26,1996
306 K

LView Pro 1.D2: Graphics viewer and editor

Files from the sim-win3 archive (since May 20,1998)

lviewp1b.zip
graphics/
Mar 31,1996
307 K

MSWindows image file editor/viewer

Tip

Most shareware files are supplied in Zip form — compressed with WinZip. To decompress them you need WinZip. Get a copy from:
http://www.winzip.com

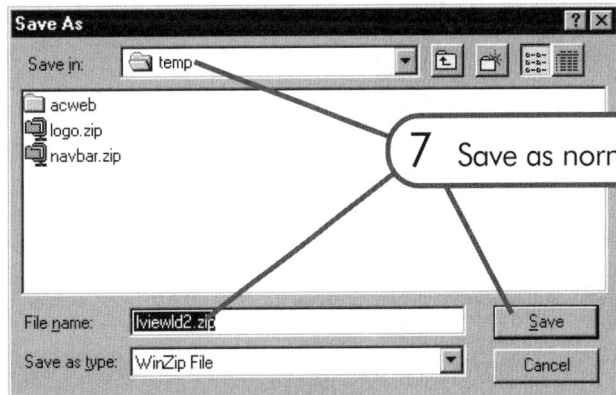

7 Save as normal

Shopping on the Web

What do they sell on the World Wide Web? You will find the kinds of goods that, five years ago, would have been sold by mail order or over the phone – the Web is a natural extension of these approaches. It is a logical place to sell specialist goods that can be difficult to find in your local high street – hobbyist materials, collectors' items, or almost anything hand-made. It is particularly good for selling anything which people buy on specification rather than by trying on, e.g. computer hardware and software, books and CDs. At Dan (below), as at many hardware suppliers, you can order a custom-built PC, checking the cost as you pick the components.

Tip

If you are buying from a US-based firm, remember that there will be VAT to add to the cost, plus the delivery charges. Check the final total before confirming the order.

A wide choice of options and clear pricing information are given at all good hardware suppliers

Shop safely

The Internet has its fair share of crooks, but if you observe a few sensible precautions, you should be able to buy goods and services on-line as safely as you can by mail order or in the high street.

Too good to be true?

It is cheaper to trade on the Internet than it is in the high street, or even by by mail order or telephone, so you should expect to get a better deal, a faster service or a lower price. But if an offer sounds too good to be true, it probably is!

Who are these people?

Don't deal with people you don't know or with those that you can only contact over the Internet. If a firm is new to you, check that they really exist by looking up their address at Yell, in the Electronic Yellow Pages (page 69), or the Companies lists at Yahoo.

It's not just credit card fraud

In fact credit card fraud makes up less than 20% of Internet fraud. Most victims paid by cheque, cash, money orders or bank debits.

You are as safe paying by credit card over the Internet as you are over the phone – which is not completely safe. Make sure that the *SSL security checking* is enabled on your browser – on the **Advanced** panel of the **Internet Options**. This ensures that the transactions you have with the firm cannot be 'eavesdropped' over the Internet.

Take note

In 1998, on-line fraud cost Internet users around £200 million. The most common types of fraud were auctions, online purchase and the provision of Internet services.

Tip

If you want to know more about fraud, go to Yahoo and work through the menus to *Computers and Internet – Internet – Business and Economics – Fraud*, or head for Internet Fraud Watch at: http://www.fraud.org

Finding the shops

Basic steps

There's no high street on the Internet, but shops are not hard to find. Most portals and directories have a shopping area, with links to online stores. Yahoo's are very good – and try Yahoo UK (if you live in the UK) first, as a local supplier should mean lower delivery costs.

1 Go to Yahoo shopping at:
shopping.uk.yahoo.com

2 Select the category.

3 Follow the links.

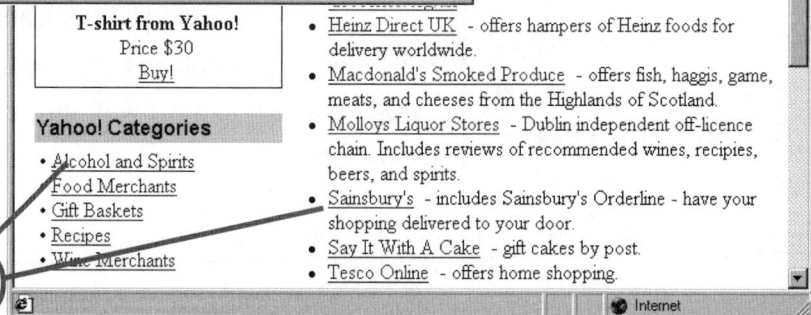

1 Go to Yahoo shopping

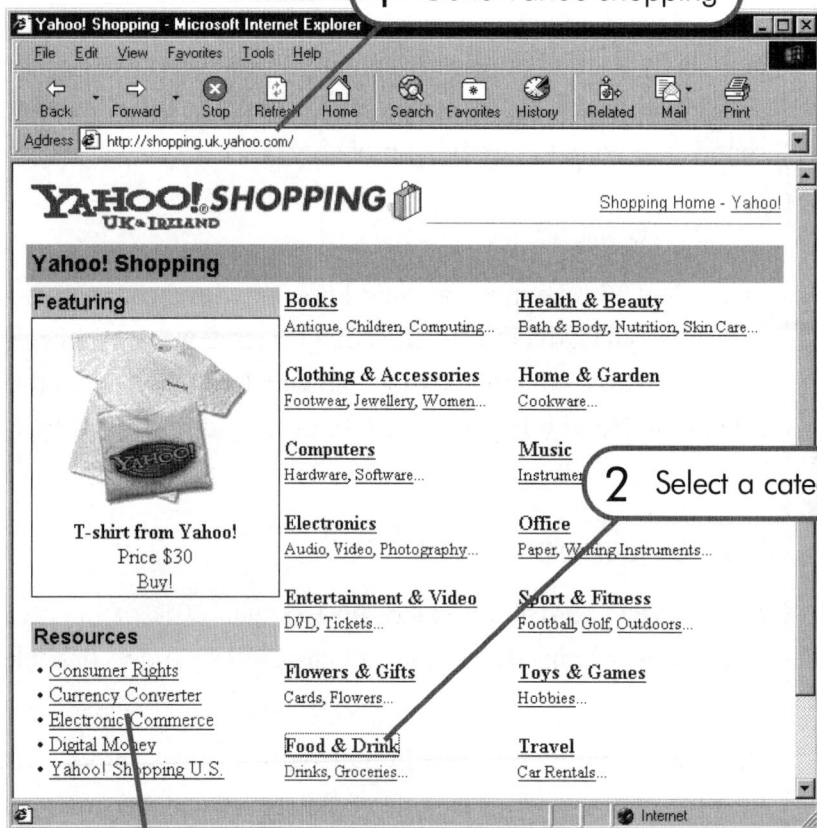

Yahoo! Shopping - Microsoft Internet Explorer

File Edit View Favorites Tools Help

Back Forward Stop Refresh Home Search Favorites History Related Mail Print

Address http://shopping.uk.yahoo.com/

YAHOO! SHOPPING
UK & IRELAND

Shopping Home - Yahoo!

Yahoo! Shopping

Featuring

T-shirt from Yahoo!
Price $30
Buy!

Resources

- Consumer Rights
- Currency Converter
- Electronic Commerce
- Digital Money
- Yahoo! Shopping U.S.

Books
Antique, Children, Computing...

Clothing & Accessories
Footwear, Jewellery, Women...

Computers
Hardware, Software...

Electronics
Audio, Video, Photography...

Entertainment & Video
DVD, Tickets...

Flowers & Gifts
Cards, Flowers...

Food & Drink
Drinks, Groceries...

Health & Beauty
Bath & Body, Nutrition, Skin Care...

Home & Garden
Cookware...

Music
Instrumen...

2 Select a category

Related Mail Print

Office
Paper, Writing Instruments...

Sport & Fitness
Football, Golf, Outdoors...

Toys & Games
Hobbies...

Travel
Car Rentals...

Internet

The Currency Converter is handy when shopping overseas

T-shirt from Yahoo!
Price $30
Buy!

Yahoo! Categories

- Alcohol and Spirits
- Food Merchants
- Gift Baskets
- Recipes
- Wine Merchants

r beer from the comfort of your PC.
s from around the globe.
order wine and champagne online.
wrapped champagnes, wines and

- experience the luxurious tradition of
from home.

- Heinz Direct UK - offers hampers of Heinz foods for delivery worldwide.
- Macdonald's Smoked Produce - offers fish, haggis, game, meats, and cheeses from the Highlands of Scotland.
- Molloys Liquor Stores - Dublin independent off-licence chain. Includes reviews of recommended wines, recipies, beers, and spirits.
- Sainsbury's - includes Sainsbury's Orderline - have your shopping delivered to your door.
- Say It With A Cake - gift cakes by post.
- Tesco Online - offers home shopping.

Internet

3 Follow the links

Online banking

For keeping track of your money, paying bills and moving cash between accounts, online banking is as convenient as telephone banking and offers greater control. You can *see* what you are doing while you online, and – if you have suitable software – you can download your account information for further work offline.

If you want a mortgage, pension, ISA or insurance, check out the Web. Most companies now run sites where you can, at the very least, read about their services. At more interactive sites, you can get instant quotations or calculations. While you don't want to rush into long-term financial commitments, it's good to be able to get high-quality information online.

Online banking is very cost-effective, and this should be reflected in better interest rates – it is at egg

Welcome to Egg - Microsoft Internet Explorer

File   Edit   View   Favorites   Tools   Help

Back   Forward   Stop   Refresh   Home   Search   Favorites   History   Related   Mail   Print   Edit

Address http://www.egg.co.uk/

egg: Individual Money Matters

Net a great rate
with an Egg Savings Account.

With 5.85% gross p.a./AER from just £1. It's the smart way to manage your money.

Apply Now

June 9, 1999   News from Egg

Internet Offer
Find out about Egg's new free Internet service.

PC Offers
A Pentium III PC installed in your home from only £889.00

Tailored Loans
A fast decision with competitive rates and the flexibility to choose your repayment period.

Savings Online
Now you can keep an eye on your savings online, day or night. Get a Mini-statement, transfer funds or request stationery.

Internet

Summary

❏ All manner of games are supported on the Web in one form or another. If you want to play games online, try MSN's Gaming Zone.

❏ Chat rooms are where people can get together in real-time to exchange ideas and gossip.

❏ With Microsoft Chat, you can chat in a comic strip.

❏ You can listen to radio stations around the world through your browser.

❏ There are thousands of programs and other files available for download at the shareware sites.

❏ A wide range of goods can now be bought over the Internet and delivered to the door.

❏ There are risks in purchasing goods and services over the Internet, but take sensible precautions and it should be no riskier than buying by mail or in the high street.

❏ Cheaper running costs should enable Internet-based traders to offer god deals – but amazing bargains are often a sign of a con man at work.

❏ You can find shops through Yahoo and other portals.

❏ Many banks now offer online banking – try it, it's a more convenient alternative to telephone banking.

6 Electronic Mail

Outlook Express

Internet Explorer does not handle e-mail and news. For this you need different software, and the default program is Outlook Express (or Outlook if you have Microsoft Office installed).

If you prefer to use another e-mail application, you can link it into IE 5 through the Tools – Internet Options – Programs panel.

1 Select a Mail option

Mail
Read Mail
New Message...
Send a Link...
Send Page...
Read News

3 Start work

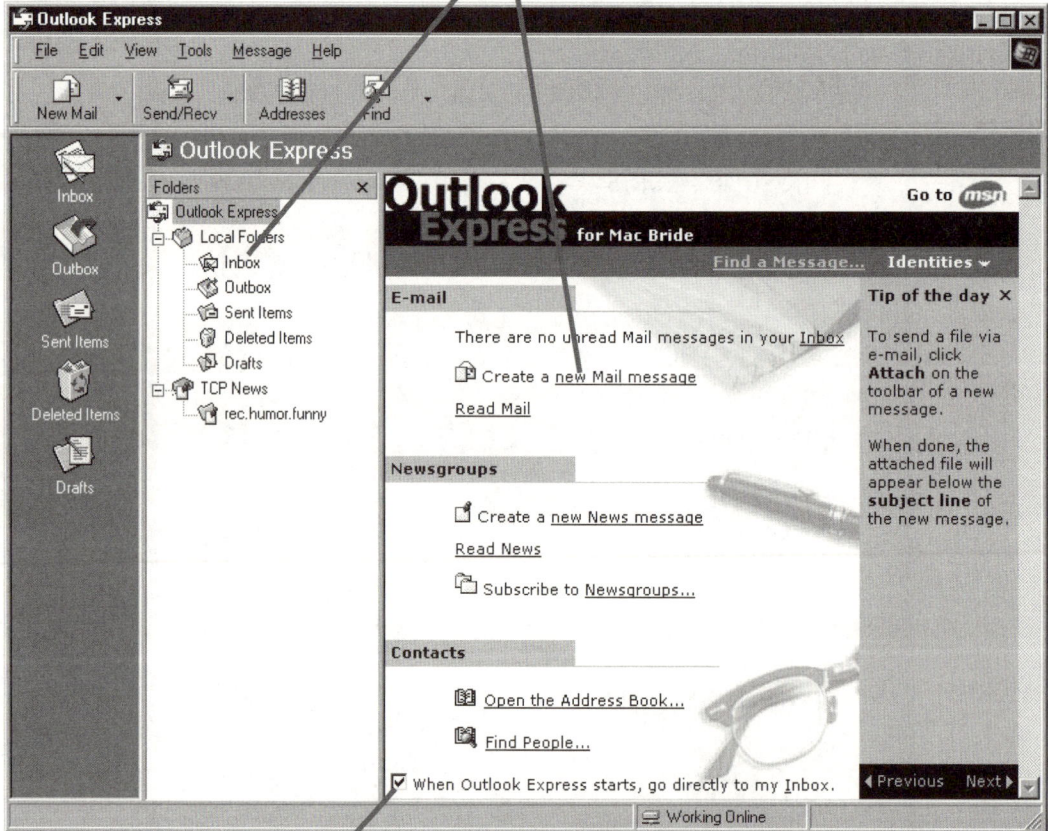

Set this option to skip the 'contents' display and go straight to your Inbox in future

Outlook Bar   Folder List   Toolbar   Preview pane header

Views   Folder Bar   Header list   Preview pane

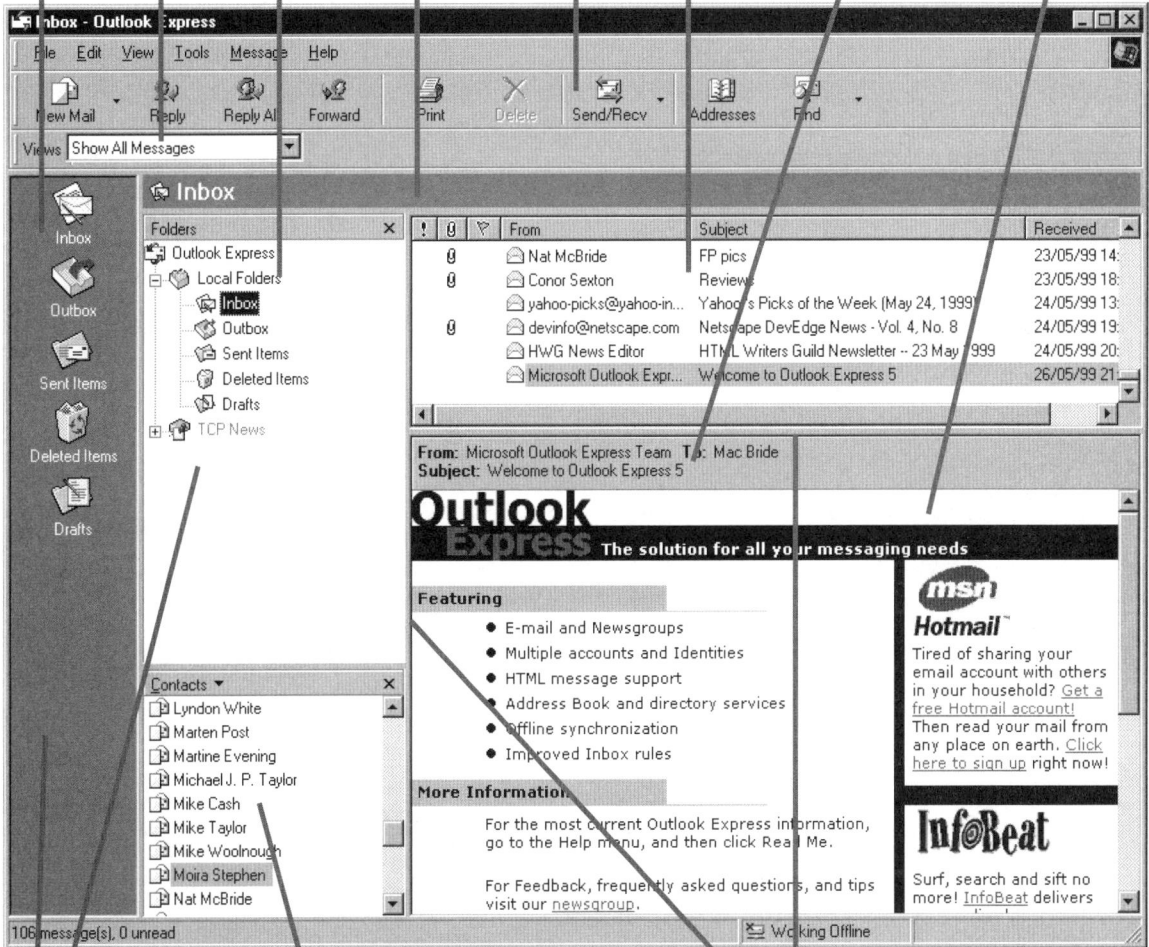

The Outlook Bar and Folder List are both
used for switching between folders – you
do not need them both (see next page).

The dividing lines between the
panes can be dragged to
change their relative sizes

Display options

These can be set from the View menu.

- The **Layout** panel defines the contents of the Outlook Express window;

- The **Columns** routine lets you choose which items from the headers to include in the message lists.

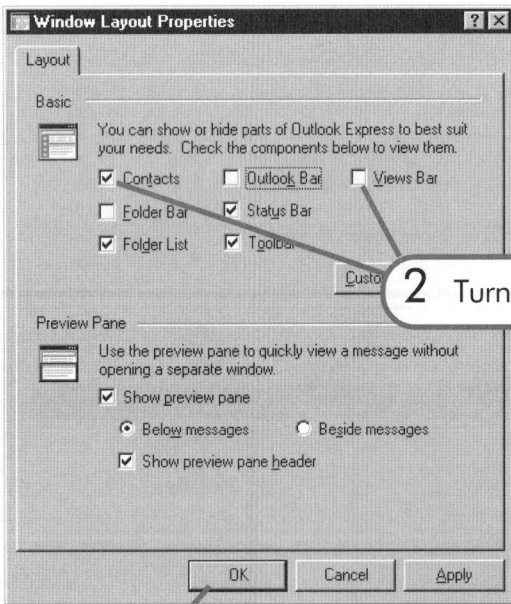

❑ Layout options

1 Open the View menu, select Layout...

2 Tick to turn an item's display on or off.

3 Click OK.

❑ Selecting header items

4 Open the View menu, and select Columns...

5 Select an item from the Displayed list and click Show to include.

6 Select an item from the Displayed list and click Hide to remove from display.

7 Adjust the positions with the Move buttons – Up moves a column to the left; Down moves it to the right.

Window Layout Properties

Layout

Basic

You can show or hide parts of Outlook Express to best suit your needs. Check the components below to view them.

☑ Contacts   ☐ Outlook Bar   ☐ Views Bar
☐ Folder Bar   ☑ Status Bar
☑ Folder List   ☑ Toolbar

Custo...

2 Turn items on or off

Preview Pane

Use the preview pane to quickly view a message without opening a separate window.

☑ Show preview pane

⦿ Below messages   ○ Beside messages

☑ Show preview pane header

OK   Cancel   Apply

3 Click OK

Columns

Check the columns that you would like visible in this view. Use the Move Up and Move Down buttons to reorder the columns however you like.

☑ Priority
☑ Attachment
☑ Flag
☑ From
☑ Subject
☑ Received
☐ Account

Move Up
Move Down
Show
Hide
Reset

7 Adjust positions

The selected column should be 110 pixels wide.

OK   Cancel

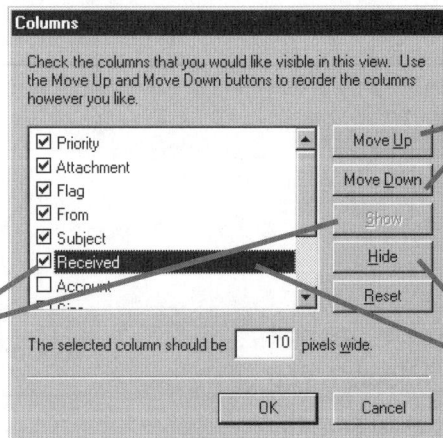

5 Show the column

6 Hide the column

Basic steps

1 Open the Tools menu and select Options...

2 Clear the Send and Receive...box, if you have a dial-up line.

3 On Send, only check Save copy of sent... if you really need copies.

4 Clear Send immediately if you compose messages off-line.

cont...

These options are entirely that – optional! The only crucial options are on the Server panel, and they will have been set up by the Connection Wizard (page 26). These pages cover some of the key options that you should consider.

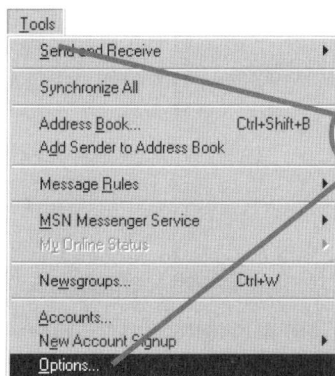

Tools

Send and Receive ▶
Synchronize All
Address Book...   Ctrl+Shift+B
Add Sender to Address Book
Message Rules ▶
MSN Messenger Service ▶
My Online Status ▶
Newsgroups...   Ctrl+W
Accounts...
New Account Signup ▶
Options...

1 Use Tools – Options

3 Clear Save copy of sent

Options

| Security | Connection | Maintenance |
| General | Read | Send | Compose | Signatures | Spelling |

Sending

☐ Save copy of sent messages in the 'Sent Items' folder

☐ Send messages immediately

☑ Automatically put people I reply to in my Address Book

☑ Automatically complete e-mail addresses when composing

☑ Include message in reply

☑ Reply to messages using the format in which they were sent

International Settings...

Mail Sending Format

◉ HTML   HTML Settings...   Plain Text Settings...
○ Plain Text

News Sending Format

○ HTML   HTML Settings...   Plain Text Settings...
◉ Plain Text

OK   Cancel   Apply

4 Clear Send immediately

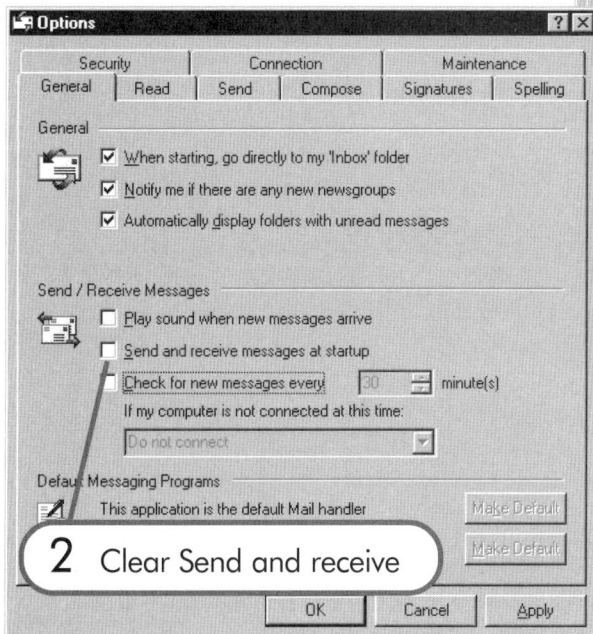

Options

| Security | Connection | Maintenance |
| General | Read | Send | Compose | Signatures | Spelling |

General

☑ When starting, go directly to my 'Inbox' folder

☑ Notify me if there are any new newsgroups

☑ Automatically display folders with unread messages

Send / Receive Messages

☐ Play sound when new messages arrive

☐ Send and receive messages at startup

☐ Check for new messages every [30] minute(s)

If my computer is not connected at this time:

[Do not connect ▾]

Default Messaging Programs

This application is the default Mail handler   Make Default

Make Default

2 Clear Send and receive

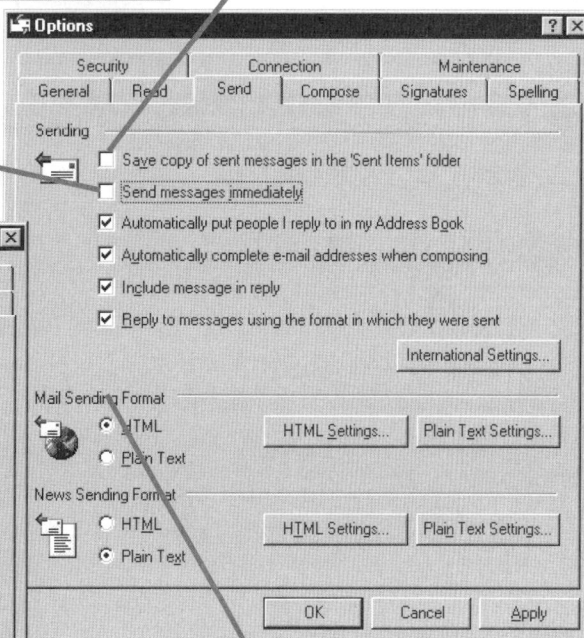

OK   Cancel   Apply

If your recipients can view HTML formatted mail, click here – and format your messages!

You can turn off the automatic Spellcheck and
only run it when you feel the need.

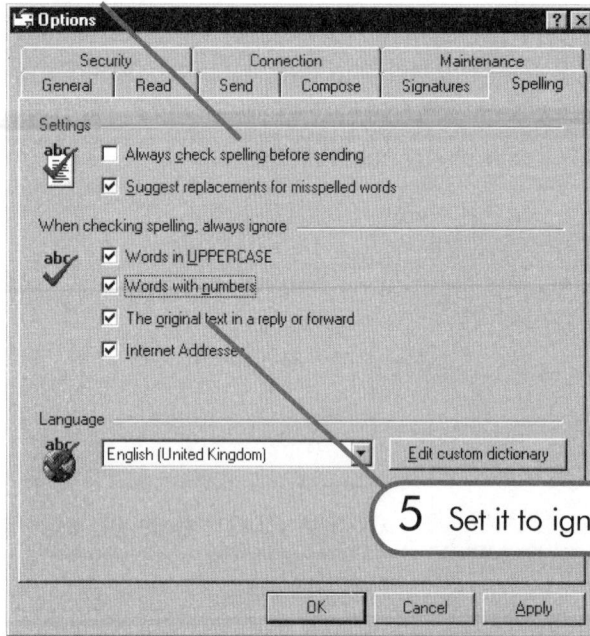

...cont

5 On Spelling, turn on all
the Ignore options.

6 On Security, if you want
to be able to send
secure e-mail, get your
Digital ID – these cost
and are only worth
bothering with if confi-
dentiality is important.

7 On Dialup, select when
the connection is to be
made and closed.

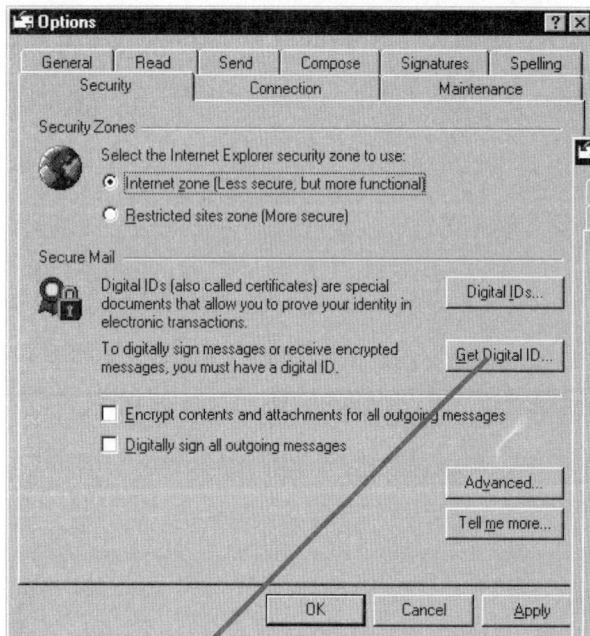

5 Set it to ignore all these

7 When do you want to connect?

6 Get a Digital ID?

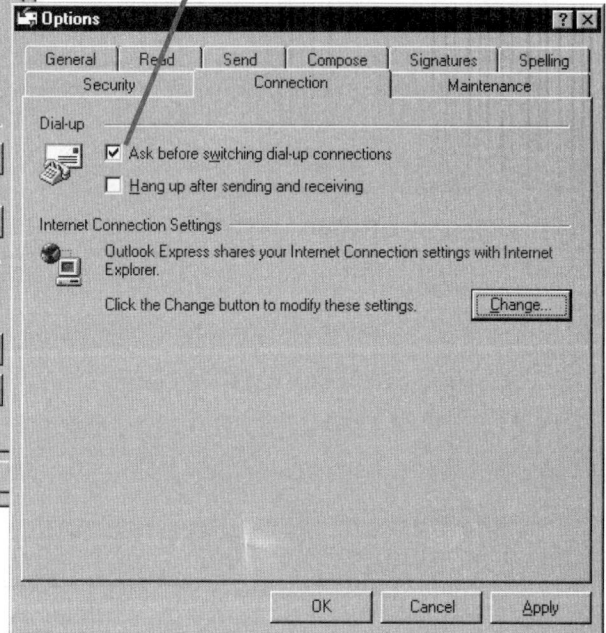

News options

The options on the Read and Maintenance panels are mainly related to newsgroup messages. You may prefer to leave these at their defaults until you have been using the newsgroups for a while.

Take note

Newsgroups are covered in the next chapter.

Some newsgroups have hundreds of messages, so that downloading their headers (subject and sender details) can take a while – set a limit.

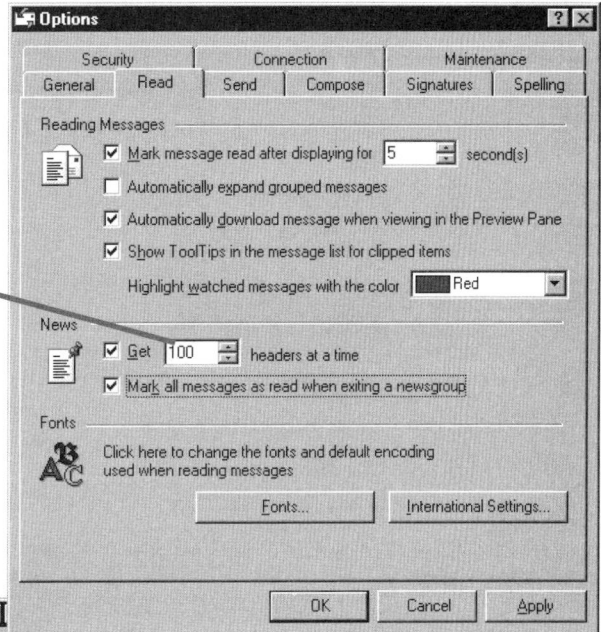

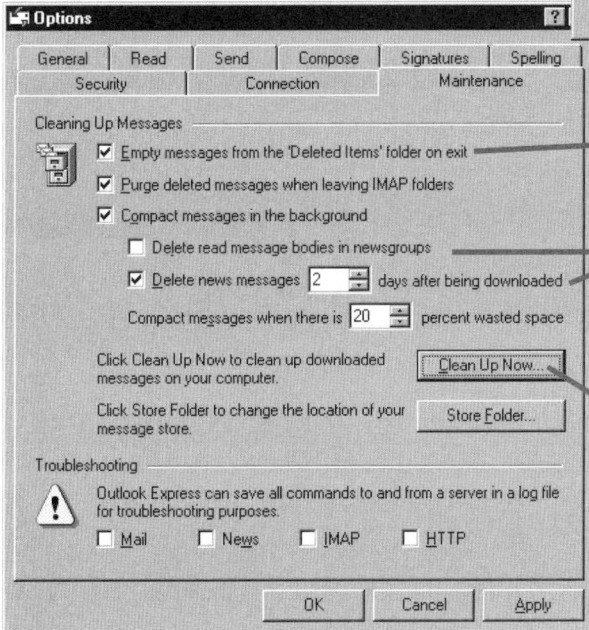

'Deleted' messages are stored in the 'Deleted Items' folder – check this box to clear the folder on exit.

Use these options to delete Newsgroup messages automatically either after reading, or after a few days

If you are running short of disk space, click Clean Up Now and remove unwanted files

Sending messages

To send e-mail, all you need is the address – and something to say! Messages can be composed and sent immediately if you are on-line, or composed off-line and sent later. If you are writing to someone who can read HTML formatted messages (i.e. an Outlook or Netscape user), you can liven them up by using stationery (see page 94).

Just click New Mail for a plain message

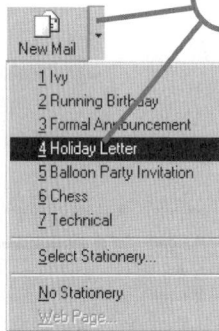

New Mail

1 Ivy
2 Running Birthday
3 Formal Announcement
4 Holiday Letter
5 Balloon Party Invitation
6 Chess
7 Technical

Select Stationery...

No Stationery
Web Page...

1 Select a format from the New Mail list

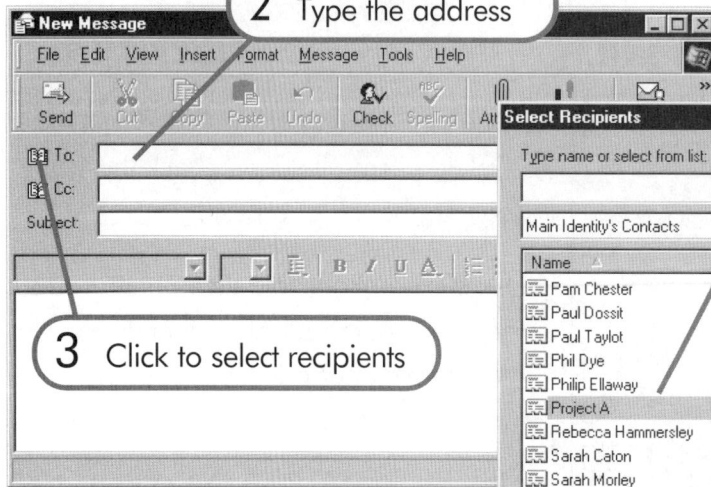

2 Type the address

3 Click to select recipients

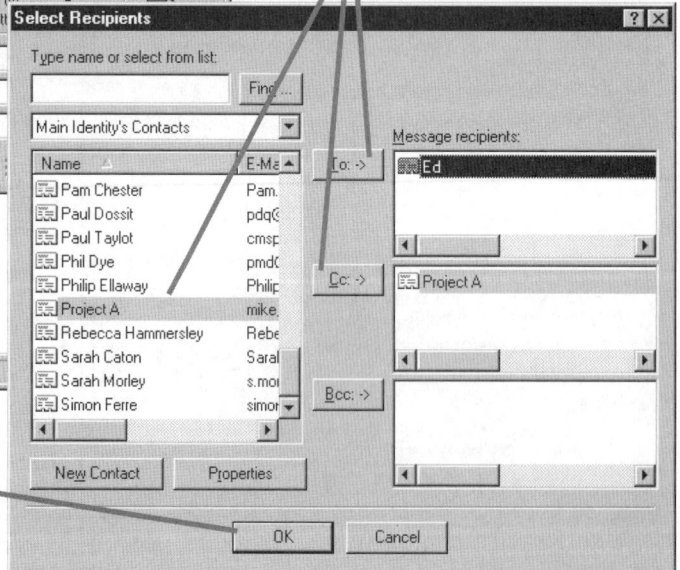

4 Select and click

5 Click OK

Basic steps

1 Open the Compose menu and select New Message or drop down the New Mail list and pick your 'stationery' (see page 94).

2 Type the To: address.

or

3 Click 📧 beside To: to open the Select Recipients panel.

4 Select the names and click the To-> or Cc-> buttons to copy them to the recipients lists.

New Message

File   Edit   View   Insert   Format   Message   Tools   Help

Send   Cut   Copy   Paste   Undo   Check   Spelling   Att

To:
Cc:
Subject:

Select Recipients

Type name or select from list:

Find...

Main Identity's Contacts

Name	E-Ma
Pam Chester	Pam.
Paul Dossit	pdq@
Paul Taylot	cmsp
Phil Dye	pmd(
Philip Ellaway	Philip
Project A	mike.
Rebecca Hammersley	Rebe
Sarah Caton	Sarah
Sarah Morley	s.mor
Simon Ferre	simor

New Contact   Properties

To: ->   Message recipients: Ed

Cc: ->   Project A

Bcc: ->

OK   Cancel

5 Click OK.

6 Type a Subject.

7 Type your message.

8 If you are using HTML, select text and format it as required.

9 Click 🖳 to send the message.

❏ If you have turned on the *Send immediately* Option, you should now see it go.

6 Type the Subject

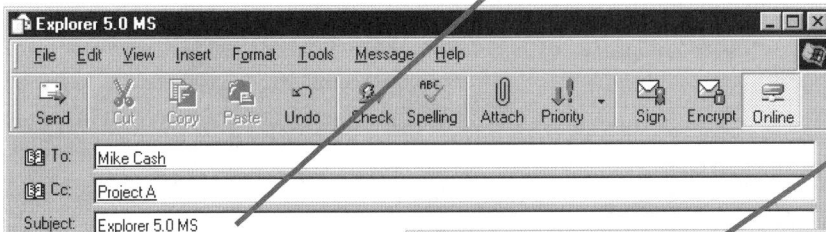

Use the Format menu to switch between HTML and Plain Text

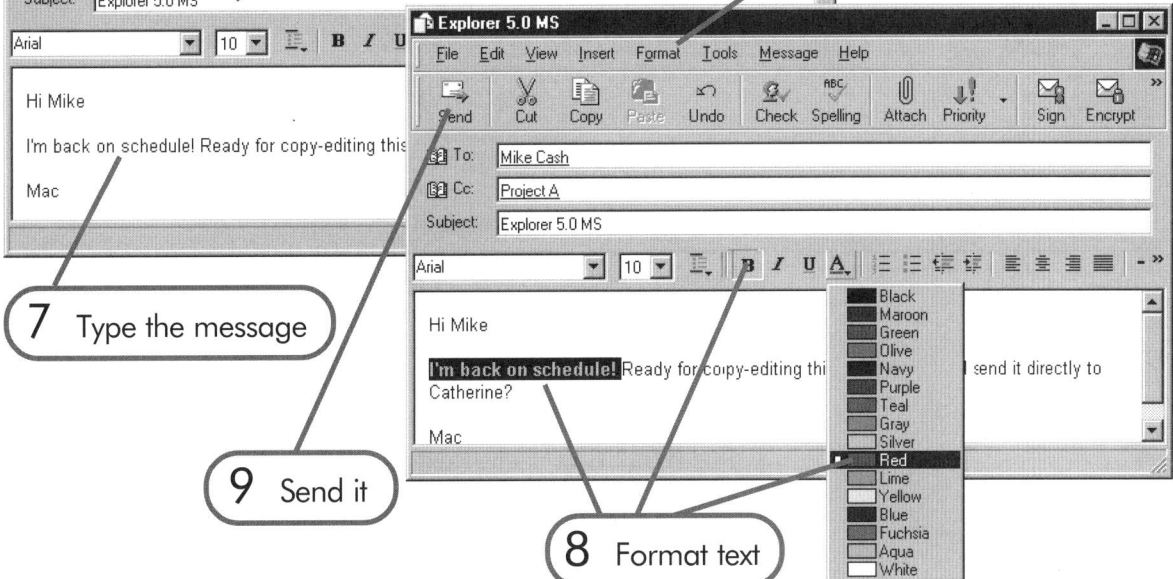

Explorer 5.0 MS

File Edit View Insert Format Tools Message Help

Send Cut Copy Paste Undo Check Spelling Attach Priority Sign Encrypt Online

To: Mike Cash

Cc: Project A

Subject: Explorer 5.0 MS

Arial 10 B I U

Hi Mike

I'm back on schedule! Ready for copy-editing this

Mac

7 Type the message

Explorer 5.0 MS

File Edit View Insert Format Tools Message Help

Send Cut Copy Paste Undo Check Spelling Attach Priority Sign Encrypt

To: Mike Cash

Cc: Project A

Subject: Explorer 5.0 MS

Arial 10 B I U A

Hi Mike

I'm back on schedule! Ready for copy-editing thi   send it directly to Catherine?

Mac

Black
Maroon
Green
Olive
Navy
Purple
Teal
Gray
Silver
Red
Lime
Yellow
Blue
Fuchsia
Aqua
White

9 Send it

8 Format text

Stationery

There is a collection of ready-made stationery – HTML files with images and formatted text – on which you can write your messages. The drop-down list holds recently-used styles, and there are more in the stationery cupboard!

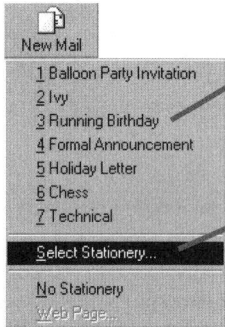

1 Select a style.

or

2 Select More Stationery and open a file, prewiewing it in the Preview Pane.

3 Enter your text where indicated, or in any blank area.

New Mail

1 Balloon Party Invitation
2 Ivy
3 Running Birthday
4 Formal Announcement
5 Holiday Letter
6 Chess
7 Technical

Select Stationery...

No Stationery
Web Page...

1 Select a style

2 Open a Stationery file

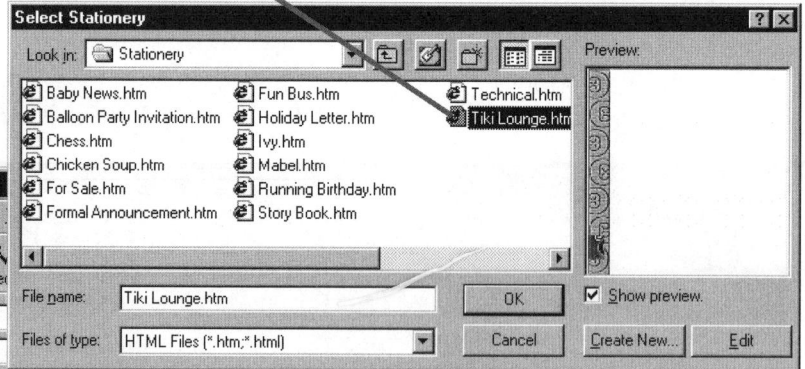

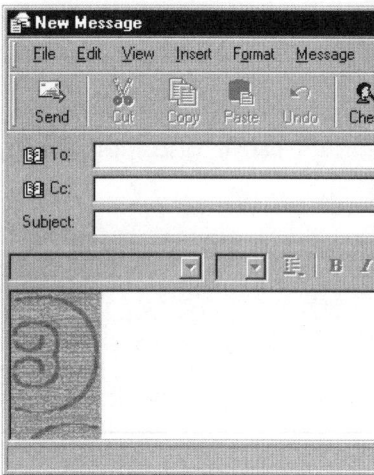

Select Stationery

Look in: Stationery

Baby News.htm   Fun Bus.htm   Technical.htm
Balloon Party Invitation.htm   Holiday Letter.htm   Tiki Lounge.htm
Chess.htm   Ivy.htm
Chicken Soup.htm   Mabel.htm
For Sale.htm   Running Birthday.htm
Formal Announcement.htm   Story Book.htm

Preview:

File name: Tiki Lounge.htm   OK   ☑ Show preview.

Files of type: HTML Files (*.htm;*.html)   Cancel   Create New...   Edit

New Message

File   Edit   View   Insert   Format   Message

Send   Cut   Copy   Paste   Undo   Chec

To:
Cc:
Subject:

B *I* U A

3 Add your text

Take note

Any HTML file can be used as stationery – though obviously, those designed for the job tend to work better. You can create your own if you like – see Chapter 8 for more on HTML.

Handling incoming mail

1 Select the message.

2 Click a toolbar button.

3 When *replying*, the address will be copied in for you – when *forwarding* you must enter the address.

4 Add your own text.

5 Delete any of the copied in text that you don't want.

6 Send the message as normal.

Most of the buttons on the toolbar are there to deal with incoming messages. Click on one to:

Reply to the sender;

Reply to the sender and all who received a copy;

Forward the message to another person;

Delete it.

When you reply to, or forward a message, its text is copied into the Compose window for editing.

2 Click a button

1 Select the message

6 Click Send

3 Enter the address if forwarding

4 Add new text as required

5 Delete unwanted text

Hi Moira

Thanks for the warning - I'll make sure I'm around for the postie tomorrow.

----- Original Message -----
From: Moira Stephen
To: Mac
Sent: Tuesday, May 18, 1999 10:31 PM
Subject: Access 2000 Made Simple

In the post - sent this afternoon.

Message Rules

Swamped by too much mail? Message Rules can help to filter out the junk and to focus on the important messages.

A Message Rule has two components:

● The **Condition** identifies it. This may be based on who sent it, keywords in the subject or text, its priority, size, the presence of attachments or other features.

● The **Action** tells Outlook what to do with the message. This could be to flag or colour it or move it to a special folder for easier finding, or delete it automatically.

The simplest way to set up a new rule is to base it on an existing message of the type that you want the rule to pick up.

1 Select a message of the right type.

2 Open the Message menu and select Create Rule from Message…

3 Tick one or more Conditions to identify the messages.

4 Tick the Action to apply to messages of this type.

5 If the Condition or Action needs further definition, click on the underlined value.

6 Enter the details as needed and click OK.

7 Give it a meaningful Name and click OK.

3 Tick the Condition(s)

4 Select an action

New Mail Rule

Select your Conditions and Actions first, then specify the values in the Description.

1. Select the Conditions for your rule:

☐ Where the From line contains people
☐ Where the Subject line contains specific words
☑ Where the message body contains specific words
☐ Where the To line contains people

2. Select the Actions for your rule:

☐ Move it to the specified folder
☑ Copy it to the specified folder
☐ Delete it
☐ Forward it to people

3. Rule Description (click on an underlined value to edit it):

Apply this rule after the message arrives
Where the message body contains specific words
Copy it to the specified folder

4. Name of the rule:

New Mail Rule #1

OK   Cancel

6 Enter the details

Type Specific Words

Type specific words or a phrase, and click Add.

project   Add

Words:

Where the message body contains
'work'
or 'job'

Remove
Options...

OK   Cancel

7 Name it

5 Edit values

Managing Rules

1 Open the Tools menu, point to Message Rules and select Mail.

2 Select the rule.

3 Use the buttons to Modify, create a New rule or Remove an unwanted one.

Or

4 Click Move Up or Move Down to set the order.

The Message Rules dialog box can be used to edit or delete existing rules, or to create new ones from scratch. You can also adjust the order in which rules are applied. This won't normally matter, but there could be circumstances where you want to set up exceptions. For instance, you might have a rule to delete chain letter junk, by checking for 'chain' in the message, but not want to miss your monthly e-mail from a specialist cycle parts supplier – which may also contain the word 'chain'. The solution here is to set up a rule which stops processing rules when it finds a message from the parts supplier, and to place this above your chain letter deleter.

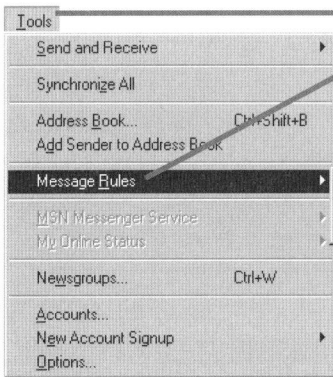

1 Use Tools – Message Rules – Mail…

2 Select the rule

3 Edit as needed

4 Set the order

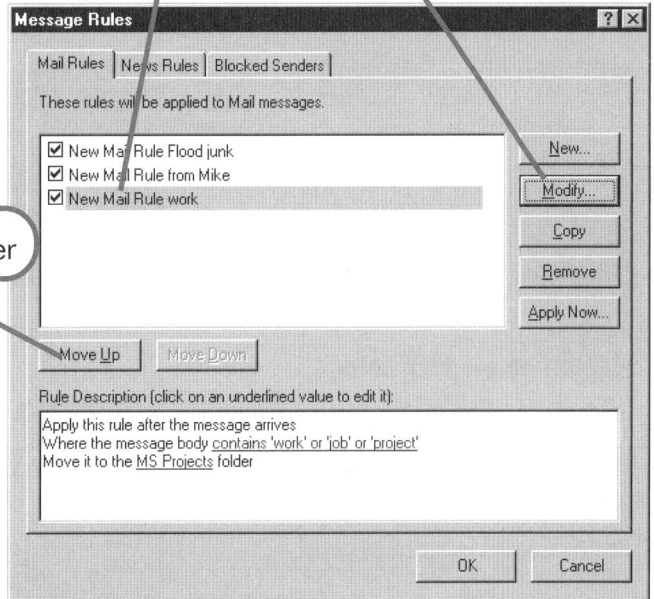

Tools

Send and Receive ▶

Synchronize All

Address Book...   Ctrl+Shift+B

Add Sender to Address Book

Message Rules ▶   Mail...
                    News...
                    Blocked Senders List...

MSN Messenger Service ▶
My Online Status ▶

Newsgroups...   Ctrl+W

Accounts...
New Account Signup ▶
Options...

Message Rules   ? ✕

Mail Rules | News Rules | Blocked Senders

These rules will be applied to Mail messages.

☑ New Mail Rule Flood junk
☑ New Mail Rule from Mike
☑ New Mail Rule work

New...
Modify...
Copy
Remove
Apply Now...

Move Up   Move Down

Rule Description (click on an underlined value to edit it):

Apply this rule after the message arrives
Where the message body contains 'work' or 'job' or 'project'
Move it to the MS Projects folder

OK   Cancel

Take note

You can also apply Message Rules to newsgroups – see page 122.

The Address Book

If you are going to write to someone, you must have their e-mail address – and if you are going to write to them often, you should keep the address in your Address Book. This can hold not only e-mail addresses, but also *snail-mail* (normal) addresses, phone numbers and other details.

There are two ways to get an address into your book:

● Write it into the book at any time, on- or off-line;

● The easy way – if the person has written to you, start to reply and let the system extract the address from the To: entry.

1 Open the Tools menu and select Address Book... or click 📖.

2 At the Address Book window, open the File menu or click the New button and select New Contact.

3 On the Personal panel type the person's First, and Last (and Middle?) names and e-mail address.

1 Use Tools – Address Book...

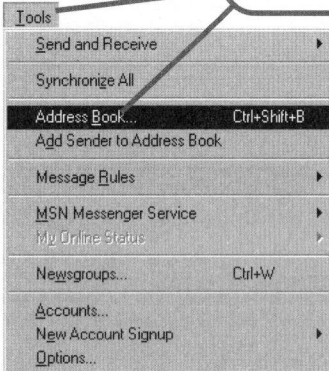

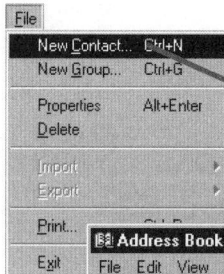

Tools
Send and Receive	▶
Synchronize All	
Address Book...	Ctrl+Shift+B
Add Sender to Address Book	
Message Rules	▶
MSN Messenger Service	▶
My Online Status	▶
Newsgroups...	Ctrl+W
Accounts...	
New Account Signup	▶
Options...	

File
New Contact...	Ctrl+N
New Group...	Ctrl+G
Properties	Alt+Enter
Delete	
Import	▶
Export	▶
Print...	
Exit	

2 Set up a New Contact

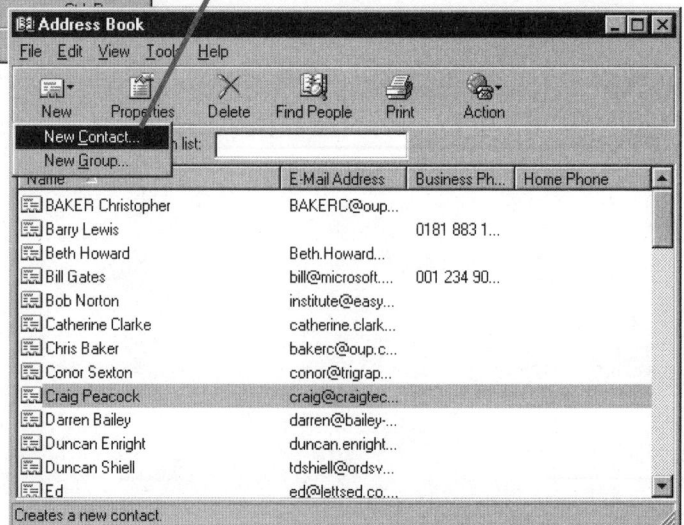

Tip

To edit an existing entry, select it then click the Properties button to open the panel.

Address Book

File Edit View Tools Help

New   Properties   Delete   Find People   Print   Action

New Contact...
New Group...

Name	E-Mail Address	Business Ph...	Home Phone
BAKER Christopher	BAKERC@oup...		
Barry Lewis		0181 883 1...	
Beth Howard	Beth.Howard...		
Bill Gates	bill@microsoft....	001 234 90...	
Bob Norton	institute@easy...		
Catherine Clarke	catherine.clark...		
Chris Baker	bakerc@oup.c...		
Conor Sexton	conor@trigrap...		
Craig Peacock	craig@craigtec...		
Darren Bailey	darren@bailey-...		
Duncan Enright	duncan.enright...		
Duncan Shiell	tdshiell@ordsv...		
Ed	ed@lettsed.co...		

Creates a new contact.

4 If they have several addresses, click Add and enter the others, Adding each one.

5 Go to the other panels to add further details.

6 Click OK.

Double check the address – it's easy to get them wrong!

If there are several addresses, set one as the Default.

3 Type the name and address

4 Click Add

Bill Gates Properties

Personal | Home | Business | Other | NetMeeting | Digital IDs

Enter personal information about this contact here.

Name

First: Bill   Middle: Last: Gates

Display: Bill Gates   Nickname:

E-Mail Addresses

Add new: billgates@aol.com   Add

billgates@aol.com (Default E-Mail)   Edit

Remove

Set as Default

☐ Send E-Mail using plain text only.

OK   Cancel

5 Add other info

Bill Gates Properties   ? X

Personal | Home | Business | Other | NetMeeting | Digital IDs

Enter business-related information about this contact here.

Company: Microsoft   Job Title: Chairman

Street Address: Department:

Office:

City: Phone: 001 234 900 100

State/Province: Fax: 001 234 900 200

Zip Code: Pager:

Country: IP Phone:

Business Web Page:

http://www.microsoft.com/bill   Go

6 Click OK

OK   Cancel

Tip

You could just type a person's whole name into any of the Name slots, but if you split it into First and Last, they will be listed in alphabetical order (by first or last name — your choice) in the Address Book.

Capturing an address

If someone has written to you and you want to add their name to your Address Book, start to reply and capture their address from the *To:* slot of the Compose Window. If you do not actually want to reply at that point, just close the window to abandon the message.

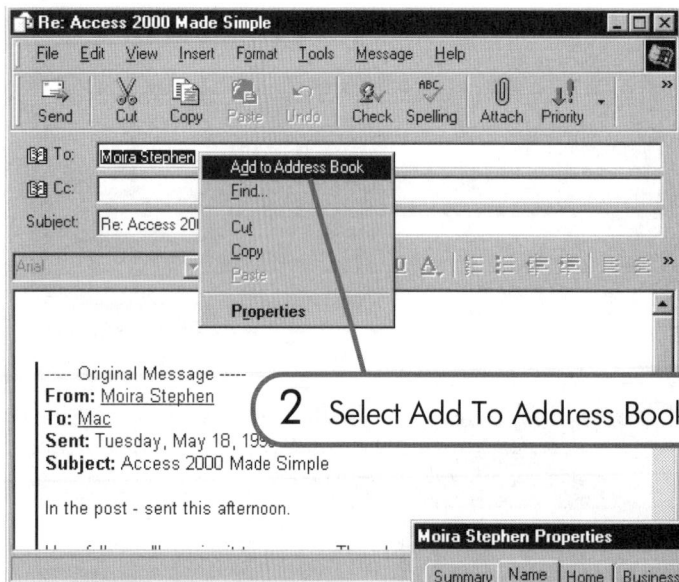

1 Start to reply to a message from the person whose address you want.

2 Right-click on the name and select Add To Address Book.

3 Enter or edit the First/ Last names.

4 Click OK.

5 Cancel the new message if you do not want to reply at this time.

Re: Access 2000 Made Simple

File   Edit   View   Insert   Format   Tools   Message   Help

Send   Cut   Copy   Paste   Undo   Check   Spelling   Attach   Priority

To: Moira Stephen

Add to Address Book
Find...

Cc:

Cut
Copy
Paste

Subject: Re: Access 20

Properties

Arial   U A   ≡ ≡ ≡ ≡ | ≡ ≡

----- Original Message -----
From: Moira Stephen
To: Mac
Sent: Tuesday, May 18, 199
Subject: Access 2000 Made Simple

In the post - sent this afternoon.

2 Select Add To Address Book

5 Cancel?

Moira Stephen Properties

Summary   Name   Home   Business   Personal   Other   NetMeeting   Digital IDs

Enter name and e-mail information about this contact

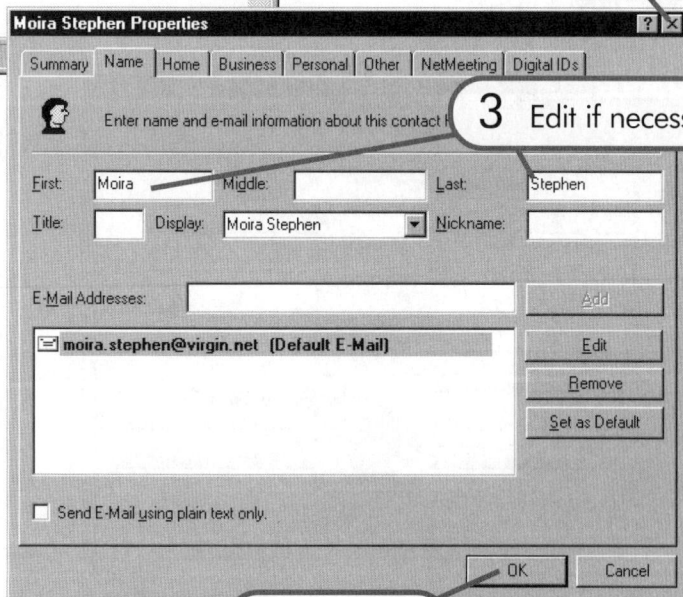

3 Edit if necessary

First: Moira   Middle: Last: Stephen

Title: Display: Moira Stephen ▼ Nickname:

E-Mail Addresses: Add

moira.stephen@virgin.net (Default E-Mail)   Edit

Remove

Set as Default

☐ Send E-Mail using plain text only.

OK   Cancel

4 Click OK

Take note

Sometimes you will get the e-mail address in the First name slot (as well as in the address box). Type in the real name.

Mail groups

1 In the Address Book click New and select New Group.

2 Type in a Group Name.

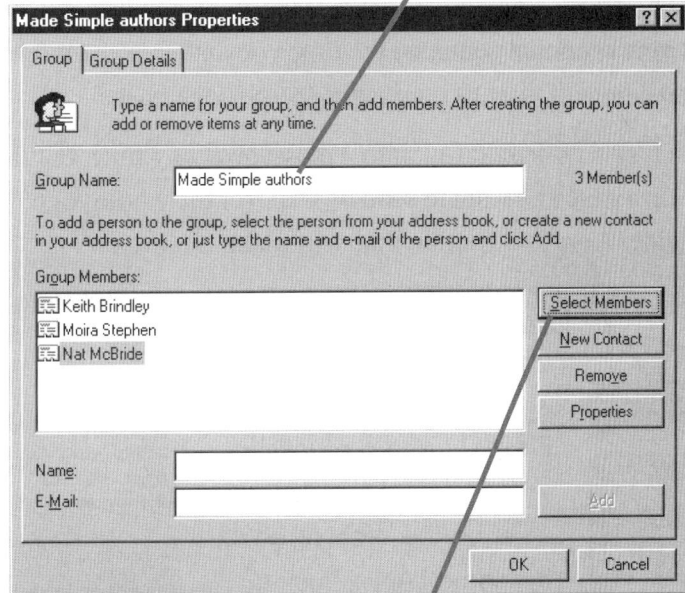

3 Click Select Members.

4 At the Select Group Members dialog box, select a name from the list and click Select->.

5 Repeat Step 4 for each member.

6 Click OK to close Select, then again at the Properties box.

If you regularly send messages to the same set of people, you can create a mail group. One message composed to the group will then be sent to all.

2 Type a Group Name

Made Simple authors Properties ? X

Group | Group Details

Type a name for your group, and then add members. After creating the group, you can add or remove items at any time.

Group Name: Made Simple authors   3 Member(s)

To add a person to the group, select the person from your address book, or create a new contact in your address book, or just type the name and e-mail of the person and click Add.

Group Members:

Keith Brindley
Moira Stephen
Nat McBride

Select Members
New Contact
Remove
Properties

Name:
E-Mail: Add

OK   Cancel

4 Add each person

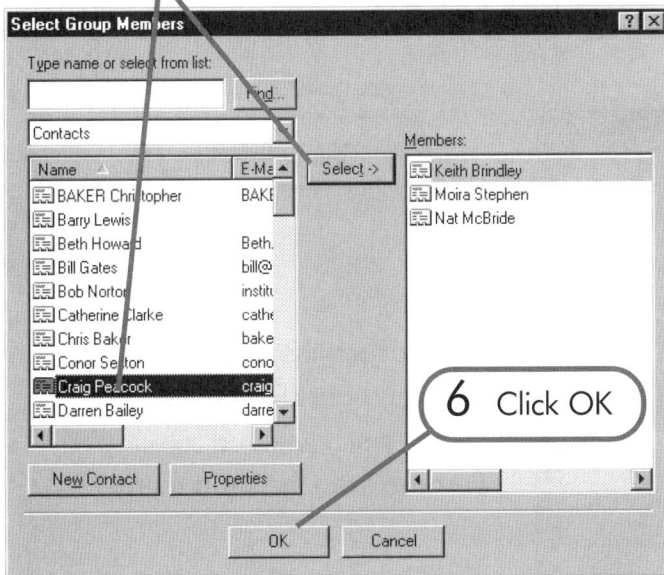

Select Group Members ? X

Type name or select from list:

Find...

Contacts

Name	E-Ma
BAKER Christopher	BAKE
Barry Lewis	
Beth Howard	Beth.
Bill Gates	bill@
Bob Norton	instit
Catherine Clarke	cathe
Chris Baker	bake
Conor Sexton	cono
Craig Peacock	craig
Darren Bailey	darre

Select ->

Members:
Keith Brindley
Moira Stephen
Nat McBride

New Contact   Properties

OK   Cancel

3 Click Select Members

6 Click OK

Take note

If you also contact people by phone or NetMeeting, add those details. You will then be able to use the **Actions** button to **Dial** a number or place an **Internet Call**.

Files by mail

Files of any type – documents, graphics, audio clips – can be attached to messages and sent by e-mail. Compared to sending them on paper or disk by post, e-mail is often more reliable, quicker and cheaper. The larger the file, the longer it takes to get through, and the greater the chance of errors – increasing transmission time. Somewhere over 2Mb (local contacts, much more for international contacts) the time you and your recipient spend on-line will start to outweight the postage costs.

You can type a hypertext link into a message at any time, but if you are on a page and want to send its URL (or the whole page!) to someone, there is a routine that will make it simple.

Basic steps

1 Write your message.

2 Open the Insert menu and select File Attachment or click [Attach].

3 Browse for the file.

4 Click Attach. The file will be listed in the Attach line above the message area.

2 Use Insert – File Attachment

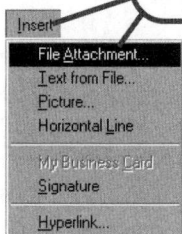

If the file is in a place that your recipient can reach – i.e. on the Web or on the same LAN – just send a Shortcut

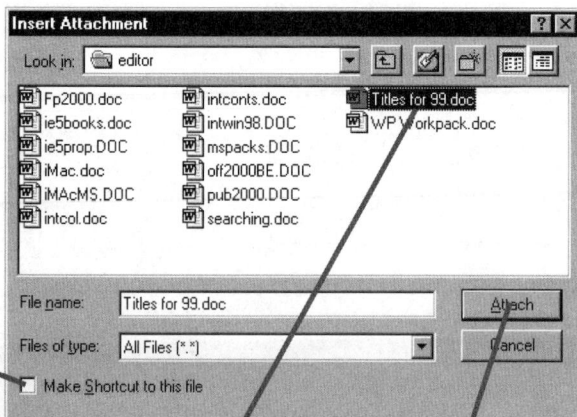

Insert menu
File Attachment...
Text from File...
Picture...
Horizontal Line
My Business Card
Signature
Hyperlink...

Insert Attachment

Look in: editor

Fp2000.doc	intconts.doc	Titles for 99.doc
ie5books.doc	intwin98.DOC	WP Workpack.doc
ie5prop.DOC	mspacks.DOC	
iMac.doc	off2000BE.DOC	
iMAcMS.DOC	pub2000.DOC	
intcol.doc	searching.doc	

File name: Titles for 99.doc [Attach]

Files of type: All Files (*.*) [Cancel]

☐ Make Shortcut to this file

3 Select the file

4 Click Attach

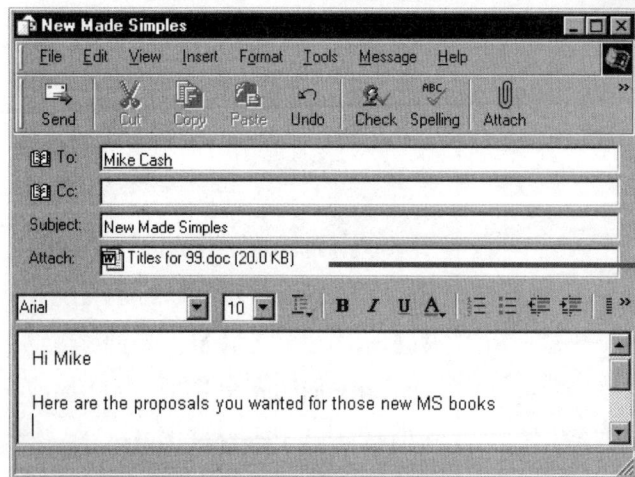

New Made Simples

File Edit View Insert Format Tools Message Help

Send | Cut | Copy | Paste | Undo | Check | Spelling | Attach

To: Mike Cash
Cc:
Subject: New Made Simples
Attach: Titles for 99.doc (20.0 KB)

Arial 10 B I U A

Hi Mike

Here are the proposals you wanted for those new MS books

If you attach the wrong file by mistake, right-click on its name in the Attach line and select Remove from the short menu

❏ To attach a link

5 Go to the page.

6 Open the File menu, point at Send, then select Link by E-mail.

Or

7 Click the Mail button, and select Send a Link.

8 The page title will be in the Subject line and the URL will be given in the Attach line and as a link in the message area. Enter the recipient and add your message text as normal.

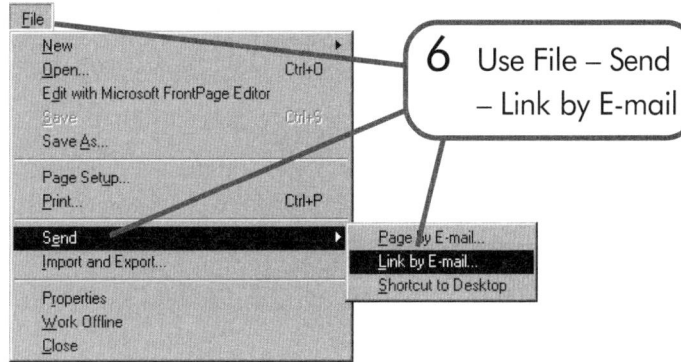

You can also send the page as the message – editing it or adding your own text to it, if required

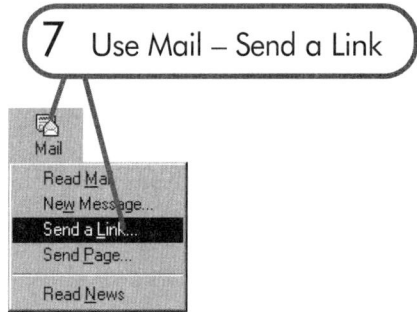

File menu:
New ▶
Open...   Ctrl+O
Edit with Microsoft FrontPage Editor
Save   Ctrl+S
Save As...

Page Setup...
Print...   Ctrl+P

Send ▶
Import and Export...

Properties
Work Offline
Close

Send submenu:
Page by E-mail...
Link by E-mail...
Shortcut to Desktop

> 6 Use File – Send – Link by E-mail

> 7 Use Mail – Send a Link

Mail
Read Mail
New Message...
Send a Link...
Send Page...
Read News

> 8 Add the recipient and your message

The Kadmium Ignatious Crew _ □ ✕
File Edit View Insert Format Tools Message Help

Send   Cut   Copy   Paste   Undo   Check   Spelling   Attach   Priority »

To: Nat McBride
Cc:
Subject: The Kadmium Ignatious Crew
Attach: The Kadmium Ignatious Crew.url (184 bytes)

Arial   ▼ 10 ▼   B I U A, ⋮≣ ≣ 镊 镊 ≣ ≣ »

URL links are also placed in the message

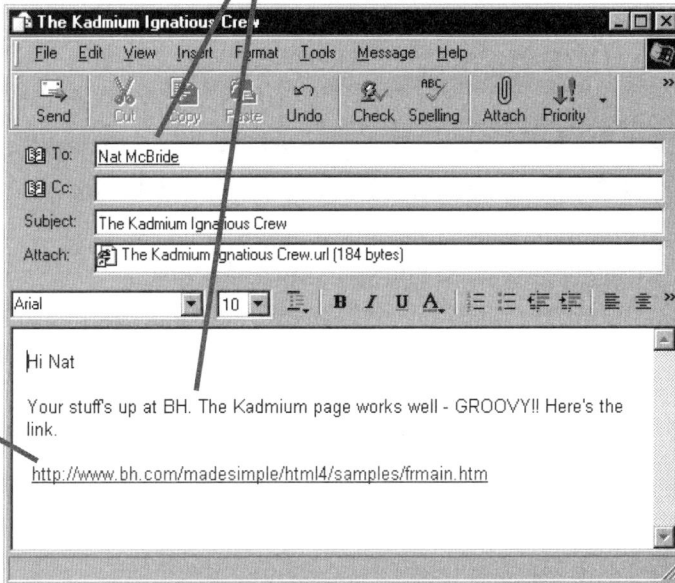

Hi Nat

Your stuff's up at BH. The Kadmium page works well - GROOVY!! Here's the link.

http://www.bh.com/madesimple/html4/samples/frmain.htm

Tip

If you receive an attached file in your mail, treat it as you would a file in the news (page 124).

Mail folders

There arc initially five mail folders:

Inbox where new mail arrives;

Outbox for messages awaiting delivery;

Sent for copies of outgoing mail;

Deleted where messages are stored after deletion;

Drafts for holding messages not yet ready for sending.

Messages in **Deleted** are removed at the end of the session if you turn on **Empty messages from 'Deleted Items'...** (page 91).

It is useful to set up one or more new folders for long-term storage. You might have one for each project, topic or set of contacts – at the very least, you should have an *Old Mail* folder so that your Inbox doesn't get too cluttered.

Basic steps

❑ Creating a new folder

1 Open the File menu, point to New and select Folder...

2 Select the folder in which it is to be created – select Local folders for a top-level folder.

3 Give it a name.

4 Click OK.

Tip

Use the File –Folder – Compact All Folders command regularly. This reclaims the space that had been taken by deleted messages.

The default folders cannot be moved or deleted – but the ones you create can be.

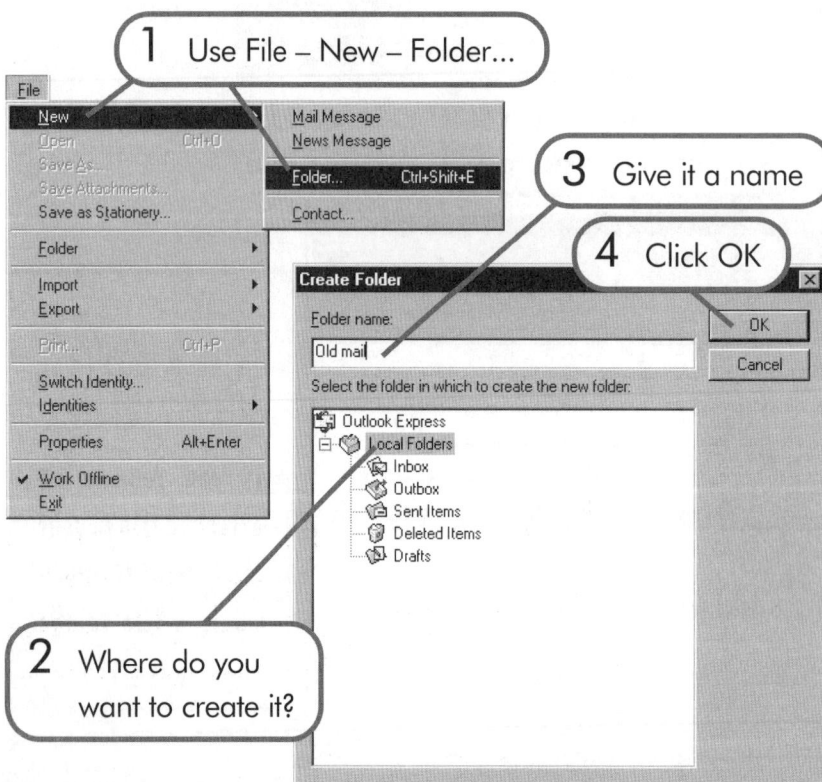

1 Use File – New – Folder...

3 Give it a name

4 Click OK

2 Where do you want to create it?

❑ Moving messages

5 Select the message and drag it across to the target folder.

❑ Copying messages

6 Right-click on the message to open the short menu or open the Edit menu, and select Copy to Folder.

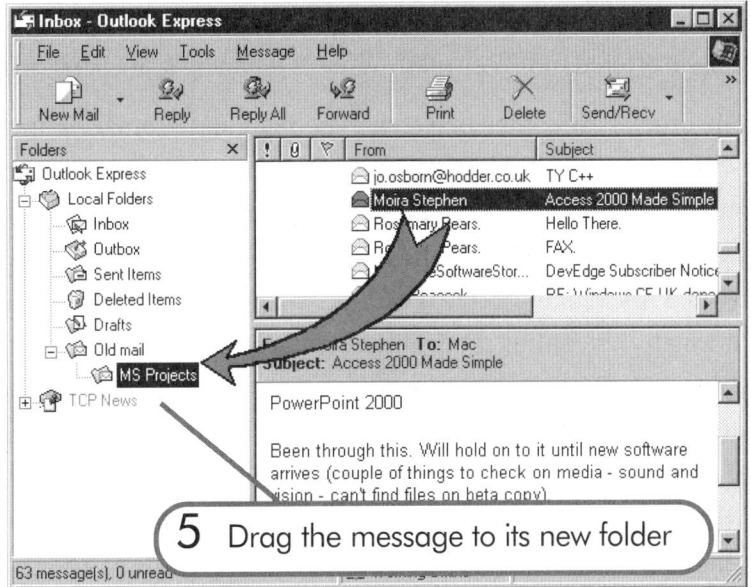

7 Select the target folder and click OK.

5 Drag the message to its new folder

7 Select the target folder

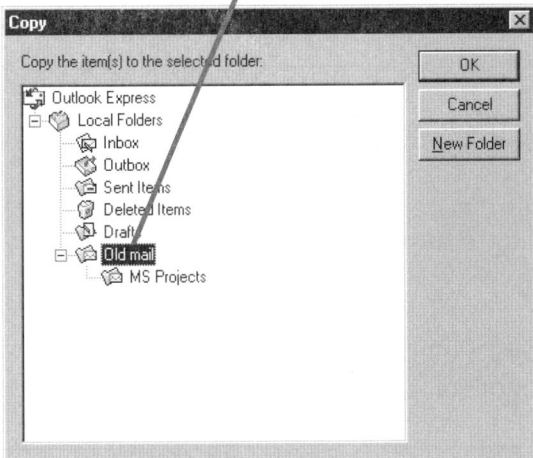

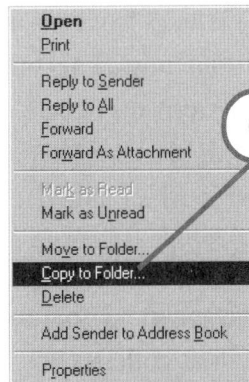

6 Select Copy to Folder

Tip

Go through your old mail now and then and delete stuff that is no longer relevant.

Web mail

Go to almost any of the major directories and portals and you will be offered free Web mail. What is it and how does it work?

The crucial difference between Web mail and ordinary e-mail is that your mail folders, where you store your messages, are online. With ordinary e-mail, you only need to be online while you are sending and receiving messages – they can be read and written, moved and deleted offline. With Web mail, you must (normally) be online the whole time that you are dealing with your mail. (It is possible to download messages for reading and storage, and upload the text of messages that you have written in a word-processor.) As a result, dealing with the mail is slower – and more costly if you are paying for the online and telephone time.

The big advantage of Web mail – apart from the fact that it is free – is that you can access your mailbox from anywhere as long as you can get into the Internet somehow. This may be through a terminal in a public library, from a friend's or colleague's desktop anywhere in the world, or through your own (temporary) account at your place of work or study.

A Web mail address is worth having if:

● you are a student and want to be able to keep in touch when you are at home or at college;

● your job takes you to places where you cannot easily access your normal Internet account;

● you are likely to be changing your job/college/Internet Access Provider and don't want the disruption of a change of address.

Web mail providers

❑ There are some specialist providers, and Web mail is offered as a service at most of the big directories and portals. Key providers include:

MailCity
www.mailcity.com

Excite
mail.excite.co.uk
mail.excite.com

Yahoo
mail.yahoo.co.uk
mail.yahoo.com

Netcenter
home.netcenter.com

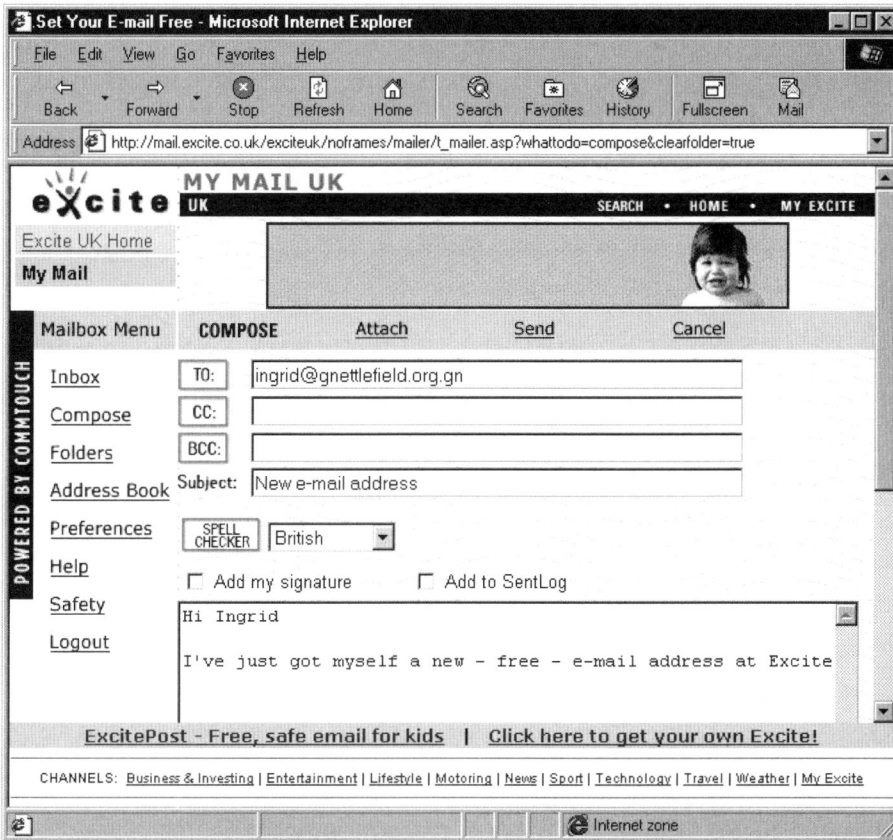

Screenshots from Excite's mail service – the Inbox, Compose (left), Folders and Address book are almost identical to those of Oultook Explorer, but you can only write plain text messages.

Junk e-mail can be a problem for anyone – anything which helps keep it under control is worth using!

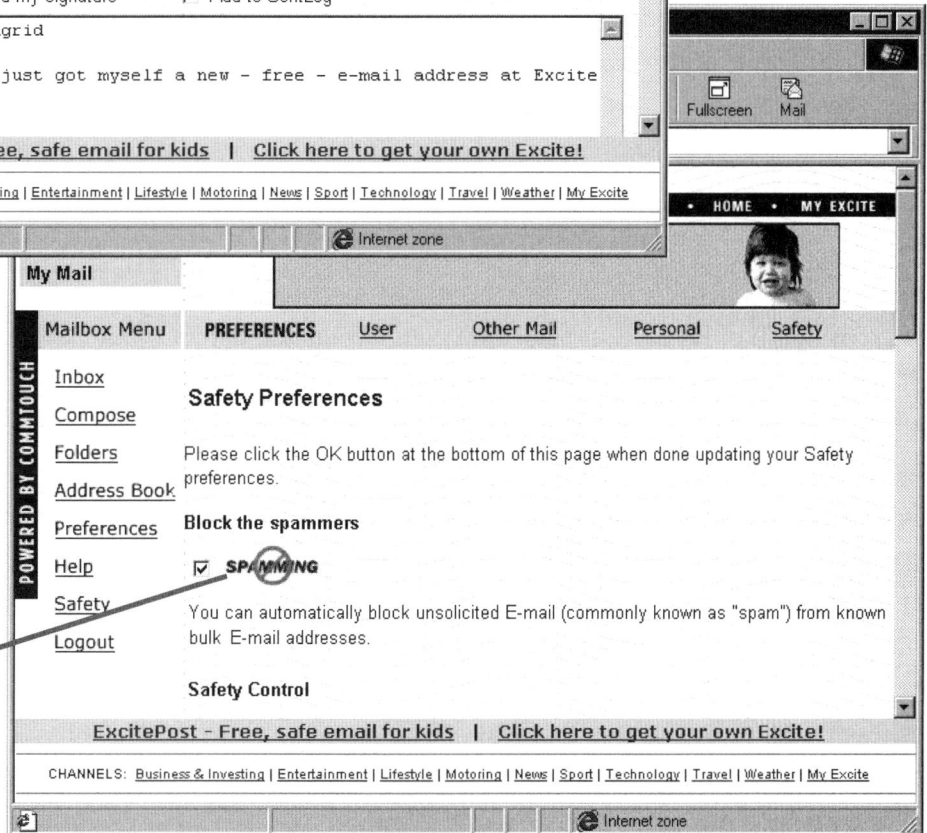

E-mail etiquette

When you send someone a paper letter, you know that what they receive will be the same as you send, and if you enclose lots of material, you will pay the extra postage. E mail is different. Your recipients actively download your messages, which takes time and can cost money. Further, if they are using an older or simpler, text-based e-mail application, it can affect the appearance – and sometimes the *delivery* – of your messages.

Text and data files

A lot of business users, and some individuals, have e-mail systems that can only handle plain text. If you want to send files to these people, the files must first be converted to text. That is easy for you – just set the option when attaching the file. However, there are several formats for sending data files as text, and your recipient must have a suitable converter to extract the file at the other end. Send a small test file first to check that they can handle your files.

Size

Some e-mail systems set a limit to the size of messages; 1,000 lines (roughly 60Kb) is a typical maximum. You are hardly likely to write this much, but an attached file can easily push the message size over the limit. Even where there is no limit, file size is still a factor. The larger the file, the longer it takes to download, and the higher your recipients' phone bills. With a good modem and a standard phone line, e-mail usually comes in at around 3Kb per second, or 1Mb in 5 minutes. Use the standard WinZip (or PKZip) software to compress data files before attaching them. Document files can be reduced to 10% or less of their original size this way. Some graphics formats compress well, others – such as GIFs and JPEGs – have built-in compression and often are not worth ZIPping.

E-tiquette rules

❏ Small is beautiful. Short messages are quick and cheap to download.

❏ Test first. When sending anything other than plain text, try a short test file first to make sure that the other person can receive it properly.

❏ Zip it up! If you are sending files, compress them with WinZip.

❏ Subject matters! Always type a Subject line so that the other person can identify the message.

❏ Short signatures. If you have a signature, keep it short – no more than half a dozen lines. Long files, no matter how clever, are an irritating waste of space.

Signatures

1 Open the Tools menu
and select Options…

2 Switch to the Signatures
tab.

3 Click New.

4 Tick Text and type in
your signature.

Or

5 Tick File and browse for
your signature file.

6 Set the Add options as
required.

7 Click OK.

A signature can be added to the end of every message. You can write your signature directly into the Options panel or link in a signature file. This must be a plain text file, containing your name, e-mail address and any other contact details you want to give. People's signatures often also contain a favourite quote, advert, or a picture or name created from ASCII characters. e.g.

```
    _
   \ \              _  _       ,----------------------------,
    \**\ _ _ _    V \..............| COME FLY WITH ME |
  X*#####*+~~\_\            '----------------------------'
    o/\ \
      \_\
```

1 Use Tools – Options

2 Go to Signatures

3 Click New

6 Add to which messages?

4 Type a Text signature

5 Link to a file

7 Click OK

Finding people

Finding people on the Internet can be very difficult. Users get online through hundreds of access providers or thousands of businesses – and there is no one 'controlling' organisation. However, there are sites that are compiling directories of e-mail addresses, and the best of these people-finding site be reached through Outlook Express.

● Don't expect too much from this. You are more likely to succeed if the person is in the States or uses one of the major access providers.

1 Open the Edit menu, point to Find and select People …

2 Enter the name.

3 Click Find Now. After a few moments, the lower panel will open to display the results.

4 If you have no luck there, select another site from the Look-in list and try again.

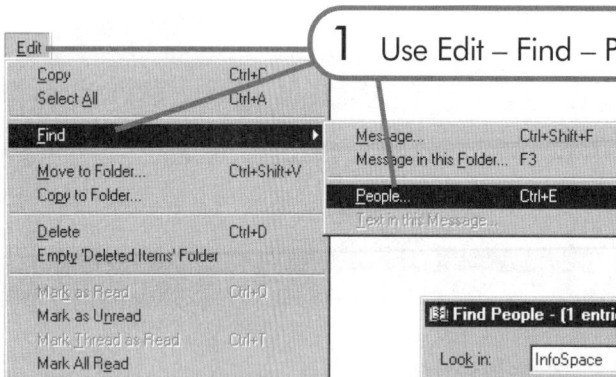

Edit

Copy	Ctrl+C
Select All	Ctrl+A
Find	▶
Move to Folder...	Ctrl+Shift+V
Copy to Folder...	
Delete	Ctrl+D
Empty 'Deleted Items' Folder	
Mark as Read	Ctrl+Q
Mark as Unread	
Mark Thread as Read	Ctrl+T
Mark All Read	

Message...	Ctrl+Shift+F
Message in this Folder...	F3
People...	Ctrl+E
Text in this Message...	

1 Use Edit – Find – People

2 Type the name

3 Click Find Now

Find People - (1 entries found)

Look in: InfoSpace

People | Advanced

Name: Tony Blair

E-mail:

People

Name	E-Mail Address	
Tony Blair		

Web Site...
Find Now
Stop
Clear All
Close
Properties
Delete
Add to Address Book

This is not *the* Tony Blair, by the way!

Tip

If you want other people to be able to find you more easily, go to each of the people finding sites and add your address to their directory.

5 If you get too many results, click Web site.

6 At the site, look for the Advanced search option (most offer one) and specify your search more closely.

There is no 'best' people-finding site – none are complete, and all have a slightly different set of people.

4 Try another site

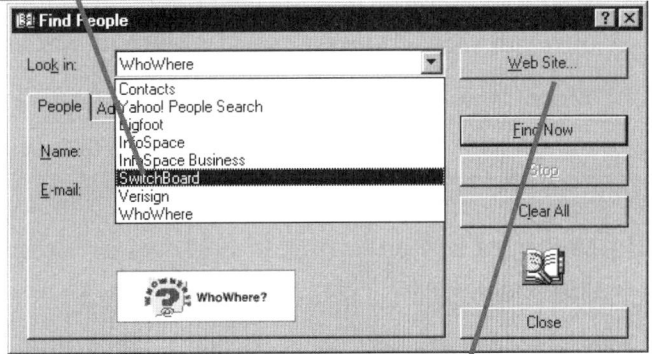

5 Go to the site

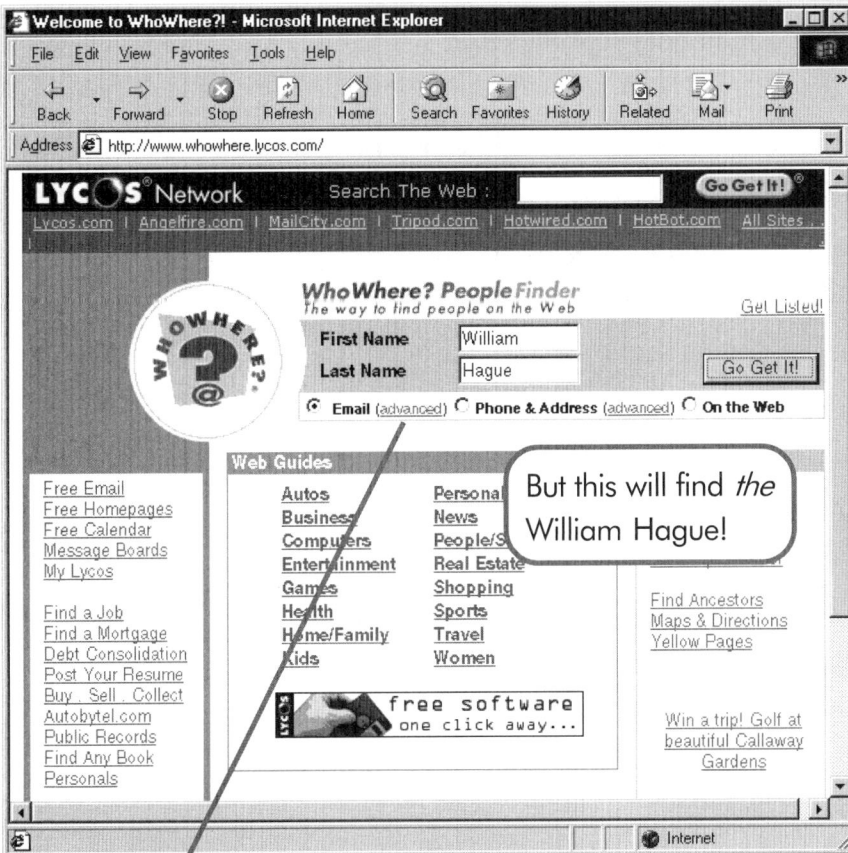

But this will find *the* William Hague!

6 Try an Advanced Search

Tip

You can also get Phone numbers, real addresses and other information at most people directories.

Summary

❑ Outlook Express handles both e-mail and newsgroups.

❑ With the Options, you can set up the system to suit how you work. They can be changed at any time.

❑ When sending messages, start by selecting who they will go to. You should always write the nature of the message in the Subject line.

❑ Messages can be formatted and sent on decorative stationery.

❑ You can easily reply to incoming mail, or forward it to a third person.

❑ Message rules allow you to automate your message handling.

❑ The easiest way to manage e-mail addresses is to store them in the Address Book.

❑ Mail groups are useful where you regularly send the same message to a number of people.

❑ Documents and other files can be sent by mail.

❑ New mail folders can be created to store old mail. Messages can be easily moved between folders.

❑ If you want a mailbox that you can access from any computer anywhere, sign up for a Web mail account.

❑ E-mail etiquette is based on not wasting other people's time (and phone bills). Mail should be kept short, and should have a clear Subject line.

❑ Signatures can add something extra to your mail – and long ones can add far too much!

❑ If you want to know an e-mail address, you can often find people at one or other of the people directories.

7 Newsgroups

Newsgroups

These have developed from e-mail, but instead of articles being mailed directly to you, they are sent in bulk to your news server, and you download from there those articles that you want to read. At the last count there were around 30,000 groups, each dedicated to a different interest – professions and obsessions, programming languages and TV programmes, hobbies, politics, sports, fan clubs and all the rest.

- The quality and volume of the articles vary enormously. Some newsgroups circulate large quantities of interesting and relevant articles; some carry few articles, and even they are hardly worth reading.

- Some newsgroups are moderated, i.e. they have someone who checks all incoming articles before broadcasting them to the members. This reduces the quantity of irrelevant and/or boring post.

- Some groups are mainly for discussions, others are more like open help-lines, where people can ask for – and get – solutions to technical problems.

- Not all newsgroups are available on all servers.

- As newsgroups bring together people who share an interest, they can be a good place to make new friends.

- If you subscribe to a group, it is added to your news folder, for easy access. If you do not subscribe, you have to find it in the full list every time you want to read its articles.

- You can just download the message headers, containing the subject, author and other details, then select individual messages and download their text. This can save wasting a lot of phone time and hard disk space on unwanted messages.

Take note

Most newsgroups are part of USENET – the Users Network –a loose collection of individuals and organisations. Other old networks also brought their own newsgroups into the Internet, and many more have been added over the years. New newsgroups keep appearing all the time.

Newsgroup names

Tip

If you are new to the Internet, there is a group specially for you. It's called:

news.announce.newusers

Newsgroups are organised into a branching structure, with major sections sub-divided by topic. Their names reflect this structure.

For example, **comp.lang.basic.visual.database** is in the **compu**ter section, which amongst other things covers programming **lang**uages, including **basic**, and this has a **visual** subsection containing four groups, one of which is concerned with **database** programming.

You can see the full list of the newsgroups available on your server, by clicking the Newsgroups button to open this dialog box. You can find groups on particular topics, when you want to select one to subscribe or sample (page 116), but one day – when you have a spare hour or two – work through the whole list just to see what's there.

Used for finding the newsgroups on a topic – see page 116

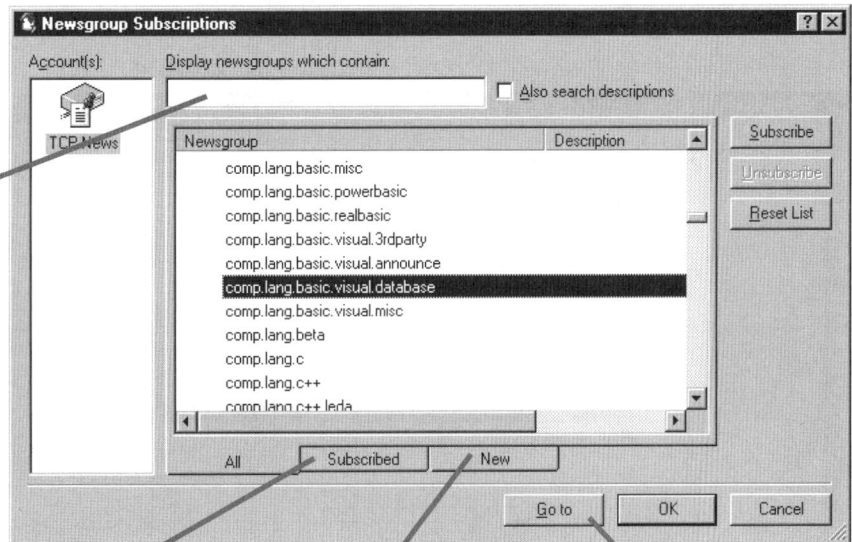

Groups to which you subscribe are listed in this panel

When the server takes on new groups, they will be listed here

Lets you dip into a newsgroup

Getting the newsgroups

Once you get into the newsgroups, reading and writing messages is almost identical to handling e-mail, but first you have to get into the groups! There are two approaches: you can subscribe to groups if you want to read their messages regularly, or dip into them, much as you might surf the Web.

Subscribing costs nothing and commits you to nothing. It simply place the group in the folder list for easy access.

If you want to read the occasional article in different newsgroups, without cluttering up the folder list, you can use the **Go to** option to pick up the current articles.

Whether you are subscribing or sampling, newsgroups are selected from the **Newsgroups** panel. Rather than struggle with the full list, filter it with one or more words that are likely to be in the name.

1 From the Tools menu, select Newsgroups... or click [Newsgroups...] in the top panel of the newsgroups window.

2 Open the All groups panel.

3 Type a word to filter the list – if there are still too many, type a second word.

4 Select a group.

5 See what's there by clicking Go to.

or

6 Join the group by clicking Subscribe.

---

3 Type a word or two

4 Select a group

6 Click Subscribe

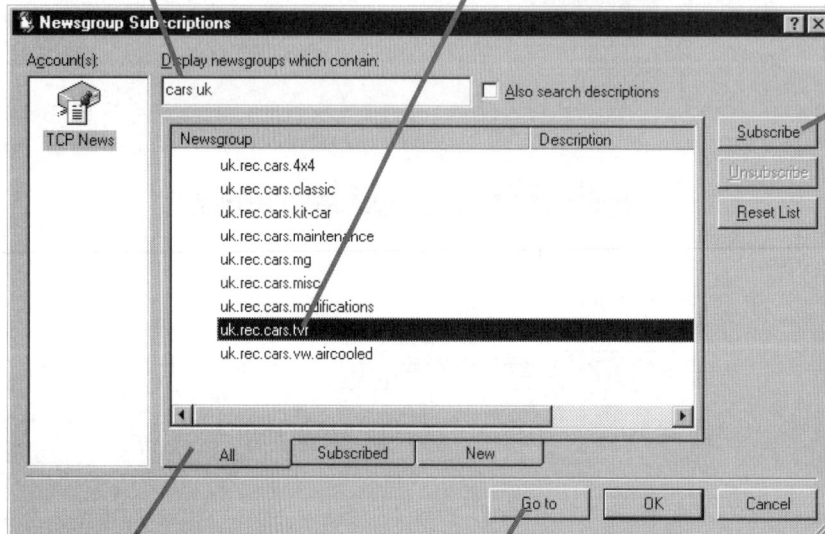

Newsgroup Subscriptions ? ☒

Account(s): Display newsgroups which contain:

cars uk   ☐ Also search descriptions

TCP News

Newsgroup	Description
uk.rec.cars.4x4	
uk.rec.cars.classic	
uk.rec.cars.kit-car	
uk.rec.cars.maintenance	
uk.rec.cars.mg	
uk.rec.cars.misc	
uk.rec.cars.modifications	
uk.rec.cars.tvr	
uk.rec.cars.vw.aircooled	

Subscribe
Unsubscribe
Reset List

All | Subscribed | New

Go to | OK | Cancel

2 Open All

5 Click Go to

Take note

When you first connect to your news server, you must download the list of groups — be patient, it's a long list!

Downloading

1 Select each group in
turn, click [Settings ▼]
and set the messages
or header option.

2 Select the group(s) that
you want to synchro-
nise or use Tools –
Synchronize All.

3 Click [Synchronize Account]

4 When the messages
start to download, if
you want to read
offline, tick Hang up
when finished.

If you *Go to* a group, Outlook will immediately download its
headers, and you can then download those messages which look
interesting.

If you *Subscribe* to a group, you control what comes in. The
Settings define whether to downloaded new or all messages or
just headers – collecting selected messages later. **Synchronise**
lets you choose which groups to download and when.

● To keep online time to a mimimum, synchronise the
headers only, then hang up. Go through the headers and
mark the messages you want to read, then go online again
to download the marked messages (see page 119).

Settings ▼

● Don't Synchronize

All Messages
New Messages Only
Headers Only

**1 Get messages or
just headers?**

3 Click Synchronize Account

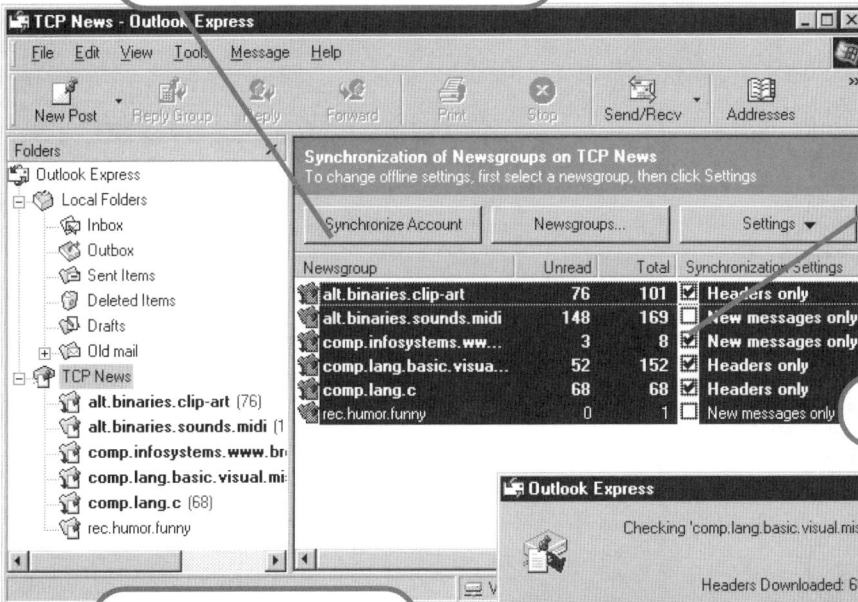

TCP News - Outlook Express

File   Edit   View   Tools   Message   Help

New Post   Reply Group   Reply   Forward   Print   Stop   Send/Recv   Addresses

Folders

Outlook Express
  Local Folders
    Inbox
    Outbox
    Sent Items
    Deleted Items
    Drafts
    Old mail
  TCP News
    alt.binaries.clip-art (76)
    alt.binaries.sounds.midi (1
    comp.infosystems.www.br
    comp.lang.basic.visual.mi
    comp.lang.c (68)
    rec.humor.funny

Synchronization of Newsgroups on TCP News
To change offline settings, first select a newsgroup, then click Settings

[Synchronize Account]   [Newsgroups...]   [Settings ▼]

Newsgroup	Unread	Total	Synchronization Settings
alt.binaries.clip-art	76	101	☑ Headers only
alt.binaries.sounds.midi	148	169	☐ New messages only
comp.infosystems.ww...	3	8	☑ New messages only
comp.lang.basic.visua...	52	152	☑ Headers only
comp.lang.c	68	68	☑ Headers only
rec.humor.funny	0	1	☐ New messages only

**Clear the box if you
don't want the
group this time**

2 Select the groups

Outlook Express

Checking 'comp.lang.basic.visual.misc' for new messages.

Headers Downloaded: 68 (of 100)

[Hide]
[Stop]
[Details >>]

☑ Hang up when finished

4 Go offline after?

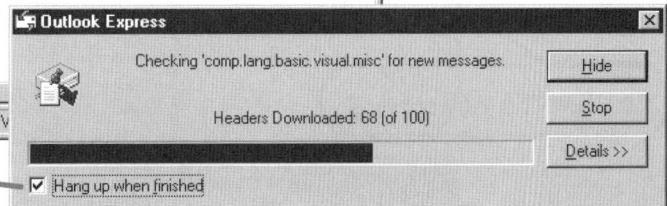

Reading the news

There are three possibilities here.

● You have downloaded all (or new) messages – this is a sensible option only with newsgroups which have few new messages and where most are likely to be of interest.

● You have downloaded only the headers but are online.

● You have downloaded the headers only, then hung up.

Reading is simple and much the same for the first two, but the third involves a little more. In this case you must first scan through the headers, marking the messages you want to read. Next you need to download them, and then you can read them.

One of the key differences between news and e-mail is that in newsgroups, a message can start a 'conversation' – a sequence of replies. These are marked by ⊞ beside the first message.

1 Open the news folder and select a group.

❑ Messages downloaded

2 Select a message and read it in the lower pane.

❑ Headers, but online

3 Select a message and wait for it to download into the lower pane.

2 Select an article and read

---

comp.infosystems.www.browsers.ms-windows - Outlook Express

File   Edit   View   Tools   Message   Help

New Post | Reply Group | Reply | Forward | Print | Stop | Send/Recv | Addresses | Find

Folders

Outlook Express
└ Local Folders
  ├ Inbox
  ├ Outbox
  ├ Sent Items
  ├ Deleted Items
  ├ Drafts
  └ Old mail
└ TCP News
  ├ alt.binaries.clip-art (76)
  ├ alt.binaries.sounds.midi (1
  ├ **comp.infosystems.www.br**
  ├ comp.lang.basic.visual.mi
  ├ comp.lang.c (68)
  └ rec.humor.funny

Subject

IE5 page and graphics loading problem
⊞ Stack error in Opera 3.60 16bit
Re: Netscape and Deleting Web Sites from Address Field?
Opera
Re: Is there a way to save real audio streams while listen to it
netscape preferences

From: Sam To: comp.infosystems.www.browsers.misc,comp.infosystems.www.browsers.ms-win...
Subject: IE5 page and graphics loading problem

Anyone else find that IE5 doesn't always load pages the first time, and that some graphics don't load? I get an 'Error' message, as if the page URL is wrong, but when I reload the page again it comes up properly, and similarly I have to click 'show picture' to make some (but not all) pics come up because they don't at first. I have checked the settings and have got pictures enabled so I don't know why it does this, it's irritating. IE4 never used to do it.

Cheers,
Sam.

---

8 message(s), 2 unread   Working Offline

1 Select a newsgroup

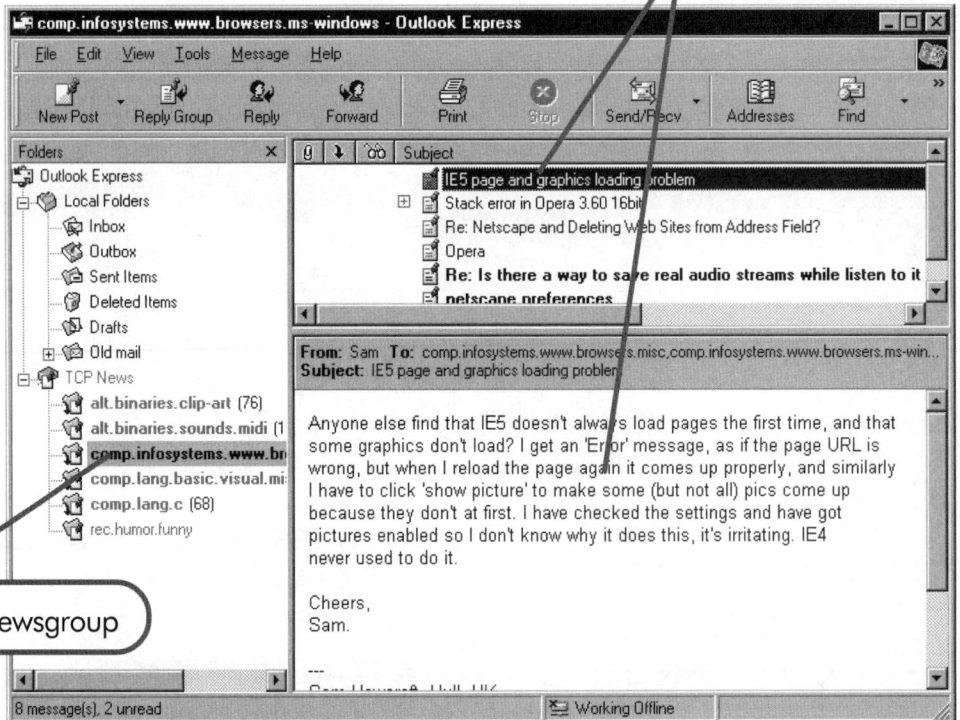

❑ Working offline

4 Scan the headers, clicking into the 🔽 column to mark those you want to read.

5 Open the Tools menu and select Synchronize Newsgroup.

6 Tick Get messages marked for download and click OK.

7 Download, hang up and read the messages.

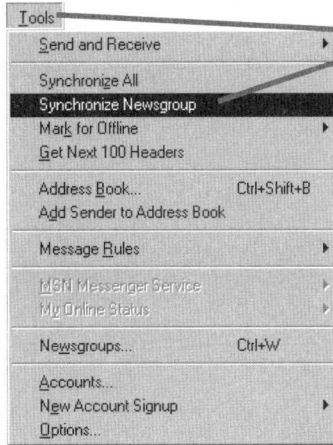

Tools
Send and Receive ▶
Synchronize All
Synchronize Newsgroup
Mark for Offline ▶
Get Next 100 Headers

Address Book...   Ctrl+Shift+B
Add Sender to Address Book

Message Rules ▶

MSN Messenger Service ▶
My Online Status ▶

Newsgroups...   Ctrl+W

Accounts...
New Account Signup ▶
Options...

5 Use Tools – Synchronize Newsgroup

You can get any other new messages or headers at the same time, if wanted

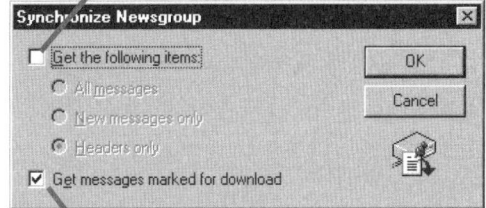

Synchronize Newsgroup ☒
☐ Get the following items:
  ○ All messages
  ○ New messages only
  ● Headers only
☑ Get messages marked for download
  [OK] [Cancel]

4 Mark for downloading

6 Tick Get messages...

comp.lang.c - Outlook Express   _ ☐ ☒
File   Edit   View   Tools   Message   Help

New Post   Reply Group   Reply   Forward   Print   Stop   Send/Recv   Addresses   Find

Folders   ✕   ⑧   🔽   👓   Subject
🗐 Outlook Express   🔽   📄 Re: free()
  ⊟ 🖥 Local Folders   ⊞ 📄 dynamic linked list + dynamic struct members
    📬 Inbox   📄 Re: using findnext command
    📪 Outbox   ⊞ 📄 Calculator Source Code
    📩 Sent Items   🔽   ⊟ 📄 realloc and calloc
    🗑 Deleted Items   📄 Re: realloc and calloc
    📝 Drafts   ⊞ 📄 [Answer] pointer to struct
  ⊞ 📁 Old mail
  ⊟ 📰 TCP News   From: To:
    📰 alt.binaries.clip-art (76)   Subject:
    📰 alt.binaries.sounds.midi (1
    📰 comp.infosystems.www.browse   ℹ️ **Message unavailable while offline**
    📰 comp.lang.basic.visual.misc
    📰 comp.lang.c   Outlook Express is unable to display this message when
    📰 rec.humor.funny   you are not connected to the Internet.

68 message(s), 0 unread   📶 Working Offline

First message in a conversation – click + to see the others

In a conversation the Subjects are identical but with 'Re:' at the front

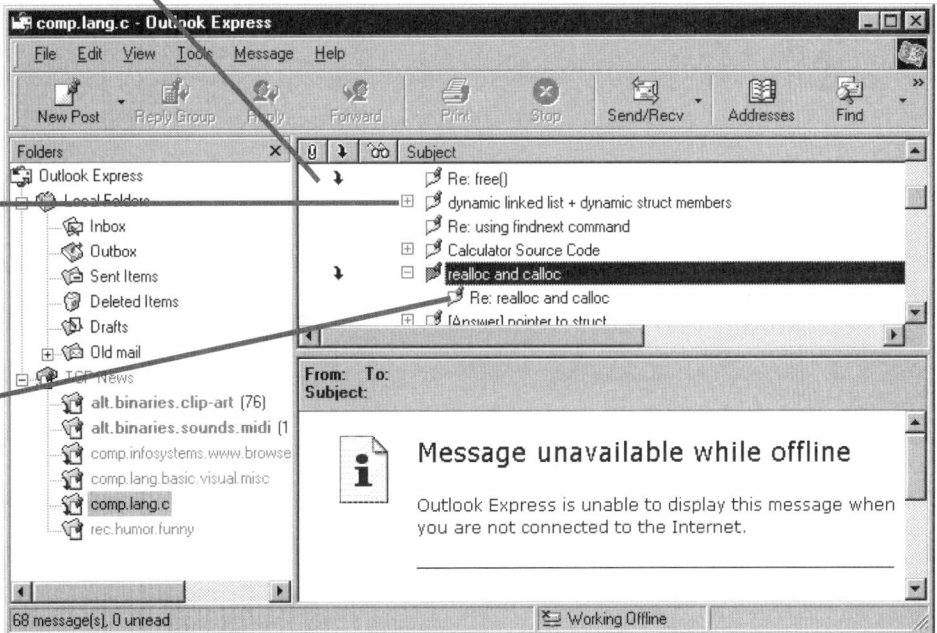

Posting and replying

Posting articles to a newsgroup is very similar to sending mail, but with a couple of significant differences:

● When posting to a newsgroup, your message goes to thousands of people – observe the netiquette (page 172).

● When responding to an article, you can reply to the author only (i.e. send a personal e-mail), or post to the whole group, or reply to both at once.

If your message is *truly* relevant to several groups, you can write other group names in the Cc: slot

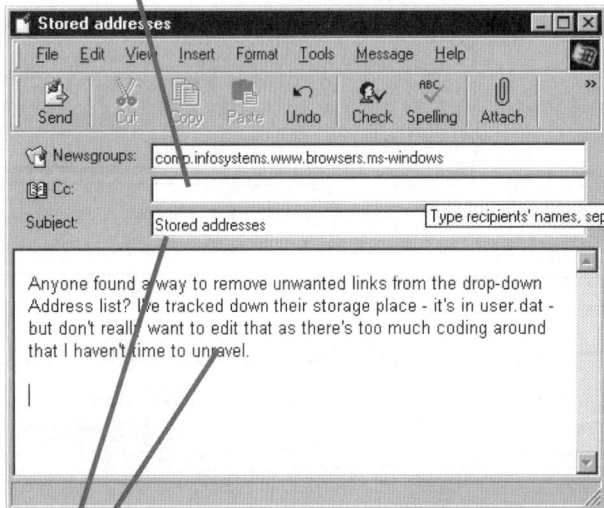

Stored addresses

File   Edit   View   Insert   Format   Tools   Message   Help

Send   Cut   Copy   Paste   Undo   Check   Spelling   Attach

Newsgroups: | comp.infosystems.www.browsers.ms-windows
Cc: |
Subject: | Stored addresses

Type recipients' names, sep

Anyone found a way to remove unwanted links from the drop-down Address list? I've tracked down their storage place - it's in user.dat - but don't really want to edit that as there's too much coding around that I haven't time to unravel.

3 Enter the Subject and message

Message

New Message	Ctrl+N
New Message Using	▶
Reply to Sender	Ctrl+R
Reply to All	Ctrl+Shift+R
Reply to Group	Ctrl+G
Forward	Ctrl+F
Forward As Attachment	
Cancel Message	
Create Rule From Message...	
Block Sender...	
Flag Message	
Watch Conversation	
Ignore Conversation	
Unscramble (ROT13)	
Combine and Decode...	

5 Reply to sender, group or all?

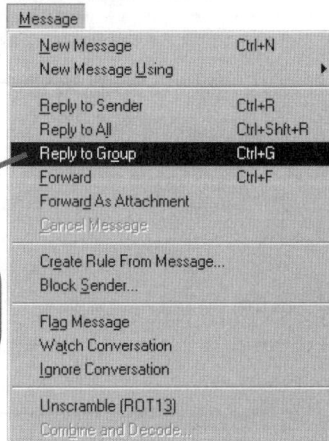

Basic steps

❑ Posting articles

1 From the news folder, select the one in which you want to post.

2 Click 📝 ▾ or use Message – New Message.

3 The group's name will be in the Newsgroups: slot. Enter the Subject, and type the message.

❑ Responding to articles

4 Select the article.

5 Use the Message menu to Reply to All.

Or

6 Use the buttons to reply to the Sender 📨 or to the Group 📧.

7 Edit unwanted lines from the quoted article.

8 Type your reply.

9 Click the Send button.

comp.infosystems.www.browsers.ms-windows - Outlook Express

File   Edit   View   Tools   Message   Help

| New Post | Reply Group | Reply | Forward | Print | Stop | Send/Recv | Addresses |

Folders

- Outlook Express
- Local Folders
  - Inbox
  - Outbox
  - Sent Items
  - Deleted Items
  - Drafts
  - Old mail
- TCP News
  - alt.binaries.clip-art (7
  - alt.binaries.sounds.m
  - comp.infosystems.www.b
  - comp.lang.basic.visual.m
  - comp.lang.c (1)
  - rec.humor.funny

| Subject |
| IE5 page and graphics loading problem |
| Stack error in Opera 3.60 16bit |
| Re: Netscape and Deleting Web Sites from Address Field? |
| Opera |
| Re: Is there a way to save real audio streams while listen to it ? |

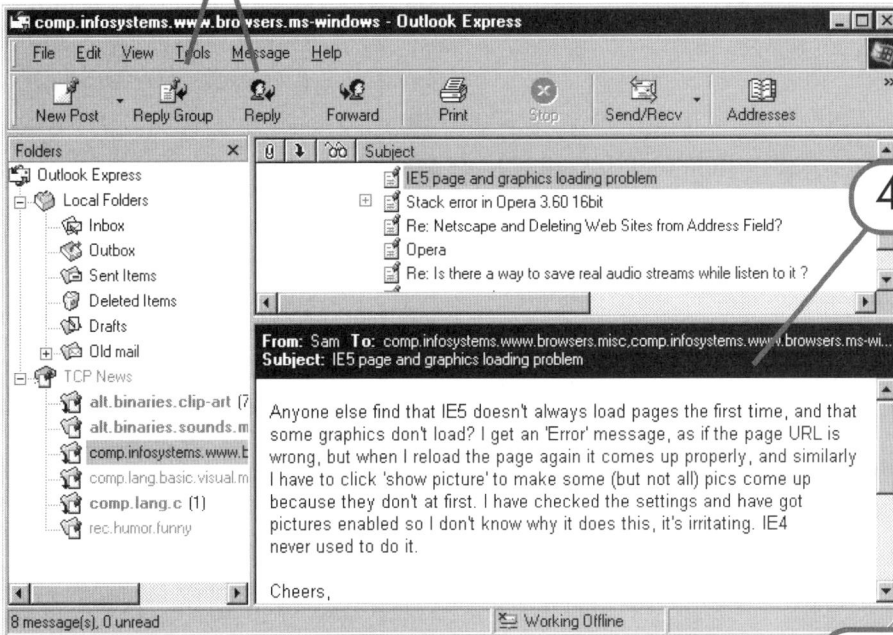

4 Select the article

From: Sam **To:** comp.infosystems.www.browsers.misc,comp.infosystems.www.browsers.ms-wi...
Subject: IE5 page and graphics loading problem

Anyone else find that IE5 doesn't always load pages the first time, and that some graphics don't load? I get an 'Error' message, as if the page URL is wrong, but when I reload the page again it comes up properly, and similarly I have to click 'show picture' to make some (but not all) pics come up because they don't at first. I have checked the settings and have got pictures enabled so I don't know why it does this, it's irritating. IE4 never used to do it.

Cheers,

8 message(s), 0 unread   Working Offline

7 Snip out excess text

9 Send it

Re: IE5 page and graphics loading problem

File   Edit   View   Insert   Format   Tools   Message   Help

| Send | Cut | Copy | Paste | Undo | Check | Spelling | Attach | Sign | Online |

Newsgroups: comp.infosystems.www.browsers.misc,comp.infosystems.www.browsers.ms

Cc:

Subject: Re: IE5 page and graphics loading problem

Sam <s.j.haycroft@NOSPAMenglish.hull.ac.uk> wrote in message
> Anyone else find that IE5 doesn't always load pages the first time, and that
> some graphics don't load? I get an 'Error' message, as if the page URL is
<snip>

Phew, I though it was my mouse finger failing! Yes, it happens odd times. It would be worth recording when it happens to see if there is any pattern to it.

8 Type your message

Tip

Before you ask for help, look for and read the group's FAQs (Frequently Asked Questions) file. Long-term members can get impatient with newbies who keep on asking the same questions.

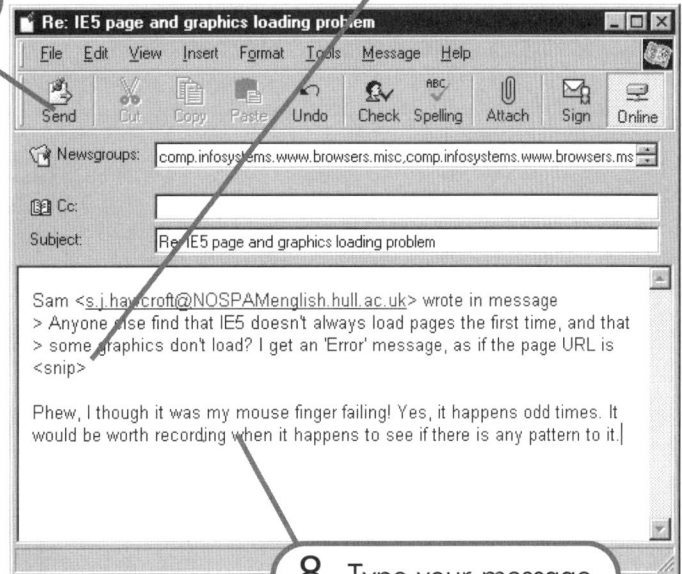

Message Rules

Rules can be used to sort and filter newsgroup messages, just as they can with e-mail. There is a different, smaller range of Conditions, reflecting the slightly different natures of newsgroups and personal messages.

Rules are particularly useful for picking up specific topics in groups that tend to generate large numbers of messages. Set up a rule to scan the subject for keywords, then mark messages for download, and you can save yourself quite a bit of time.

Basic steps

1 Select a message.

2 Open the Message menu and select Create Rule from Message...

3 Tick one or more Conditions to identify the messages.

4 Tick the Action to apply to messages of this type.

5 Click on any under-lined values.

6 Select or enter details as needed.

7 Give it a meaningful Name and click OK.

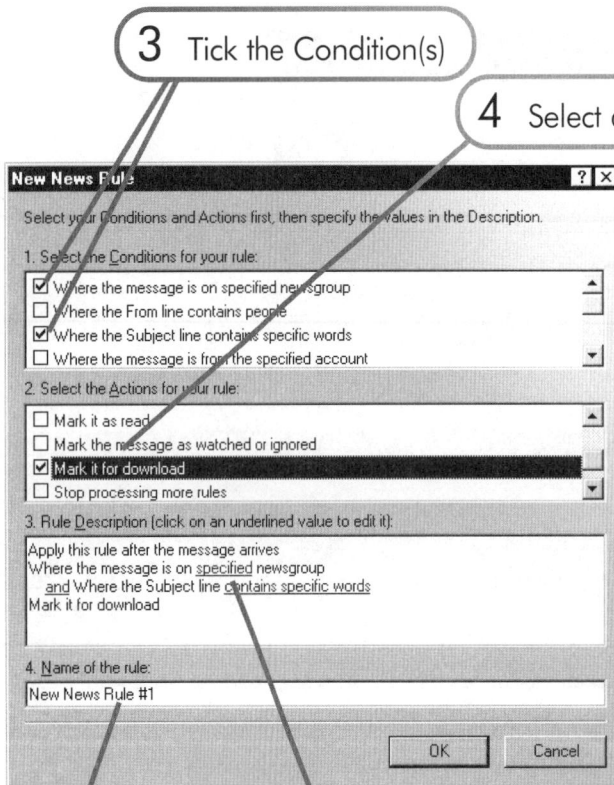

3 Tick the Condition(s)

4 Select an action

7 Name it

5 Click to specify

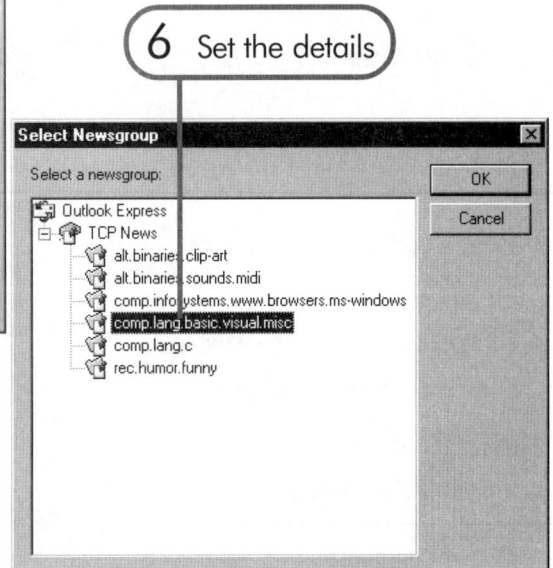

6 Set the details

Newsgroup netiquette

The rules are mainly aimed at not wasting other people's time (and connection charges!), but there is also a large element of trying to encourage a fruitful and co-operative atmosphere within the groups.

● DO write a very clear Subject entry so that others will know what the article is about.

● DO keep articles brief and to the point.

● DO trim unnecessary lines out of quotes when posting replies to articles.

● DO 'lurk' (read without posting) for a while before you start to post. That way you will learn the range and nature of topics that are covered by the group.

● DO read the FAQs (Frequently Asked Questions) lists before you start to post questions to a group. The answers may already be there.

● DON'T post 'off-topic'. Articles must be relevant to the newsgroups.

● DO be tolerant of others – they may be young, inexperienced or struggling with English as a foreign language.

● DON'T overreact – abusive articles do not contribute anything useful to discussions. If you do feel strongly about something someone has written, step back, calm yourself and write a reasoned response. And if that provokes an angry reply, let it drop.

● DO make it clear when you are joking, as not everyone will share your sense of humour. They can't see that you are smiling, so add a <grin> or a Smiley :-).

Files in the News

Some newsgroups circulate graphics, sounds and other binary (i.e. not plain text) files. Outlook will display (or play) these if it can, and if not, will show their presence with a paperclip icon.

The filename is usually in the Subject line

1 Open the article

Copy

Save Picture As...

Save Background As...

Select All

2 Select Save Picture As...

3 Click to open

Opens the 'flutedgl.gif (16.9 KB)' attachment.

4 Open or Save

With safe file types (e.g. sounds and images), clear this tickbox and skip the warnings in future

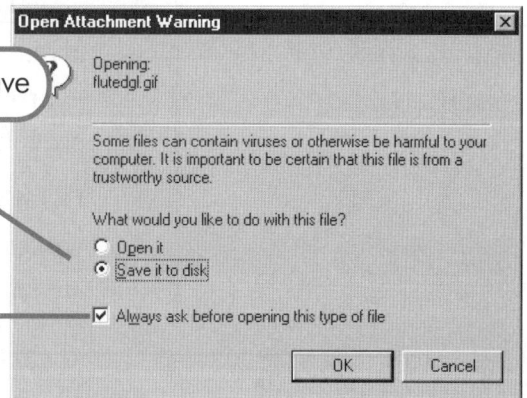

Open Attachment Warning

Opening:
flutedgl.gif

Some files can contain viruses or otherwise be harmful to your computer. It is important to be certain that this file is from a trustworthy source.

What would you like to do with this file?
○ Open it
⦿ Save it to disk

☑ Always ask before opening this type of file

OK   Cancel

1 Select the article.

2 To save a displayed image, right-click on it and select Save Picture As... from the shortcut menu.

Or

3 Click the Paperclip icon then click the filename to open the file.

4 Some files generate a warning. Choose Open to view the file or Save for offline viewing.

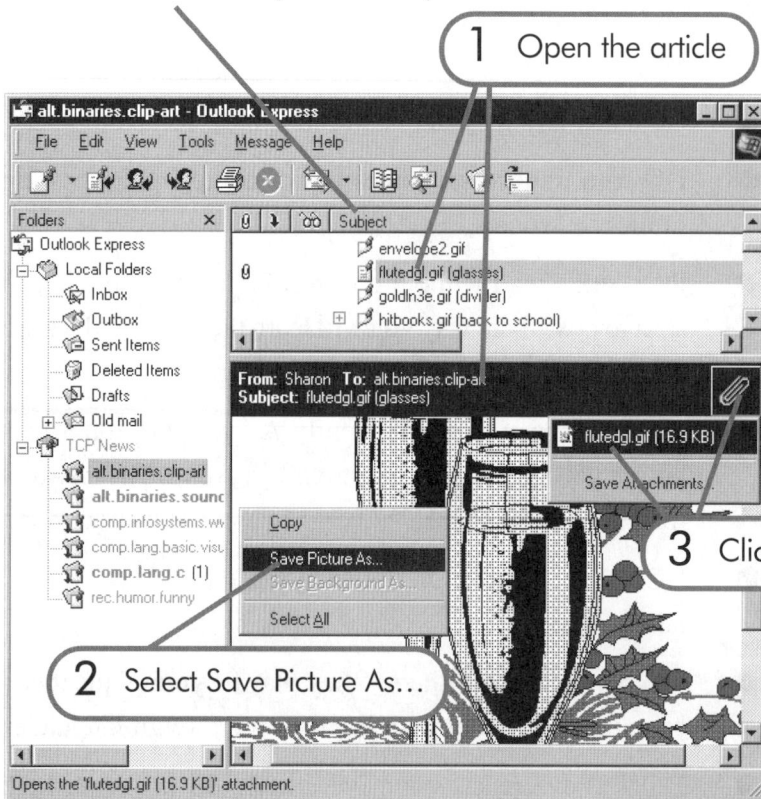

Basic steps

Multi-part files

1 Select the articles that contain parts of the file.

2 Open the Message menu and select Combine and Decode....

3 If a part is in the wrong order, drag it or select it and use Move Up or Move Down to nudge it into place.

4 Click OK.

❏ The file will appear as an attachment to the message – view or save it as normal.

The news (and e-mail) systems were designed for text messages and binary files must be specially encoding for transfer. You will rarely be aware of this as Outlook Express usually decodes them automatically. However, large binary files are sometimes split into chunks for transfer, and if you try to view a single chunk you will see only gobbledegook. Multi-part files can normally be recovered by the **Combine and Decode** tool, which detaches the parts from their messages, joins them

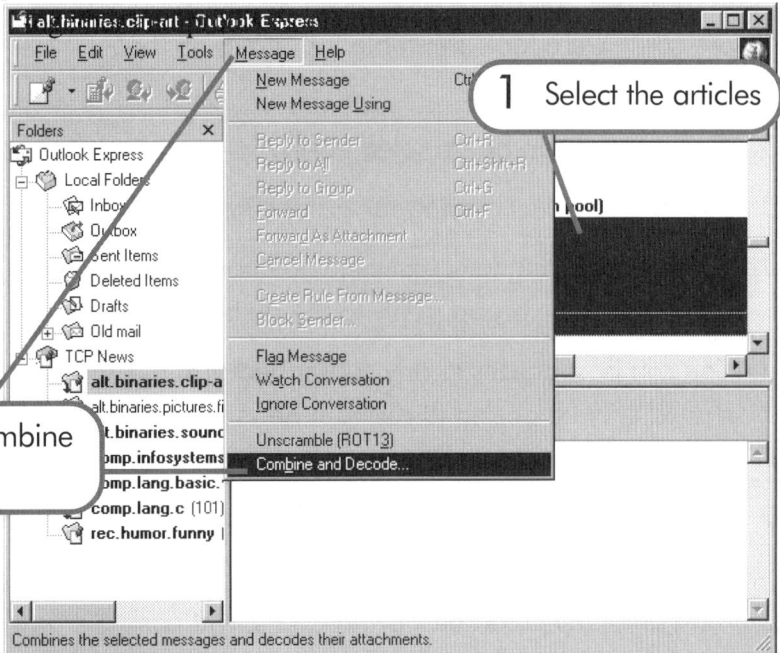

1 Select the articles

2 Use Message – Combine and Decode...

3 Drag or Move into order

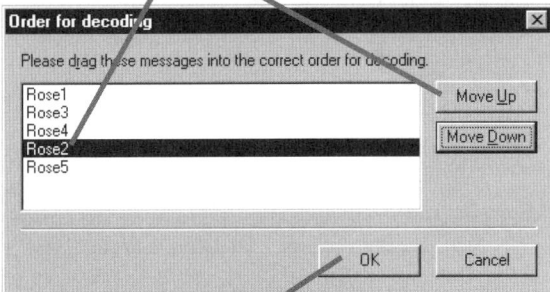

4 Click OK

Take note

Executable files (with the extension .exe) can be dangerous. Only open them if they are from a known and trusted source.

Summary

❑ There is a newsgroup for almost every conceivable interest, hobby, profession or obsession.

❑ Newsgroups are organised into a hierarchy, branching down from broad areas to highly specialised topics.

❑ The first stage in using any News system is to download the list of newsgroups from your server.

❑ In Outlook Express news articles are read and written in much the same way as e-mail messages, but there are some extra tools available for accessing the newsgroups.

❑ Newsgroups can be sampled easily.

❑ Subscribing saves hunting for groups in the full list.

❑ When responding to an article, you can post a follow-up article to the group, reply to the author, or both.

❑ You can post articles to any subscribed group. Articles should only be posted to relevant newsgroups. Off-topic postings cause offence.

❑ You can set up Message Rules to filter and organise newsgroup articles.

❑ Most binary files can be viewed and saved easily. Multi-part binary files must be joined together and then decoded – Outlook Express's Combine and Decode will do this for you.

8 FrontPage Express

Introducing FrontPage

FrontPage Express is supplied as part of the full Internet Explorer package. It is a cut-down version of FrontPage, a comprehensive Web page creation and site administration package (with additional graphics software). FrontPage Express lacks the administration and graphics software but has almost identical page-editing facilities. The good set of tools and wizards greatly simplify page creation.

File menu

New...   Ctrl+N
Open...   Ctrl+O
Close

Save   Ctrl+S
Save As...
Save All

Page Properties...

Page Setup...
Print Preview
Print...   Ctrl+P

Send...

Exit

1 Select File – New

2 Do it yourself...

3 ... or use a Wizard

New Page

Template or Wizard:

Normal Page
Confirmation Form
Form Page Wizard
New Web View Folder
Personal Home Page Wizard
Survey Form

OK
Cancel
Help

4 Click OK

Description

Create a Home Page customized to meet your needs.

Personal Home Page Wizard

This wizard helps you create a customized personal Home Page. Use it to tell friends and colleagues about yourself, and to publish links to information you are providing or have located.

Select the major sections for your Home Page:

☐ Employee Information
☑ Current Projects
☑ Hot List: Interesting Web Sites
☑ Biographical Information
☑ Personal Interests
☑ Contact Information
☐ Comments and Suggestions

Cancel   < Back   Next >   Finish

The URL of your home page – the top level one at your Web site – must normally be called 'index.htm' or 'index.html'. Check with your ISP.

Personal Home Page Wizard

The wizard needs to know what to call the new page. The Page URL is the name of the HTML file as it is stored in your web. The Page Title is what users see in a web browser. Most authors make their name part of the Home Page title.

Page URL

index.htm

Page Title

Mac's Home Page

Cancel   < Back   Next >   Finish

The editing tools

Take note

Text formatting is very easy – try it and see for yourself. We'll focus on the more interesting bits in this chapter.

The main toolbar is identical to that of Word. Use these tools to set styles, fonts, alignment, bulleted or numbered lists, idents, emphasis and colour.

The second toolbar has the usual file and cut-and-paste facilities, plus tools for inserting tables, images, links, and other components.

The Form Fields toolbar can be docked in the window frame or set to float anywhere on the window.

Navigation

Font   Link   Lists and indents

Style   Table   Image   Alignment

Form Fields toolbar (see page 138)

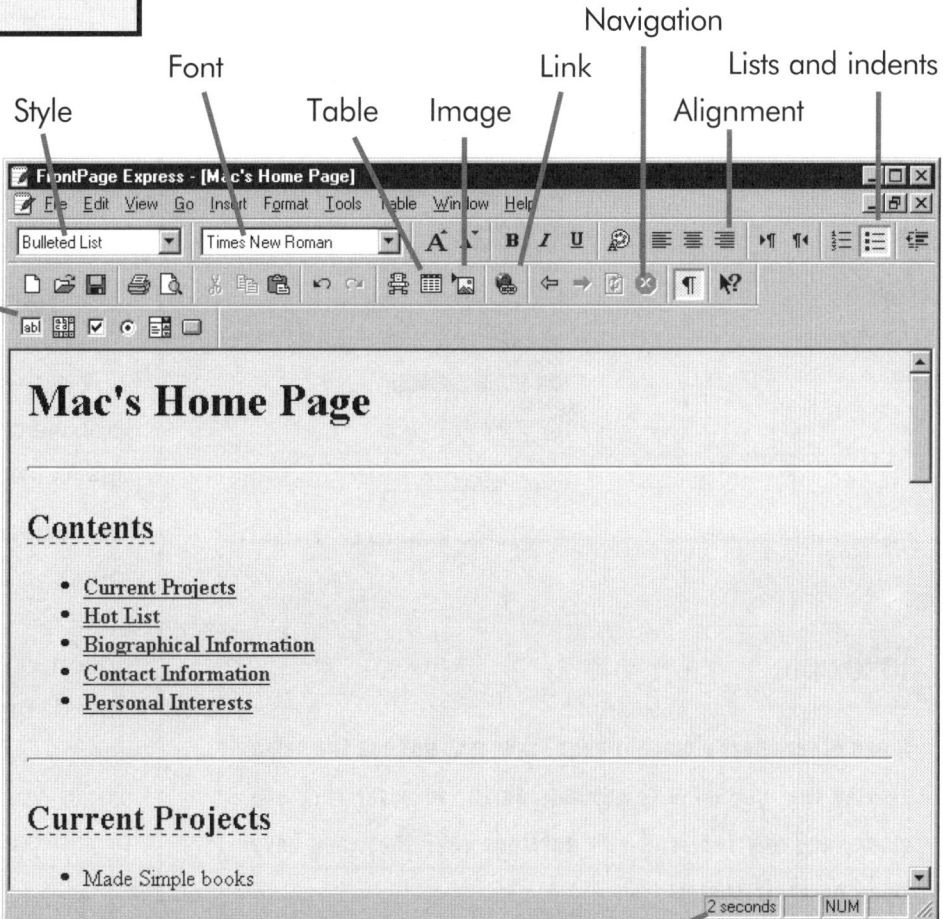

This page was started with the Home Page Wizard – the basic structure is in place, but it still needs a lot of work.

FrontPage Express - [Mac's Home Page]

File Edit View Go Insert Format Tools Table Window Help

Bulleted List   Times New Roman

Mac's Home Page

Contents

- Current Projects
- Hot List
- Biographical Information
- Contact Information
- Personal Interests

Current Projects

- Made Simple books

2 seconds   NUM

Estimated download time of page and its graphics files – keep an eye on this!

Formatting text

The simplest way to format text is to use the drop-down list of Paragraph Styles. These include:

- six levels of Headings, from 24 point down to 9 point – smaller than Normal text;

- Bulletted or Numbered Lists – and you can create lists inside lists where several levels are needed;

- Pre-Formatted, which retains a layout created with spaces and tabs – all the other styles squeeze out excess spaces;

- Address, an italic style, by convention used for your e-mail address at the bottom of your home page;

- Normal – the default.

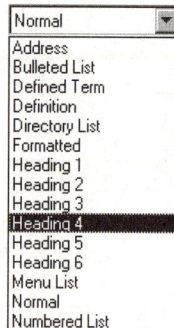

Take note

When other users view your page, they may not see the same display that you do – it depends on the browser they are using, and any font and size settings that they may have made on their system.

Tags

When you click on a tool to apply a format to some text, the editor writes HTML tags into the document for you. These are code words, written inside <angle brackets> and are usually in pairs – at the start and the end of the formatted text. To see the HTML tags, use View – HTML.

Look at the page and source opposite and try to relate the tags to the displayed text.

The text at the top of the Source code, between the <HEAD> tags, is for information only – it is not displayed on screen. This is where you write the page's title, its author and keywords for search engines to find.

For more on this, read *HTML 4.0 Made Simple* or *FrontPage Made Simple*.

FrontPage Express - [Text Styles]

File Edit View Go Insert Format Tools Table Window Help

Normal | Times New Roman | A A B I U

Text Styles

1. **Heading 1**

2. **Heading 2**

3. **Heading 3**

4. **Heading 4**

5. **Heading 5**

6. **Heading 6**

Normal

Address

- List Item 1
- List Item 2
- List Item 3

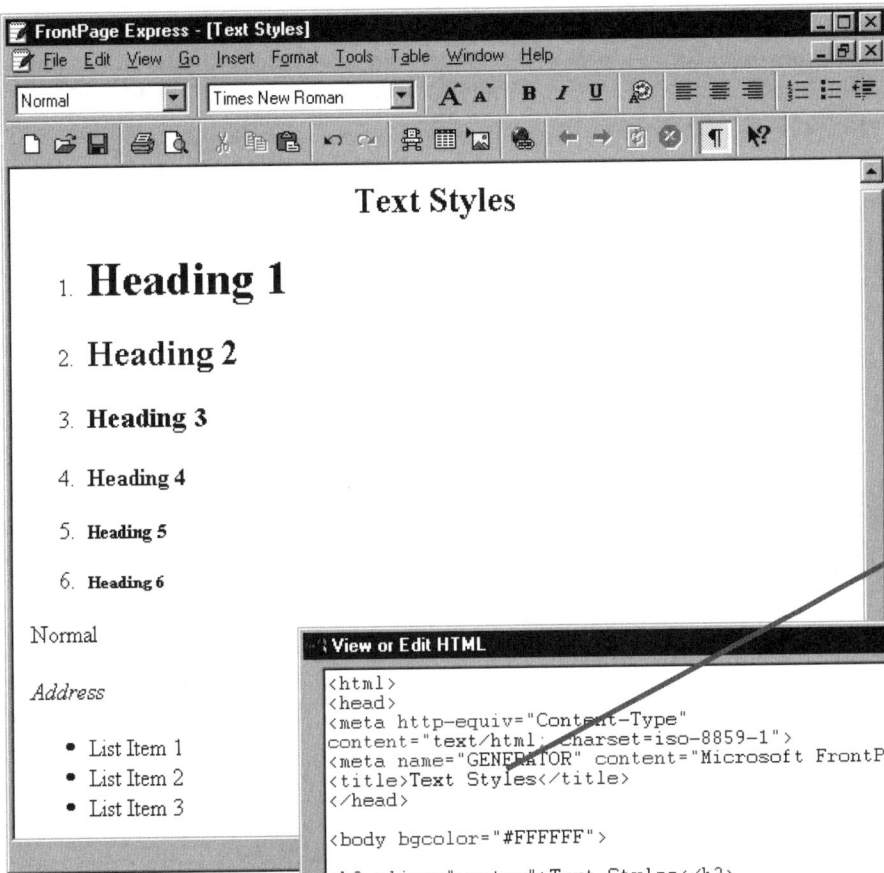

The title appears in the title bar when the page is viewed in a browser.

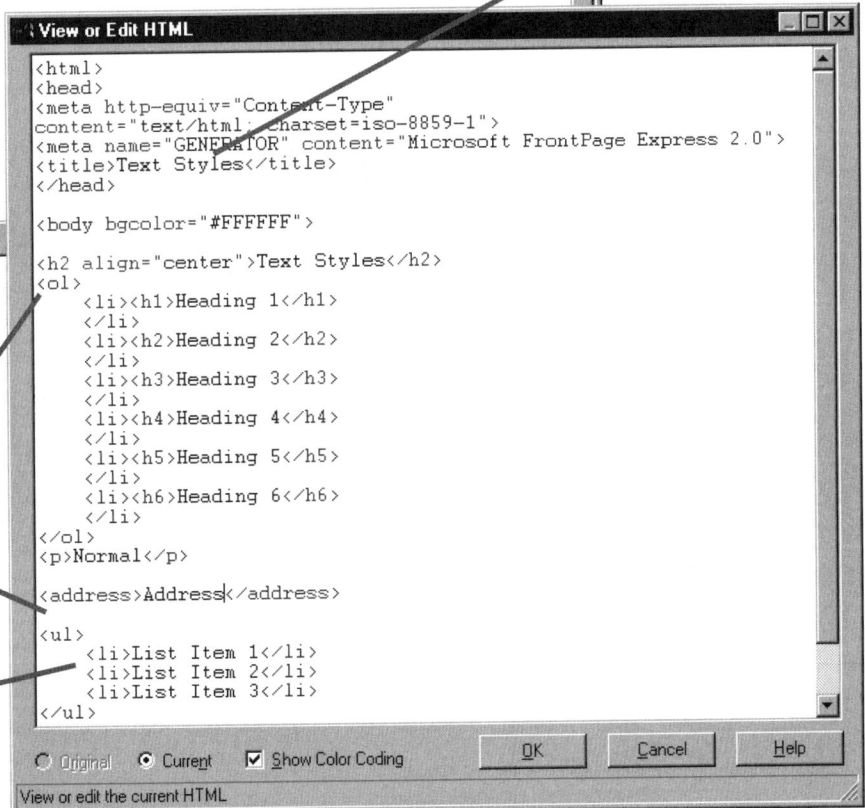

View or Edit HTML

```
<html>
<head>
<meta http-equiv="Content-Type"
content="text/html; charset=iso-8859-1">
<meta name="GENERATOR" content="Microsoft FrontPage Express 2.0">
<title>Text Styles</title>
</head>

<body bgcolor="#FFFFFF">

<h2 align="center">Text Styles</h2>
<ol>
    <li><h1>Heading 1</h1>
    </li>
    <li><h2>Heading 2</h2>
    </li>
    <li><h3>Heading 3</h3>
    </li>
    <li><h4>Heading 4</h4>
    </li>
    <li><h5>Heading 5</h5>
    </li>
    <li><h6>Heading 6</h6>
    </li>
</ol>
<p>Normal</p>

<address>Address</address>

<ul>
    <li>List Item 1</li>
    <li>List Item 2</li>
    <li>List Item 3</li>
</ul>
```

○ Original ● Current ☑ Show Color Coding   OK   Cancel   Help

View or edit the current HTML

<OL> </OL> mark numbered lists

<UL> </UL> mark bulleted lists

Each item in a list is enclosed by <LI> and </LI>.

Links

Without links there would be no Web, so spin a few of your own! There are essentially three types of links:

- to other pages on your system (and in your Web space, once they're uploaded);
- to pages or files at remote sites;
- to another part of the same page.

The first two types of link are created in the same way. For links within a page, you must create a *Bookmark* – a place to link to. (In standard HTML these are called *anchors*.)

Basic steps

❑ Links off the page

1 Select the words (or image) that will be hyperlinked.

2 Select Insert – HyperLink or click 🔗.

3 Type the page's URL – or the filename if the page is one of yours.

4 Click OK.

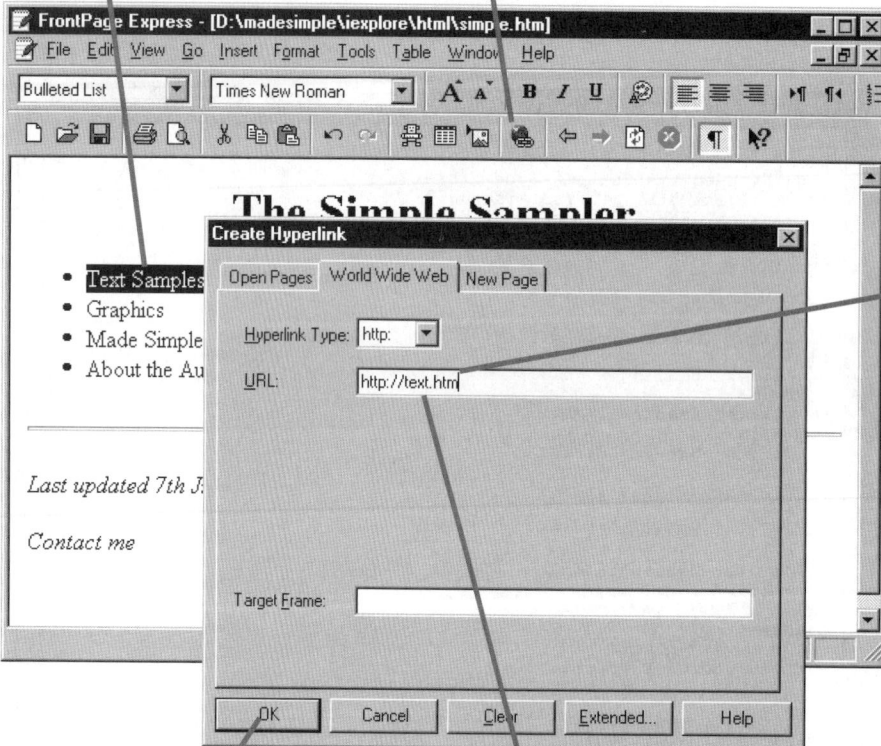

1 Select the text

2 Click Link

Use the New Page panel to create a new, linked page

3 Type the URL

4 Click OK

This URL has only the filename as the file is on the local disk

Tip

If you are writing a set of pages, store them all in one directory.

Basic steps

❑ Links within the page

1 Place the cursor where you want a Bookmark.

2 Select Edit – Bookmark.

3 Give the Bookmark a name.

4 Click OK.

5 Move to where you want to link from, select the words and click 📖.

6 Go to the Open Pages panel.

7 Select the page.

8 Select the target from the Bookmark list.

9 Click OK.

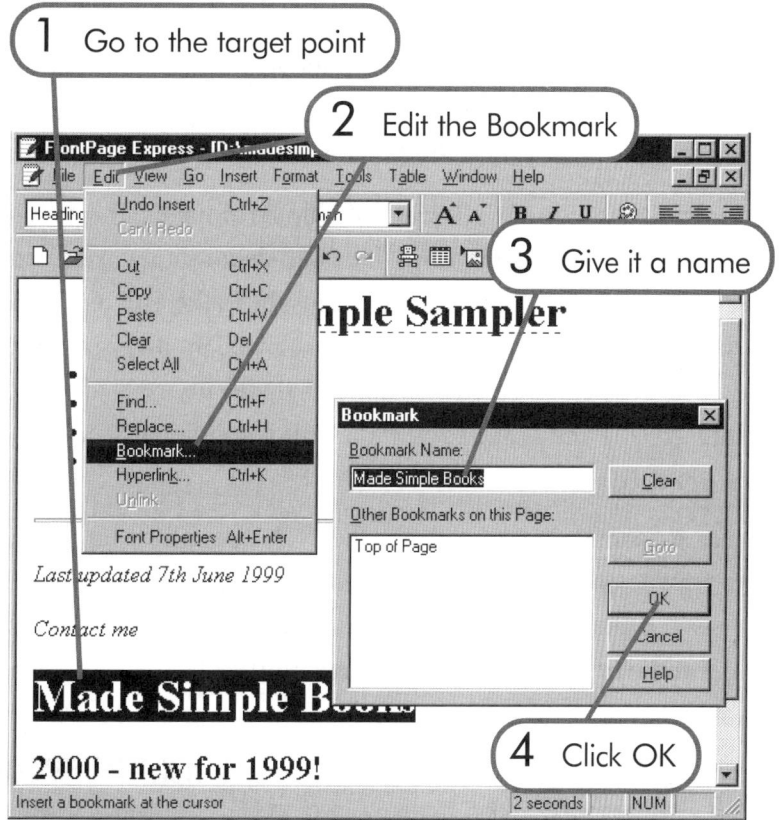

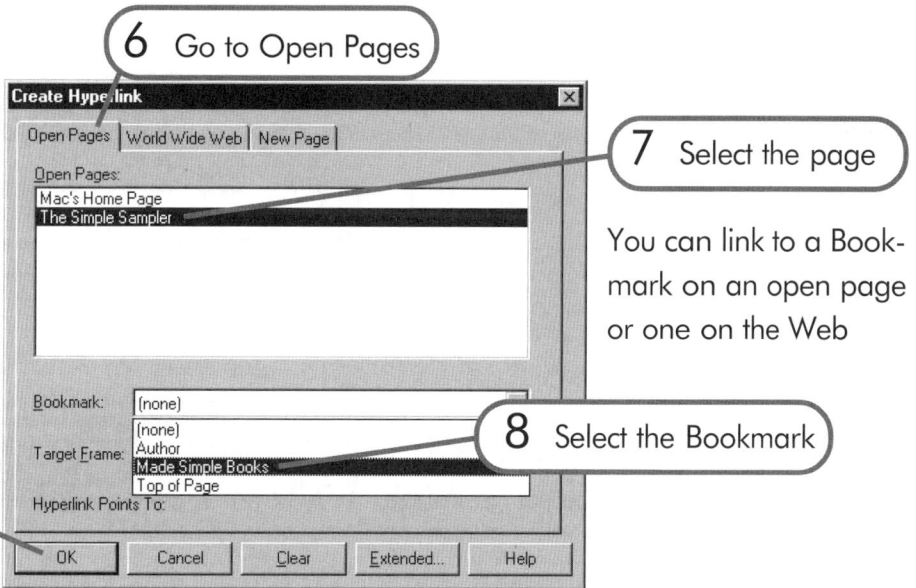

> 1 Go to the target point

> 2 Edit the Bookmark

> 3 Give it a name

> 4 Click OK

> 6 Go to Open Pages

> 7 Select the page

You can link to a Bookmark on an open page or one on the Web

> 8 Select the Bookmark

> 9 Click OK

Images

Images add a lot to Web pages – in two ways. They add to the appearance, making pages more attractive, but they also add to the download time. If you include images, they should be no larger than is necessary to do the job.

FrontPage has a good collection of Clip Art images, for use as bullets, backgrounds, dividing lines and decorations. You can also insert your own images. These must be in the GIF and JPG formats – the only types that can be viewed in all browsers. However, you can insert a bitmapped (.BMP) images – the sort produced by Paint – and FrontPage will automatically convert this to a GIF.

There are some users who access the Web through systems that can't display images, and many who choose to turn off images, for faster browsing. After inserting an image, open its Properties panel and write something in the **Alternative Text** so that they know what they are missing.

Basic steps

❑ Inserting an image

1 Place the cursor where you want the image.

2 Select Insert – Image or click 🖼.

Either

3 Open the Clip Art panel, select a set from the drop-down list then choose an image.

or

4 On the Other Location panel, click Browse and load in the file.

5 Click OK.

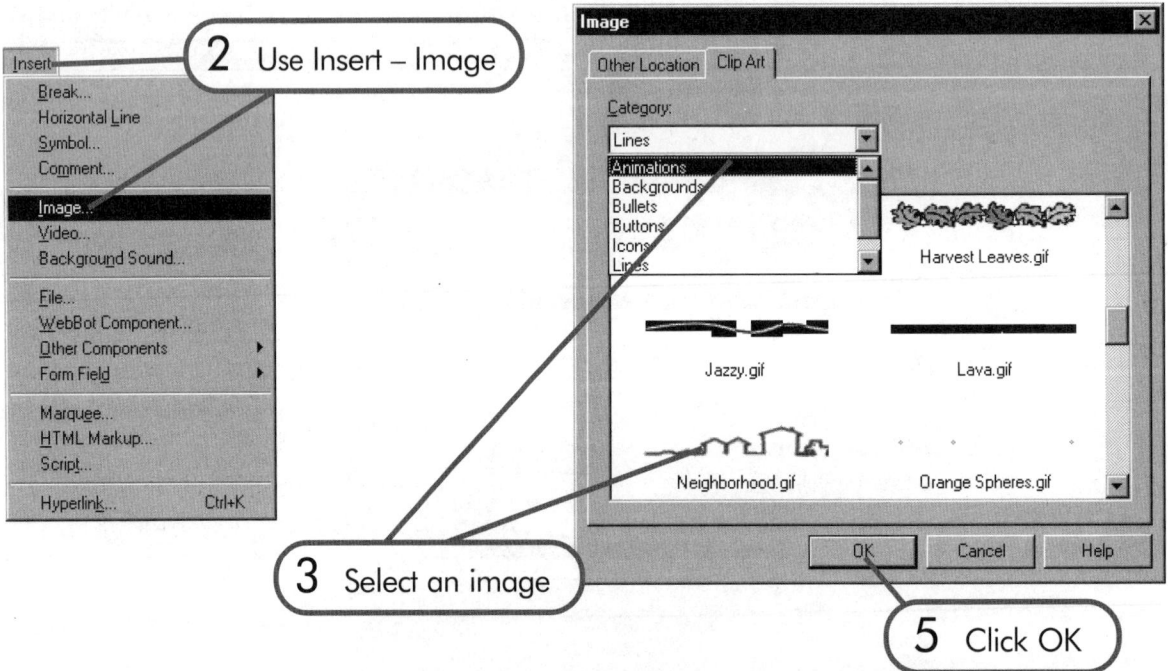

2 Use Insert – Image

3 Select an image

5 Click OK

❑ Image Properties

6 Right click on the image and select Image Properties from the context menu.

7 Type Alternative Text, for readers who don't want to or cannot view images.

8 Click OK.

With 'transparent' GIFs, the page's background shows through unpainted parts of the image

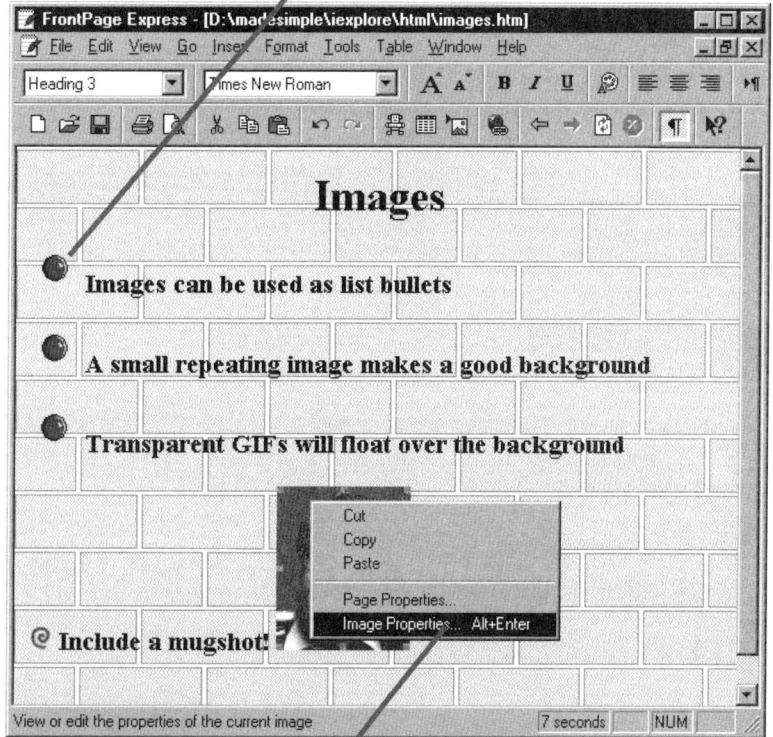

FrontPage Express - [D:\madesimple\iexplore\html\images.htm]

File Edit View Go Insert Format Tools Table Window Help

Heading 3   Times New Roman

Images

Images can be used as list bullets

A small repeating image makes a good background

Transparent GIFs will float over the background

| Cut |
| Copy |
| Paste |
| Page Properties... |
| Image Properties... Alt+Enter |

Include a mugshot

View or edit the properties of the current image   7 seconds   NUM

7 Type Alternative Text

Image Properties

General | Video | Appearance

Image Source
mymug.gif   Browse...

Type
● GIF   ☐ Transparent   ○ JPEG   Quality: 75
        ☐ Interlaced

Alternative Representations
Low-Res: Browse...

Text: Author's mugshot

Default Hyperlink:
Location: Browse...

Target
Frame:

Extended...

OK   Cancel   Help

6 Right-click and select Image Properties

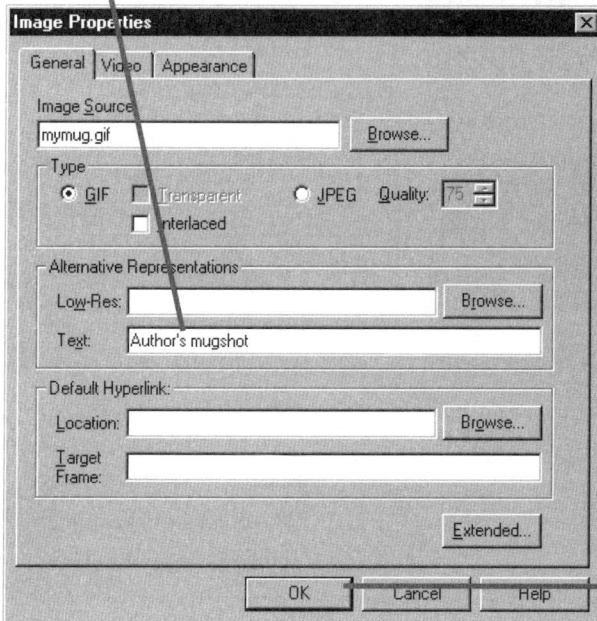

Take note

You can add a hyperlink to a picture. Either set it on the Properties or select the image and use Insert – Hyperlink as you would with text.

8 Click OK

135

Backgrounds

If you want a background picture, use a small one that can be repeated, tile-fashion, to fill the page. These are added through the Background panel.

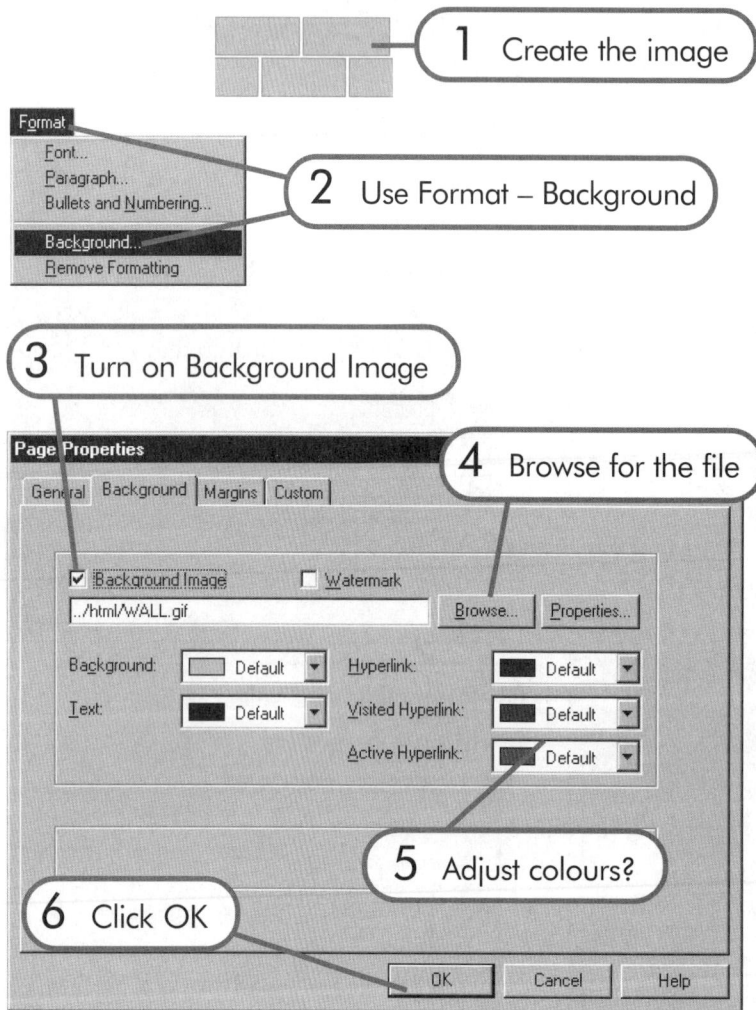

1 Create the image

2 Use Format – Background

Format
Font...
Paragraph...
Bullets and Numbering...
Background...
Remove Formatting

3 Turn on Background Image

Page Properties

General | Background | Margins | Custom |

☑ Background Image   ☐ Watermark
..html/WALL.gif   Browse...   Properties...

Background: Default   Hyperlink: Default
Text: Default   Visited Hyperlink: Default
                               Active Hyperlink: Default

4 Browse for the file

5 Adjust colours?

6 Click OK

OK   Cancel   Help

The background picture is repeated across and down the page. You can create vertical stripes using a thin, but wide picture – the one used here is 800 pixels wide, by 35 high.

Basic steps

1 If you want your own background, create a small image in a graphics program.

2 Open the Format menu and select Background.

3 Turn on the Background Image checkbox.

4 Click Browse and locate your file or select Clip Art from the Background set.

5 If necessary, change the text colours to suit your new background.

6 Click OK.

Take note

If you turn on **Watermark**, the background image will stay still with text scrolling over it when the page is viewed through IE4 or 5. The effect is not visible in FrontPage – or in other browsers.

Basic steps

1 Type in suitable text, such as *Mail to me* and select all or part of it.

2 Click 🖳.

3 Select *mailto:* from the Hyperlink Type list.

4 Enter your e-mail address as the URL.

5 Click OK.

If you want readers to be able to get in touch with you, include a mailing link. This should have *mailto:* followed by your e-mail address as the URL. When a reader clicks on this link, the New Message window will open in their browser, with your address already in the Mail To slot.

● Your e-mail address will normally take this form, but check with your access provider:

username@access.provider

Tip

To test the link, preview the page in the browser and click on the link. You should get a New Message window with your e-mail address in the To slot.

Tip

If you want a form to collect data from visitors, you can create one quickly using the Form Wizard when you start a new page.

1 Select the link text

2 Click Insert Link

FrontPage Express - [D:\madesimple\iexplore\html\simple.htm]

File Edit View Go Insert Format Tools Table Window Help

Address   Times New Roman

The Simple Sampler

• Text Samples
• Graphics
• Made Sim
• About the

3 Select mailto:

Create Hyperlink

Open Pages | World Wide Web | New Page

Hyperlink Type: mailto:

URL: mailto:macbride@tcp.co.uk

Last updated 7t...

Contact me

4 Type your address

Target Frame:

Made S

2000 - new

For Help, press F1

OK   Cancel   Clear   Extended...   Help

5 Click OK

Forms

Writing your own HTML code to create a form can take time. The Form Fields toolbar in FrontPage simplifies the job, though you still have to do some work to ensure that when the form is sent back to you, you can identify the items your visitors entered and the selections they made.

● Every Form Field must have a name.

● Text boxes can have sample text in them.

● Check boxes can be set *on* or *off* and need labels to tell the visitor what they're for.

● Radio buttons must have a Value (for feedback) and a text prompt.

● Drop-down menus need Choices (menu items) and Values (for feedback).

Basic steps

1 Type a label (if needed) and position the cursor for the first field.

2 Select the field type from the Form Field toolbar.

3 Right-click on the field and select Form Field Properties.

4 Set the Name and Value as required.

5 Click OK.

Keep all the fields within the outline – unless you want to have several separate forms on the page.

The Form Fields

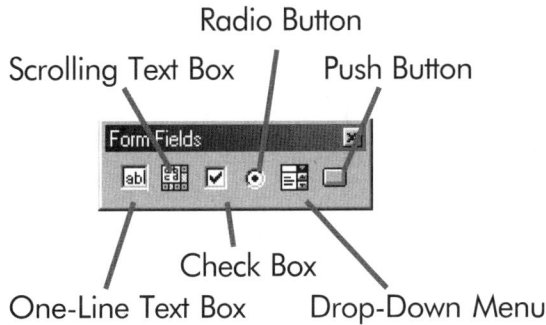

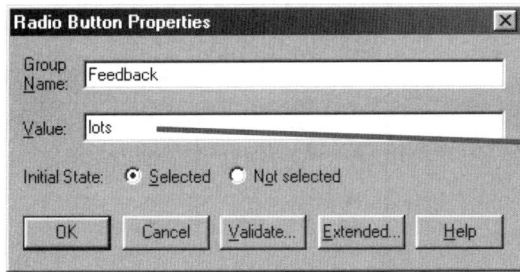

Scrolling Text Box
Radio Button
Push Button

One-Line Text Box
Check Box
Drop-Down Menu

Buttons are simple – use Submit for one to send the form, or Reset to clear the values. No Name is needed.

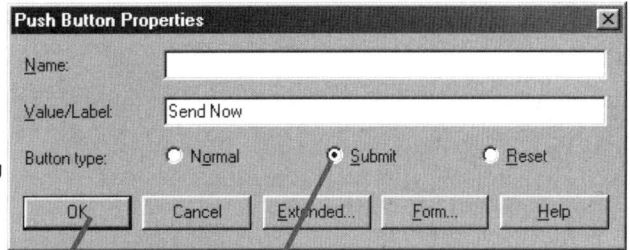

Push Button Properties

Name:

Value/Label: Send Now

Button type: ○ Normal ● Submit ○ Reset

[OK] [Cancel] [Extended...] [Form...] [Help]

Radio Button Properties

Group Name: Feedback

Value: lots

Initial State: ● Selected ○ Not selected

[OK] [Cancel] [Validate...] [Extended...] [Help]

5 Click OK

4 Set Properties as needed

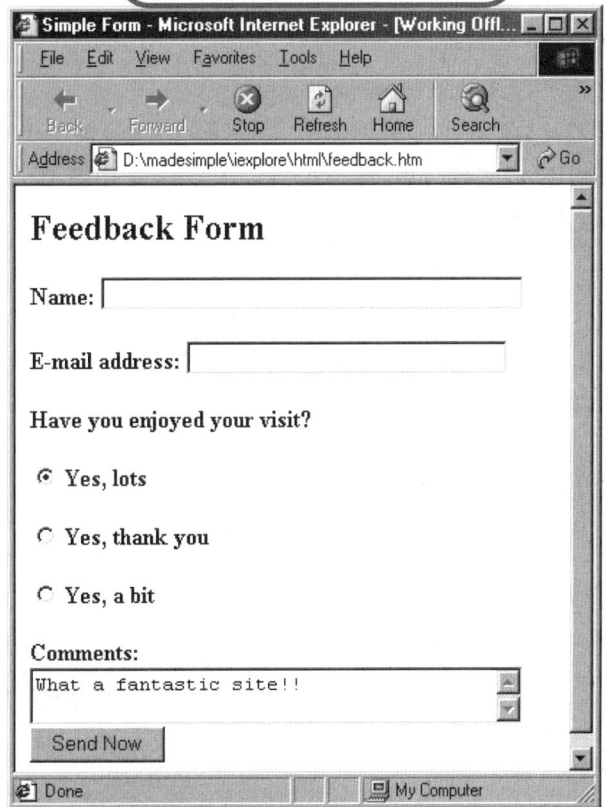

• Radio buttons need a Group Name – the same for all buttons in the set – and a different Value for each one. When the form is sent back to you, it will have an entry such as 'Feedback = lots' to show which button was selected.

Simple Form - Microsoft Internet Explorer - [Working Offl...

File Edit View Favorites Tools Help

Back Forward Stop Refresh Home Search

Address D:\madesimple\iexplore\html\feedback.htm Go

Feedback Form

Name:

E-mail address:

Have you enjoyed your visit?

● Yes, lots

○ Yes, thank you

○ Yes, a bit

Comments:

What a fantastic site!!

[Send Now]

Done My Computer

The Form as it appears in the browser

Take note

There is a lot more to forms than this. See *FrontPage Made Simple* or *HTML 4.0 Made Simple.*

Tables

Like Netscape's editor, FrontPage makes light work of the chore of setting up tables. The Insert table tool will give you the basic structure. You can then work your way round the cells, inserting text, images – or even other tables. Formats can be applied to the whole table, or to selected rows, columns or individual cells. The overall size of the table can be fixed in pixels, or set as a percentage of the window (see the Tip opposite).

(see the Tip opposite)

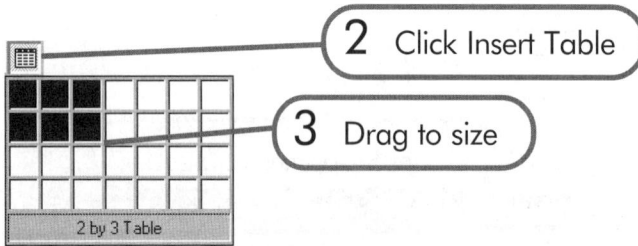

2 Click Insert Table

3 Drag to size

2 by 3 Table

1 Place the cursor where the table is to go.

2 Click 🖽.

3 Drag across the grid (and beyond if needed) to set the size.

4 Enter and format your text and images.

5 Right-click on the table to get the short menu.

6 Select Table Properties

7 Adjust settings as required.

8 Click OK.

1 Position the cursor

4 Enter and format contents

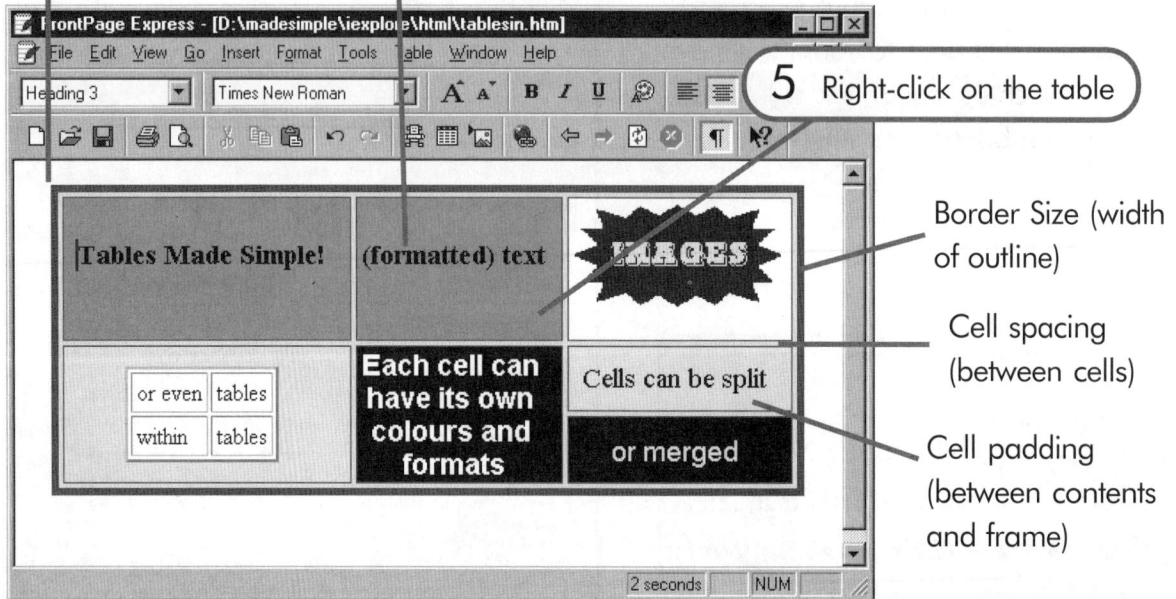

5 Right-click on the table

Border Size (width of outline)

Cell spacing (between cells)

Cell padding (between contents and frame)

140

6 Select Table Properties

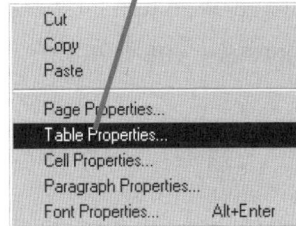

Cut
Copy
Paste

Page Properties...
Table Properties...
Cell Properties...
Paragraph Properties...
Font Properties...   Alt+Enter

7 Set format options

How big?

8 Click OK

Alignment of table across the screen

See screenshot opposite

Background colour

Set Light and Dark Borders for 3D effect

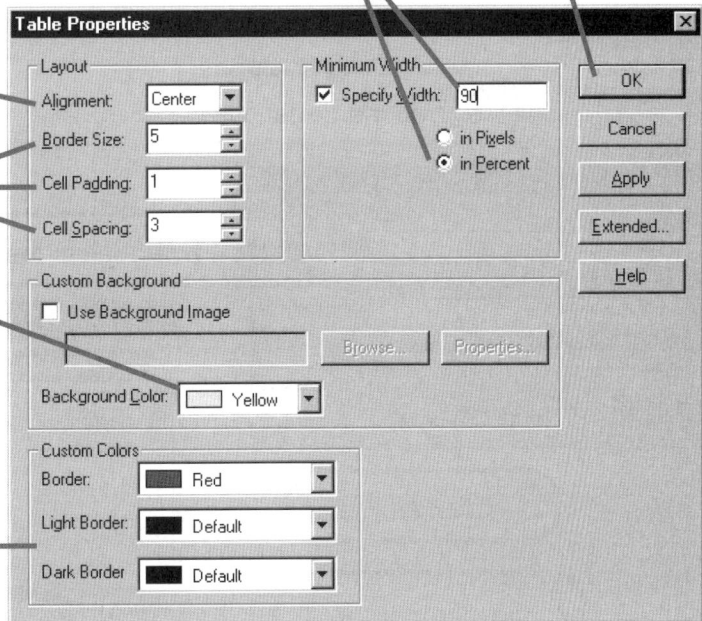

141

Saving and publishing

The full version of FrontPage contains site management facilities, and could be used for running an intranet (within an organisation) or an extensive Web site. Aspects of this show through in FrontPage Express – you'll notice it in the saving routines.

Saving

Where most applications assume that you will save your files onto your hard disks, FrontPage assumes that they will be saved – as pages – directly to your Web site. While you are still developing your pages, you are better saving them as files on your hard disk.

1 Open the File menu and select Save As...

2 Edit the Page Title if required.

3 Click As File...

4 Select the folder.

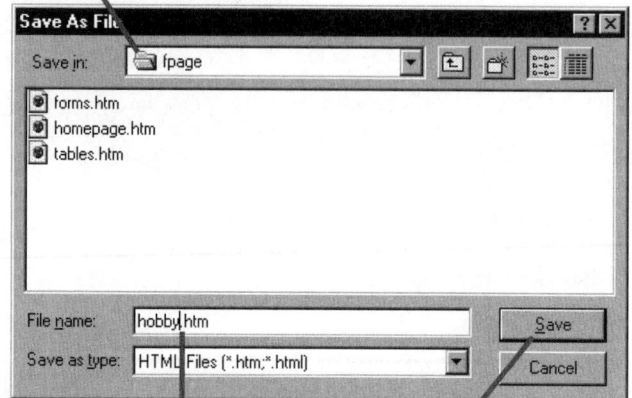

5 Edit the File name if required.

6 Click Save.

7 If the page contains images, you will be asked if you want to save them to the same folder – click Yes.

2   Edit the Page Title?

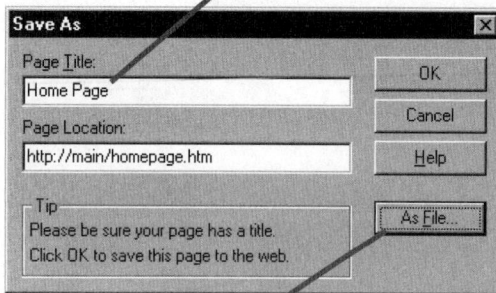

Save As

Page Title:
Home Page

Page Location:
http://main/homepage.htm

OK

Cancel

Help

Tip
Please be sure your page has a title.
Click OK to save this page to the web.

As File...

3   Click As File...

4   Select the folder

Save As File

Save in: fpage

forms.htm
homepage.htm
tables.htm

File name: hobby.htm

Save as type: HTML Files (*.htm;*.html)

Save

Cancel

7   Save images in the same folder

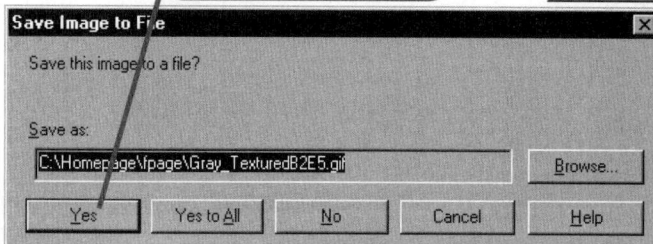

6   Click Save

5   Edit the File name?

Save Image to File

Save this image to a file?

Save as:
C:\Homepage\fpage\Gray_TexturedB2E5.gif

Browse...

Yes   Yes to All   No   Cancel   Help

Publishing

1 Open the File menu and select Save As...

2 Click OK and save any images if asked.

❑ The Web Publishing Wizard should start – if it doesn't, then run it from the Start menu.

3 Browse for the folder containing your files.

4 Select your server if you have set one up, otherwise click New.

5 Give the URL for your home page – your provider will tell you it.

6 Complete the Wizard.

The Web Publishing Wizard handles most of this. Before you run it, make sure that all the files – including any images and sounds – are all in one folder, and that this folder does not contain any other files.

3 Browse for the folder

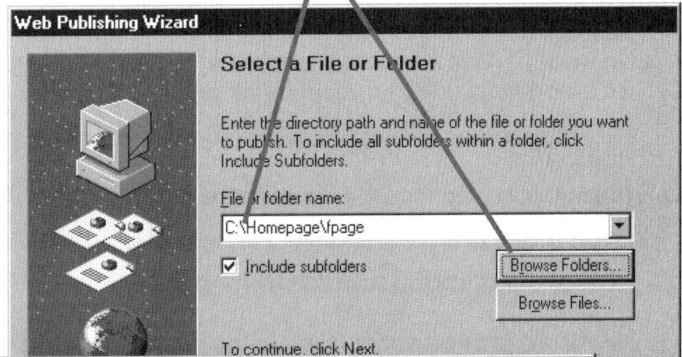

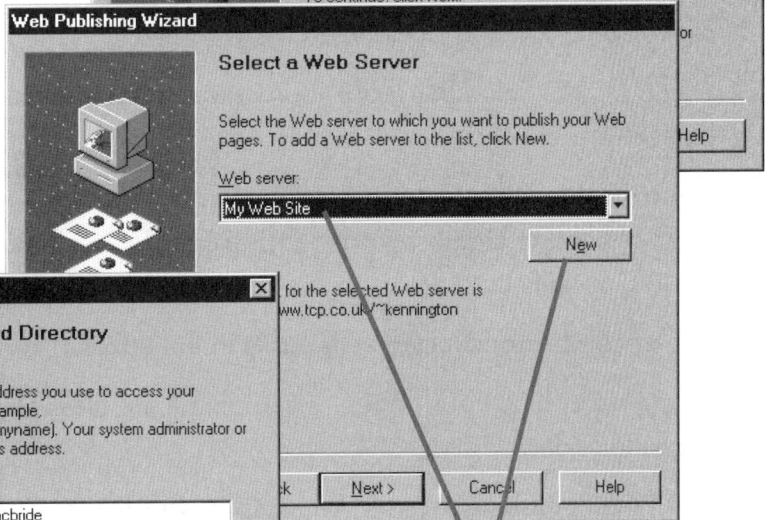

Web Publishing Wizard

Select a File or Folder

Enter the directory path and name of the file or folder you want to publish. To include all subfolders within a folder, click Include Subfolders.

File or folder name:
`C:\Homepage\fpage`

☑ Include subfolders

Browse Folders...

Browse Files...

To continue, click Next.

Web Publishing Wizard

Select a Web Server

Select the Web server to which you want to publish your Web pages. To add a Web server to the list, click New.

Web server:
`My Web Site`

New

for the selected Web server is
www.tcp.co.uk/~kennington

Help

< Back   Next >   Cancel   Help

Web Publishing Wizard

Specify the URL and Directory

Type the URL or Internet address you use to access your personal Web pages (for example, http://www.microsoft.com/myname). Your system administrator or service provider supplies this address.

URL or Internet address:
`http://www.tcp.co.uk/~macbride`

Type the local directory on your computer that will correspond to the URL entered above.

Local directory:
`C:\Homepage\fpage\`

< Back   Next >   Cancel   Help

4 Select the server

5 Set up a new server

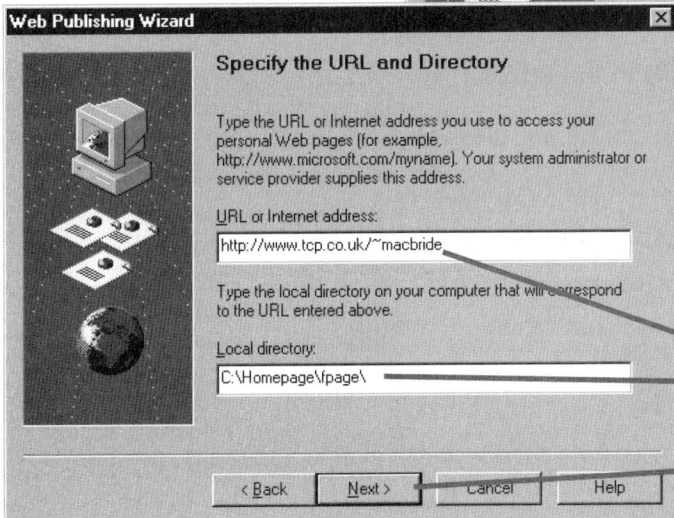

6 Complete the Wizard

Summary

- ❏ FrontPage Express makes Web page creation much easier. It can handle text formatting, lines, images, links, tables and forms.

- ❏ Paragraphs can be formatted to appear as headings, bulletted or numbered lists, or in the *address* style.

- ❏ Selected text may be made bold, italics or varied in size.

- ❏ You can add links to your other pages, to pages on remote sites or to a bookmarked point within a page.

- ❏ Images can be inserted anywhere on the page. They should be given Alternative Text for people who browse with image loading turned off.

- ❏ A picture can be set to form a background, and will be repeated across and down to fill the window.

- ❏ Add a mailto: link if you want your visitor to be able to contact you easily.

- ❏ If you want to collect information from your visitors, you will need to create a form – FrontPage Express has tools to simplify this.

- ❏ Tables can be constructed very easily in the editor.

- ❏ Before uploading your pages, assemble all the files into one folder.

- ❏ The Web Publishing Wizard will transfer your files to your service provider's server. You must give it the FTP address of your Web space, and the URL of your home page.

Index